TOWARDS A
NEW DEAL

TOWARDS A NEW DEAL

a political economy of the times of my life

ROB DAVIES

JONATHAN BALL PUBLISHERS

JOHANNESBURG ▪ CAPE TOWN ▪ LONDON

Published in South Africa in 2021 by
JONATHAN BALL PUBLISHERS
A division of Media24 (Pty) Ltd
PO Box 33977
Jeppestown
2043

ISBN 978-1-77619-093-5
ebook ISBN 978-1-77619-094-2

*Every effort has been made to trace the copyright holders and to obtain their
permission for the use of copyright material. The publishers apologise for any
errors or omissions and would be grateful to be notified of any corrections
that should be incorporated in future editions of this book.*

Photographs provided by courtesy of the author. Special thanks to
Sidwell Medupe, who took many of those pertaining to the author's time
as a minister. The photo on page 44 originally appeared in Jacques Pauw's
In the Heart of the Whore (Southern Book Publishers, 1991).

www.jonathanball.co.za
www.twitter.com/JonathanBallPub
www.facebook.com/JonathanBallPublishers

Cover photograph by Amanda's Photo Journeys
Cover design by Danny Mose Modiba
Design and typesetting by Martine Barker
Set in Adobe Garamond Pro 11.5/15

CONTENTS

LIST OF ABBREVIATIONS

The following abbreviations and acronyms are used frequently in this book:

ACP	Africa, Caribbean and Pacific (Group of States)
AfCFTA	African Continental Free Trade Area
AGOA	African Growth and Opportunity Act
ANC	African National Congress
APDP	Automotive Production and Development Programme
AU	African Union
B-BBEE	broad-based black economic empowerment
BEE	black economic empowerment
BRICS	Brazil, Russia, India, China, South Africa
CET	common external tariff
Cosatu	Congress of South African Trade Unions
DCC	Duty Credit Certificate
DTI	Department of Trade and Industry
EPA	Economic Partnership Agreement
EU	European Union
FDI	foreign direct investment
FTA	free trade area
GDP	gross domestic product
GEAR	Growth, Employment and Redistribution
GNU	Government of National Unity
IDC	Industrial Development Corporation
ICT	information and communications technology
IMF	International Monetary Fund
IP	intellectual property
IPAP	Industrial Policy Action Plan
ITAC	International Trade Administration Commission

MERG	Macro-Economic Research Group
MFN	Most Favoured Nation
MIDP	Motor Industry Development Programme
NDP	National Development Plan
NDR	National Democratic Revolution
NEC	National Executive Committee (ANC)
Nedlac	National Economic Development and Labour Council
PICC	Presidential Infrastructure Coordinating Commission
RDP	Reconstruction and Development Programme
RECs	regional economic communities
SACP	South African Communist Party
SACU	Southern African Customs Union
SADC	Southern African Development Community
SADCC	Southern African Development Coordination Conference
SARB	South African Reserve Bank
SARS	severe acute respiratory syndrome
SARS	South African Revenue Service
SOC	state-owned company
SONA	State of the Nation Address
TDCA	Trade, Development and Cooperation Agreement
TFTA	tripartite free trade area
TPSF	Trade Policy and Strategy Framework
UN	United Nations
UNCTAD	United Nations Conference on Trade and Development
VAT	value-added tax
WIPO	World Intellectual Property Organization
WTO	World Trade Organization

Introduction

This work is a memoir, but not an autobiography. It seeks to offer what could be called a political economy of the years of my life. Not being an autobiography means it does not seek to present a systematic account of my own personal role in any of the events or processes dealt with, although anecdotes are used from time to time to illustrate and emphasise points. Rather, it offers an analytical record of some of the quite extraordinary historical processes I have had the privilege, in a modest way, to participate in. These include the struggle against apartheid, particularly from the vantage point of an activist and analyst who spent many years in exile, most of them in Mozambique. I later became involved in matters of economic policy in the liberation movement. A significant number of chapters reflect in one way or another on the work I was involved in at the Department of Trade and Industry (DTI). Although this is not an autobiography, the choice of themes and issues does reflect my own experiences. As that is the case, I will offer in this introduction a brief account of my own involvement.

I did not come from a political family and had a conventional upbringing as a privileged white boy in apartheid South Africa. My father worked in the insurance business. My mother was a homemaker. From the age of nine, I attended boarding school at Kingswood College in Makhanda (then Grahamstown). My first real consciousness of issues of apartheid came while I was a student at Rhodes University between 1966 and 1969. This was in the period between the regime's smashing of the ANC underground in 1963 and the re-emergence of organisations of African workers in 1973. During that period, student politics was one of the very few significant pillars of the overt opposition left. It was also during that time that I first came to know black people in any role other than as servants.

1

While at Rhodes, I became active in the then multiracial National Union of South African Students (Nusas). I also participated in protests against various aspects of apartheid. The first of these was in 1967, when the then Prime Minister, BJ Vorster, came to lay the foundation stone of what became the 1820 Settlers National Monument building. The only route to the site then was the road that passed the Rhodes University sanatorium. I joined a small number of other students holding placards on the sanatorium wall. Long before Vorster's motorcade passed, we were picked up by the police and taken to the police station. After taking our names, the officer in charge came out to admonish us: 'I can't understand you students. Our Prime Minister comes to Grahamstown once in a lifetime, and you choose this day for a protest!' Other protests were met with a less gentle response. There was never any permission given in Grahamstown for marches, and all protest gatherings were considered illegal. I remember going to one, against some or other apartheid law, that the organisers called a 'vigil'. The change in name did not prevent it from being broken up nor those of us participating being warned that we were now known to the authorities. I also remember putting up posters in a clever two-part campaign organised by the Black Sash. In the first week posters were put up with a portrait of Vorster and the quotation from him, 'You must not try to take a man's home away from him.' Local journalists asked the police what they thought of this, leading the local spokesperson to say he could not object if people wanted to put up portraits of the Prime Minister. The next week's poster included an insert of the first with the main body graphically describing the regime's forced removals. The portrait of the Prime Minister did not stop the forced removal of these posters.

Being 'known' in a small town also had its bizarre side. At the time, there were two cinemas in the town (restricted to whites only). I recall going to a movie one Saturday evening only to encounter a local Special Branch sergeant in the gents' toilet during the interval. He said something like 'bloody communist', to which I responded with an expletive. Within seconds I found my head forced into the urinal as I was 'promised' that he would see me in jail.

With my friend Jon Stoffberg I became involved in distributing scholarship money to students at the University of Fort Hare, in Alice. Any student found accepting this money, which came ultimately from anti-apartheid support groups abroad, would have faced immediate expulsion from an institution then under a highly repressive administration. Our trips to Alice were always occasions for fascinating political discussions with students from both Fort Hare and the neighbouring Federal Theological Seminary, where we stayed over. Nusas events were another opportunity to meet and interact with other remarkable individuals and personalities. Prominent among these was Steve Biko. In the period before the establishment of Black Consciousness organisations, he was one of a small number of black students who attended Nusas activities. The first and only time I ever saw students dissecting bodies at a medical school was when, after a Nusas seminar held in Pietermaritzburg, I gave Biko and some of his colleagues a lift to what was known at the time as the University of Natal Medical School Black section in Ethekwini (then Durban).

When black former Nusas members left the organisation to form Black Consciousness, I drifted towards the more radical fringe of the white student left. The late 1960s were a period of radical student activism worldwide. Protests against the Vietnam war were erupting across campuses in the United States (US) and 1968 saw the spring uprising in Paris that eventually ended the political career of President Charles de Gaulle. This was also the year of the first student sit-in in South Africa, which took place at the University of Cape Town (UCT). An eminent black scholar, Archie Mafeje, had been recommended for appointment to the university's sociology department by the senate (the senior academic body). It was not actually illegal for the university to make such an appointment, but when it came before the university council (the executive body), that body bowed to pressure from the regime and refused to ratify it. In protest, a substantial number of UCT students occupied the administration building for around a week – until Vorster gave UCT an ultimatum to 'put its house in order', failing which, he said, he would do it for them 'and do it thoroughly'.

The second sit-in was at Fort Hare a few months later. In that case, there was no hesitation and no warnings. Instead the students were forcibly and brutally removed from the campus and sent home from various nearby railway stations. A number of white students from several campuses then decided that we would travel to Alice to continue the sit-in. I was driving one of the first cars in our convoy. We were intercepted at multiple roadblocks along the way but allowed to proceed. When we arrived at Fort Hare, we found a campus surrounded by soldiers and police. Our romantic notions of continuing the sit-in became reduced to singing 'We Shall Overcome' outside the premises.

In 1969, an incident similar to the Mafeje case unfolded at Rhodes University. A proposed appointment by the senate of Rev Basil Moore, a progressive white theologian with links to the anti-apartheid University Christian Movement, was vetoed by the council after pressure from the regime. I participated in a sit-in where we occupied the council chamber demanding that the council overturn its decision. The university administration obtained a court order, which resulted in the sheriff of the court and a cohort of police frog-marching out of the council chamber the relatively small number of us who defied the vice chancellor's ultimatum to leave. For this, I was rusticated and thereafter excluded from Rhodes University. Years later, when as a minister I spoke at a graduation ceremony at the university, the then vice chancellor, Professor Saleem Badat, offered a public apology, which I accepted.

During the time of my rustication I was introduced by faculty members, such as the philosopher Rick Turner, who had studied at the Sorbonne in Paris and was later assassinated by the regime, and the writer André Brink, to progressive and neo-Marxist literature. This included the writings of figures such as Herbert Marcuse,[1] much read by participants in the 1960s revolts on campuses in Europe and the United States. Being excluded from Rhodes, I applied to continue my studies at the University of Cape Town. My 'bad disciplinary record' from Rhodes, and my refusal to give assurances that I would not do the same again, led to a prolonged process of authorising admission. But I was allowed to attend some classes for nine months or so. During this time, I met other progressive students, including Jeremy Cronin, an extraordinarily talented individual who later became Deputy General Secretary of the South African Communist Party (SACP). During this time, we avidly read other Marxist writings, such as those of Louis Althusser and Nicos Poulantzas, as well as some of the Marxist classics. The works of Marx and Lenin were at the time banned in South Africa, but there were many loopholes in the regulations. Censors had little knowledge of contemporary Marxist work, and as long as a book or article did not have words like 'revolution' in its title, you could get it. Also, at the time, the University of Stellenbosch ran a course on (anti-)communism. Several of the works of Marx were prescribed for students on this course. All one had to do was to go to the student bookshop in Stellenbosch to buy them. Much more difficult to access was *Class and Colour in South Africa 1850–1950*, by Jack and Ray Simons.[2] A dog-eared copy was, however, passed around in our circles and sparked much interest and debate. Suffice to say it was a major stimulus to discussions on the relationship between capitalism and apartheid (see Chapter 1).

During this time, through a distant relationship to the ANC underground, I became involved in the production and distribution of underground leaflets on behalf of the movement. In the pre-digital age this required the purchase of a second-hand typewriter (then a regulated item, meaning one had to use an assumed name when purchasing it). This was used to type a wax sheet from which duplicate leaflets were clandestinely printed in the Students' Representative Council offices. The typewriter, traceable through its unique typeface, was then disposed of by throwing it into the sea. On one occasion,

I recall driving away from one of the railway stations on the Cape Flats, where we had just strewn leaflets. The only access was a single road. As we left, a police van passed us in the other direction. I sometimes wondered what would have happened if those policemen had put two and two together.

During this time, Ann Schonland Oosthuizen, the widow of Professor Daantjie Oosthuizen, an eminent Rhodes-based philosopher and early Afrikaner voice against apartheid, offered to assist in enrolling me in a postgraduate programme at the University of Southampton in Britain. I seized the opportunity and left South Africa in 1970 for what I anticipated would be a year. I travelled on the British passport I was entitled to through my parentage, and this led to my receiving a letter from the apartheid regime's Minister of the Interior declaring me a prohibited immigrant.

After completing my degree at Southampton, I spent about 18 months teaching development studies in Botswana. Thereafter I returned to Britain and undertook my first attempt at analysing the relationship between capitalism and apartheid, which was published in the *New Left Review* in 1973.[3] This led to my being invited to a conference on reconceptualising the issue at Oxford University in 1974. The conference was my first opportunity to meet in person some of the major theorists and scholars whom I knew up to then only by reputation. They included Harold Wolpe, Joe Slovo, Ruth First, Pallo Jordan, Martin Legassick and Stan Trapido. Also present were a number of my own contemporaries then enrolled at the University of Sussex. They included Dan O'Meara, Mike Morris and Dave Kaplan. I decided also to enrol at Sussex, and completed a DPhil there in 1977. My thesis, entitled 'Capital, State and White Labour in South Africa 1900–1960',[4] was published along with a number of other articles in various journals. We young white leftists saw ourselves as involved in 'theoretical practice', developing a new paradigm to deepen understanding of liberation in South Africa.

After this, as an involuntary exile from South Africa, I went to work at the Centro de Estudos Africanos (CEA, Centre of African Studies) at Eduardo Mondlane University in Maputo, Mozambique, as a *cooperante* (literally 'cooperator', the term then used for foreigners working in Mozambican institutions). Chapter 3 gives a brief sketch of some of the work carried out there – under the leadership of its Mozambican director, Aquino de Bragança, and its research director, the well-known activist-intellectual, Ruth First. As recorded in Chapter 3, I arrived in Mozambique at a time of optimism and revolutionary fervour, underpinning a sense that after centuries of brutal colonialism an alternative people-centred socialist project was being built.

Shortly after arriving in Mozambique, I formally joined the African National Congress (ANC), and a few years later was invited to join the SACP. I was not deployed to the movement's underground structures but mostly carried out what can be described as political and intelligence work.[5] Sometime in late 1980 I began a conversation with William Khanyile about participating in political education and discussion with comrades based at Matola, a suburb of Maputo. That, however, never materialised as Khanyile, along with 14 of his comrades, was killed in the January 1981 Matola raid. This was the first of several cross-border raids and assassinations carried out in Mozambique by the apartheid regime in the 1980s. Frequently, these were conducted with little concern for the 'collateral damage' caused to innocent civilians, neighbours or passers-by, and with indifference to the role actually played by those targeted.

At some stage, I was asked to assist in a few clandestine operations. These mostly involved acting as a courier. Usually, I would be asked to drive a car to Swaziland (now Eswatini). This meant clearing a usually perfunctory customs inspection at the border, and hopefully avoiding ambushes by the Resistência Nacional de Moçambique (Renamo) – the apartheid-backed armed opposition group active during the 1980s – which were becoming increasingly common on the roads out of Maputo. I accepted all the assignments given to me and never asked what had been packed or where it was in the car. But I recall one instance when a Volkswagen Beetle was delivered to my residence for me to drive to the border the following morning. Shortly before I was due to leave, I received a frantic message telling me under no circumstances to set off. I was later told that the materiel had been incorrectly packed in the area above the car's rear-mounted engine and that I would not have made it out of the city alive.

In one way or another, during my time in exile I came to meet some of the leadership figures of the ANC, whose personal qualities of integrity and self-sacrifice were inspirational and second to none. They included the President, Oliver Tambo, the Secretary-General, Alfred Nzo, Joe Slovo, Chris Hani and Mac Maharaj. Jacob Zuma was based in Maputo during much of my time there, and I became involved in a small way in some of the important work he was responsible for.

As Chapter 4 records, during the late 1980s I was drawn into the ANC's economic policy work. Little policy work on matters of the economy had been conducted before then, but by the 1980s, amid a growing number of engagements with business delegations and a sense that before too long the movement could find itself in government, this became an urgent priority. I became a regular and consistent member of the Economic Policy Committee (EPC), led by Max Sisulu (who later became Speaker of the National Assembly) and overseen from the National Executive Committee (NEC) by Sindiso Mfenyana (who later became Secretary to Parliament). At the same time, in my work at the CEA, we began to think about how the southern African region could be reconstituted and restructured after the demise of apartheid.

I returned to South Africa in August 1990, after 19 years in exile. After a short stint working at ANC headquarters in Johannesburg, I accepted an offer to take up a position as professor and co-director at the Centre for Southern African Studies (CSAS) at the University of the Western Cape (UWC). The vice chancellor, Professor Jakes

Gerwel, had defined the mission of UWC as 'the intellectual home of the left'. My co-director at the CSAS, and its founder, was Peter Vale, a highly effective organiser of research work as well as a substantial scholar on matters of international relations and foreign policy. While at the CSAS, I became involved in carrying out research work both for the ANC and for the Southern African Development Community (SADC) on issues of regional integration and cooperation after apartheid.[6]

In 1994 I was elected a member of the first democratically elected Parliament. I was drawn into the Finance, Trade and Industry and Foreign Affairs portfolio committees. In the Constitutional Assembly, I became chair of one of the subcommittees dealing with Chapter 13 (on finance), as well as provisions on the South African Reserve Bank (SARB) and the Auditor-General. In 1996 I was appointed chair of the Portfolio Committee on Trade and Industry and held that position until 2004. In 2004 I was appointed chair of the Portfolio Committee on Finance. In June 2005 President Thabo Mbeki appointed me one of two Deputy Ministers of Trade and Industry. I held the same position during the short presidency of Kgalema Motlanthe. In 2009 President Jacob Zuma appointed me minister in the same portfolio and reappointed me after the elections of 2014. I was retained in this position when President Matamela Cyril Ramaphosa took over in February 2018 until the elections in May 2019. Since 2002 I have been a member of the Central Committee of the SACP and between 2012 and 2017 served as a member of the National Executive Committee of the ANC.

This book is divided into 14 chapters. Chapter 1 sketches out the phases in the struggle against apartheid, and Chapter 2 outlines the regional dimensions of the struggle. Chapter 3 briefly looks at some of the lessons from the experience of building socialism in Mozambique. Chapter 4 examines the changing global dynamics within which South Africa's transition took place. Most of the remaining chapters deal with the evolving debate on economic policy issues, as well as the practice of implementation. I conclude with an attempt to identify the challenges and possible contours of advance of the National Democratic Revolution (NDR) over what seems certain to be an extremely challenging period that lies ahead.

1

The apartheid context

In the Introduction, I indicated that the 1970s were a period that saw a significant output of writing reconceptualising the relationship between capitalism and apartheid. Much has been written about this,[1] as well as about the broader issue of apartheid and the struggle against it, and it is not my intention to offer more than a very brief sketch here.

The essential defining characteristic of segregation and apartheid was, of course, racial discrimination and exclusion. Race became the concept around which relations to the state were defined. All people classified as white were defined as citizens of a self-governing state with basic rights of citizenship. Black people in general, and African people in particular, were excluded from these rights. This system, of course, dated back to, and had its origin in, colonial conquest and dispossession. Resistance to this system on the part of the oppressed passed through various stages. By the time of the installation of the apartheid system, the major resistance organisation was the African National Congress (allied since 1928 to the Communist Party of South Africa, CPSA). The ANC defined it as a struggle for national liberation.

The relationship between capitalism and apartheid was one of the critical questions both in the definition of the objectives of the national liberation struggle, and in the struggle over the progress of the NDR in the period following the democratic breakthrough after 1994.

Liberal discourse, which dominated much academic writing on the subject of apartheid until the mid-1970s, saw apartheid as a purely ideological creation, delinked from and antithetical to the 'economy'. Writers within this paradigm saw the history of South

Africa as being shaped by a clash between the forces of ideology and 'the economy', with the end of apartheid seen as arising from an incremental process in which economic growth and the needs of the 'economy' would erode the 'irrational' edifice of apartheid and usher in a non-racial meritocracy.[2]

In the 1970s a corpus of literature emerged challenging this paradigm.[3] Various pieces of historical research identified how many of the main discriminatory measures adopted in the period between the emergence of the mining industry in the late 19th century and 1948, and known generically as policies of segregation, were imposed to support capital accumulation. Studies showed how mining capital turned to measures such as pass laws, closed compounds, laws prohibiting trade union organisation by African workers and the migrant labour system to bring into existence a low-paid, low-skilled labour force drawn from the oppressed black population. One scholar called these types of measures 'exploitation colour bars', and showed how they in turn created competition with higher-paid, higher-skilled white workers who responded by demanding 'job colour bars'.[4]

I was one of a small number of mainly white postgraduate students who found themselves for various reasons at British universities conducting this kind of research in the 1970s. The giant among us was our mentor, Harold Wolpe. Wolpe had been a leading member of the Rivonia high command, and had been arrested, along with other members of the ANC and SACP leadership, during the raid on Liliesleaf Farm on 11 July 1963. He would certainly have been subjected to a lengthy prison term, along with Nelson Mandela, Walter Sisulu and others, had not he and Arthur Goldreich managed to engineer a dramatic escape from prison a few weeks later. Wolpe's writings sought to refine and deepen the theoretical characterisation by the ANC and SACP of apartheid as 'internal colonialism' or 'Colonialism of a Special Type'. Dan O'Meara said of Wolpe, '[His] work and actions played a fundamental role in revolutionising the way in which social scientists and activists in the struggle against apartheid both understood the workings of South African society and the appropriate ways to change it.'[5]

Wolpe's seminal contribution sought to theorise the specific form of 'articulation of modes of production' that made up the 'South African social formation'. The migrant labour system involved the 'conservation' and 'subordination' of subsistence household production in areas of origin of migrant labourers, known variously as 'reserves' or 'homelands'. Put simply, subsistence household production meant that families of migrant workers carried the costs of their own reproduction, enabling mining capital to drive down the wages of African migrant workers to levels below those that would otherwise be possible. Wolpe saw this relationship as pivotal to the entire edifice of Colonialism of a Special Type.[6] Wolpe read and critiqued the various more empirical studies emerging from the postgraduate students who converged on British universities at the time, as well as the historical contributions of Martin Legassick, who was by then a senior lecturer at the University of Warwick. From Wolpe, we learnt the importance of both theoretical and empirical rigour, and that research could be important in improving liberatory practice. Wolpe's role was that of the synthesiser and theorist who combined various insights into, among other things, perhaps the most elegant Marxist theory of the apartheid state.[7]

Apartheid emerged in the period after 1948 in the midst of a crisis of segregation affecting differentially various forces in the racially defined dominant power bloc. The Second World War had seen significant industrialisation and urbanisation. Many thousands of African workers flocked to townships around cities in search of the relatively higher wages paid in manufacturing. This deprived weaker white commercial farmers of access to the cheap labour they had become accustomed to. At the same time, white workers saw their higher wages potentially being undermined by competition from lower-paid African workers. African workers began organising in trade unions, highlighted by a major strike in the mining industry in 1946. The African National Congress, meanwhile, reinvigorated by the formation of its Youth League, was mobilising increasingly effective militant campaigns.

The election of the National Party to government in 1948 should be seen in the first instance as the electoral triumph of an alliance of those class forces that were most threatened by the weakening of the edifice of segregation.[8] These included small-scale white commercial farmers, who depended on the enforcement of influx-control regulations to secure access to cheap labour, and sections of the white working class who saw weakened job colour bars as undermining their access to employment. Beyond this was an aspirant, ethnically defined Afrikaner capital, which looked to a programme of state intervention and subsidy to carve out a niche in a bourgeoisie then dominated by foreign and 'English-speaking' settler capital – which it then caricatured as 'Hoggenheimers'. These forces were united under the banner of Afrikaner nationalism.

The first phase of the apartheid period, from 1948 to around 1960, saw the mounting of an offensive by the new regime against the oppressed black people with the aim of securing the interests of the dominant bloc in general and its own narrower support base in particular. One of the regime's first priorities was, in the words of one of its ministers, 'to bleed the (black) trade unions to death'.[9] This involved both the decisive removal of trade unions with African members from the official statutory industrial relations system and generalised repression directed against working-class leaders, trade unionists and members of the CPSA (which was banned in 1950). Strikes by black workers were also prohibited. By 1955 official statistics recorded an actual fall in average real wages paid to African workers. One researcher calculated that in 1969 the average real wage paid to black workers in the gold-mining industry was lower than it had been in 1889.[10] Other measures included a strengthening of pass laws and influx-control regulations. In 1956, African women were for the first time required to carry passes, leading to the famous march to the Union Buildings on 9 August.

This offensive did not go without challenge. The ANC launched a non-violent Defiance Campaign targeting the plethora of racially discriminatory laws and regulations. This led in turn to a steady escalation of repression by the regime. In 1955, the ANC organised a Congress of the People, which adopted the Freedom Charter, proclaiming that 'South Africa belongs to all who live in it, black and white', and that no government could claim legitimacy if was not based on 'the will of all the people'.[11] The two projects in the struggle for South Africa were henceforth clearly defined.

This first phase came to an end in 1960–1963 with the first crisis of apartheid. In March 1960 police opened fire on a crowd in Sharpeville protesting against the pass laws. Over 70 pass-burners were killed, several shot in the back as they fled the police. The shockwaves of the Sharpeville massacre reverberated around the world. Several governments and international organisations reacted by imposing boycotts and sanctions. Even South Africa's long-standing allies and partners in the West looked on anxiously, wondering whether the regime was about to fall. The regime's response was to further intensify repression. It banned the ANC as well as the breakaway Pan Africanist Congress and introduced detention without trial, among other things. The ANC saw itself at a moment where it had either to submit or fight. Under the leadership of Nelson Mandela, it set up uMkhonto we Sizwe (MK, Spear of the Nation) and launched an armed struggle, whose opening shots were a sabotage campaign. For three years uncertainty reigned, but eventually the regime gained the upper hand when it arrested the MK high command at Liliesleaf Farm, Rivonia, and consigned them to long terms of imprisonment.

The ten years from 1963 to 1973 were the 'golden years' for the beneficiaries of apartheid. The white power bloc as a whole enjoyed increasing prosperity in an economy undergoing significant growth and generating handsome profits for both domestic and foreign capital. Significant industrial development unfolded, and large domestic conglomerates emerged (some of them owned and controlled by Afrikaner capital). Foreign investment from Western countries poured in despite sanctions campaigns. The black majority, by contrast, experienced stagnant living standards amid pervasive repression.

It was in this period that the apartheid political project began to unfold. Starting under the leadership of HF Verwoerd (Prime Minister from 1958 to 1966), this envisaged the territorial division of South Africa into a permanently white-ruled area consisting of 87 per cent of the surface area of the country, with eight self-governing and eventually 'independent' African tribal 'homelands' being created in the remaining 13 per cent. All African people were to be regarded as citizens of one or other of these homelands and recognised as only ' temporary sojourners' in white South Africa. Various euphemisms were developed to replace the term 'apartheid', including 'separate development'.

It was in 1973 that the balance of forces began to turn against the white power bloc. The onset of the global economic downturn of the mid-1970s placed serious downward pressure on African living standards. Against that background, workers in Durban went on strike, demanding higher wages. In the face of the scale and determination of these strikes, both capital and the apartheid state faltered. Finding themselves unable to respond in the way they had become accustomed – dismissing strikers and replacing them with other recruits – they instead began negotiating with strikers. This spurred the resurgence, for the first time in nearly two decades, of trade union organisation among black workers.

In 1976 came the famous youth and student uprising in Soweto. At about the same time MK resumed the armed struggle inside the country, using base and transit facilities made available in neighbouring countries. By the end of the decade the regime led by BJ Vorster, who had come to office as the 'strong man' of the post-1960 repression, was looking out of control. A 'palace coup' brought PW Botha, the Minister of Defence and champion of the securocrats (an influential grouping of military and security officials), in as head of the regime, first as prime minister and later as executive president.

Under Botha, the regime underwent significant militarisation, with military-dominated security structures becoming the centre of decision-making. The securocrats devised the 'total strategy' to respond to the 'total onslaught' they saw themselves as confronting.[12] Eighty per cent of the actions under the total strategy were supposed to be political, with only 20 per cent directly security. Among the political elements of the total strategy was the creation of subordinated legislative chambers, elected by minority communities in the black population (South Africans classified as coloured and Indian) in a tricameral parliament. Long and tortuous debates about how to create supposedly representative bodies for 'urban Africans' had not proceeded beyond plans for local authorities before the demise of the regime.

In the event, none of these stratagems had much impact, and in practice the 80:20 formula was turned on its head, with most actions being security measures. Detentions proceeded apace amid the declaration of two states of emergency. Cross-border raids and military assaults in neighbouring countries became common. Towards its end, the regime resorted to assassination and extrajudicial murder on an ever-increasing scale. None of this succeeded in thwarting a liberation struggle gathering pace across all four of its pillars – armed struggle, building the underground, mass action and international isolation. By 1986 the regime was widely seen to be losing the strategic initiative. Western bankers refused to roll over loans, fearing the prospect of default rather than being motivated by solidarity. This seriously limited the regime's access to international credit and had a debilitating effect on the economy.

In 1987 a large detachment of the regime's military forces became embroiled in a major battle at Cuito Cuanavale, in Angola, after an adventurous assault deep into the southern part of that country. Massive reinforcement of Angolan forces by Cuba led to the apartheid forces losing air and ground supremacy, obliging them for the first time ever to negotiate an exit from Cuito Cuanavale.

The significance of Cuito Cuanavale is discussed more fully in Chapter 2, but, among other things, it exposed the beleaguered militaristic regime of PW Botha as having no solutions. Abandoned by his erstwhile allies in monopoly capital, Botha was ousted in another palace coup by FW de Klerk. De Klerk was positioned on the right of the National Party, but came to recognise that white minority rule could no longer be sustained without continued conflict, with damaging effects on the economy.

By the start of the 1990s, the forces of liberation had reached the point where they had made visible progress but were still far from being able to decisively defeat the apartheid enemy. Their allies in the southern African region, meanwhile, had become increasingly war-weary after being battered by apartheid destabilisation (see Chapter 2). Finally, the thawing of the Cold War created a new momentum towards seeking 'regional solutions to regional conflicts' (see Chapter 4). ANC President OR Tambo saw both the opportunities and risks in the emerging conjuncture. He conducted a major diplomatic initiative culminating in the adoption of the Harare Declaration, endorsed by the Frontline States (Mozambique, Angola, Zambia, Zimbabwe and Tanzania), defining the terms and scope of a potential negotiated transition.

In February 1990, FW de Klerk dramatically unbanned the ANC, the SACP and other proscribed organisations and announced his willingness to engage in negotiations. The stage was set for a negotiated transition.

The negotiation process lasted from 1990 to 1993, went through many ups and downs, and encountered several crises along the way. The De Klerk regime, recognising that it could no longer hold on to white minority rule, moved its focus to trying to ensure that the core interests of capital and its white electoral base would be preserved whoever eventually came into government. The formal negotiations focused on the constitutional order. The ANC insisted that the constitution of a democratic South Africa would have to be developed by an elected Constitutional Assembly, but it agreed that a pre-election process could produce an interim constitution in terms of which democratic elections would be held. After much bargaining there was also agreement that pre-defined constitutional principles would also be included in the final constitution.

The murder of SACP General Secretary and ANC leader Chris Hani in April 1993, by elements of the white far right, proved to be a major catalytic event. With the country on the brink of widespread violence in the aftermath of Hani's assassination, ANC President Nelson Mandela asserted himself as the country's de facto leader. The De Klerk regime quickly agreed to an election date, 27 April 1994, and to work in earnest to put in place the processes required to meet that deadline.

The constitutional principles were finalised in this period. They required there to be an amnesty for those who had committed acts of political violence 'on all sides'. Property would have to be protected, although there could be 'restitution' of property acquired through discriminatory practices under apartheid. There would be a justiciable constitution, a strong independent judiciary, an independent Reserve Bank, a degree of autonomy for separately elected provincial and local government and procedures to raise taxes and manage public expenditure according to prescribed norms. There was also to be a Government of National Unity (GNU), with members drawn proportionally from all parties who reached a prescribed threshold, for five years. On 27 April 1994 the country held its first democratic non-racial election. The ANC won a little less than two-thirds of the seats in a party-list proportional-vote system. Within a fortnight, Nelson Mandela was inaugurated President, with FW de Klerk one of two Deputy Presidents, the other being the ANC's Thabo Mbeki.

2

The southern African region

Living in exile in southern Africa during the decade of the 1980s led me to develop an appreciation of South Africa's position as an integral part of the African continent and of the southern African region in particular. A region, with meaning beyond a group of geographically contiguous countries, can, in fact, be identified as having come into existence in southern Africa at the end of the 19th century.[1] Once again, the development of the gold-mining industry in South Africa was pivotal in its formation.

Right from the onset of deep-level gold mining on the Witwatersrand in 1887 until the late 1970s, thousands of African migrant workers were drawn from 'labour reserves' not just inside South Africa's borders but across several of the territories of southern Africa. The colonial history of Lesotho, for example, is one of suppression by the British colonial authorities of commercial agricultural production in order to transform that territory into a labour reserve for the South African mines.[2] The Portuguese rulers of Mozambique entered into a contract with the South African Chamber of Mines allowing it to recruit Mozambican migrant workers in the area south of latitude 22 degrees south. In return, the Chamber agreed that a defined portion of wages earned by Mozambican migrant workers would be compulsorily remitted for payment back home through a transfer in gold to the Portuguese colonial authorities. When the gold exchange standard was ended in the early 1970s, and the gold price rose, this allowed the Portuguese colonial authorities to make a handsome profit at the workers' expense. Other commitments agreed to were that the South African authorities would ensure that a defined percentage of traffic to and from the Witwatersrand would pass through the port of Lourenço Marques (now Maputo). These arrangements persisted until Mozambican independence in 1975.[3] Similar arrangements allowed the Chamber to recruit migrant workers from parts of what are now Malawi, Botswana, Eswatini (Swaziland), Zambia and Tanzania.

Beyond the migrant labour system, Botswana, Lesotho and Eswatini were until their independence administered by the British High Commission in South Africa and economically incorporated into South Africa, with a customs union, monetary union and unrestricted movement of persons across national borders. Namibia (then called South West Africa) became virtually a fifth province, after being seized from the erstwhile German colonial authorities during the First World War. Although the settler population of Zimbabwe (then called Southern Rhodesia) rejected formal incorporation into South Africa in a referendum in 1923, and despite a decade-long colonial project to develop an alternative Federation of Rhodesia and Nyasaland, extensive trade and investment ties drew what are now Zimbabwe, Zambia and Malawi into what became a South Africa-centric southern African regional economy.

In addition to being forged by colonial capitalist arrangements, the region was also made by the 'informal' actions of its people. Colonial borders cut across communities, who continued to trade with each other and maintain family and clan relations. Informal intraregional trade was, and still is, not properly recorded but is generally estimated to be considerable.

Politically, all territories became subjects of either British or Portuguese colonial arrangements. In 1963, the Federation of Rhodesia and Nyasaland was dissolved as Malawi and Zambia became independent in 1964. The following year saw the self-governing settler regime in Southern Rhodesia, now calling itself simply Rhodesia, making a Unilateral Declaration of Independence (UDI) from Britain. In the following four years Botswana, Lesotho and Eswatini all became independent.

After the banning of the ANC and the arrest of its underground leadership, the organisation regrouped in exile. The formation of the Organization of African Unity (OAU) in 1963 proclaimed as its first priority support for the complete decolonisation and liberation of the entire continent. The governments of independent Tanganyika (later Tanzania), under President Julius Nyerere, and Zambia, under President Kenneth Kaunda, both placed their countries at the disposal of OAU-recognised liberation movements. Apart from the ANC and the Pan Africanist Congress, these included the Frente de Libertação de Moçambique (Frelimo), the Movimento Popular de Libertação de Angola (MPLA), the South West Africa People's Organisation (Swapo) of Namibia, the Zimbabwe African People's Union (ZAPU) and the Zimbabwe African National Union (ZANU), all of which became involved in armed struggles with the colonial regimes in their respective countries.

Up until the mid-1970s the apartheid regime's regional strategy prioritised reinforcing what it termed 'buffer states'. These were the Portuguese-ruled territories of Angola and Mozambique and the settler-ruled Rhodesia. The overall objective was to keep the liberation forces far from the borders of the South African heartland.

Portugal was the weakest link in this chain. Although the presence of the Portuguese in Africa dates back to the late 15th century, Portugal itself was never strong enough to maintain a firm hold over its colonies. One of the local beer brands in Maputo is Dois M (2 Ms). The two Ms refer to Patrice de MacMahon, who was President of France towards the end of the 19th century. MacMahon is remembered because it was he who ruled, in one of the then existing processes for resolving contending colonial claims, that parts of southern Mozambique be assigned to Portugal rather than becoming part of what is now South Africa.[4] The 'outsourcing' of this area as a recruitment ground for the Chamber of Mines reflected the inability of Portugal thereafter fully to economically exploit this territory.

After a coup in 1926, Portugal came to be ruled by a fascistic regime led initially by António Salazar and later by Marcelo Caetano. Portuguese colonies included the enclave of Goa in India, as well as East Timor and Macao in Asia, and Angola, Mozambique, Guinea-Bissau, Cape Verde and São Tomé e Príncipe in Africa. In the 1960s India reincorporated Goa into its territory with little resistance from Portugal. Ideological trickery, including the renaming of colonies as 'provinces' of a 'pluri-continental Portugal', had little or no impact in thwarting the development of liberation movements. By the late 1960s Portugal found itself embroiled in increasingly bitter military conflicts against liberation movements in several of its African colonies, as well as in East Timor. As a member of the North Atlantic Treaty Organisation (NATO), Portugal was able to rely on extensive military collaboration with its NATO allies. But by the mid-1970s these colonial wars had become increasingly costly economically, as well as unpopular among the ever-expanding number of Portuguese youth conscripted to fight in far-off 'provinces'.

In 1974, amid the failure of a major operation directed against Frelimo (called Operation Gordian Knot), a group of young military officers in Portugal overthrew the Caetano regime. Shortly thereafter, negotiations began with liberation movements. This led in quick succession to independence for Mozambique in June 1975 and for Angola in November 1975.[5]

The fall of these two former buffer states significantly changed the balance of forces in southern Africa. The apartheid regime was taken aback and had no clear idea of how to respond. Its military forces moved into Angola in November 1975, almost reaching Luanda, in the evident hope of forestalling the installation of an MPLA-led government. But these forces were withdrawn when it was made clear that such a move would not draw support from the United States (US) despite the widespread collaboration the apartheid regime apparently enjoyed from the Central Intelligence Agency (CIA) in supporting a rival movement, the União Nacional da Independência Total de Angola (Unita). According to sources widely credited in Mozambique, a similar incident occurred just before that country's independence. A force was reportedly assembled by the Bureau for State Security (BOSS) with the apparent intention of intervening to support an attempted settler coup in late 1974. This, however, was disarmed by Military Intelligence operatives loyal to then Defence Minister PW Botha, who was convinced that the coup was not viable and that any such move would lead to apartheid South Africa's further international isolation. Mozambique's independence proceeded and this also immediately opened up the eastern front in the liberation war in Zimbabwe. Within four years, the Rhodesian settler regime found itself unable to resist a transition that eventually resulted in independence for Zimbabwe, under a government led by ZANU, in 1980.

After the installation of the Botha regime, the total strategy began also to be applied in the southern African region.[6] Among its political elements was the floating of a proposal for the establishment of a Constellation of Southern African States (Consas).[7] Seeing this as some kind of loose alliance based on economic cooperation, the regime hoped to draw in Malawi, then ruled by the autocratic Hastings Banda, and some of the Southern African Customs Union (SACU) member countries, isolating the grouping that had been constituted as the Frontline States. No country, however, formally associated with Consas, leaving it stillborn. Instead the Frontline States succeeded in mobilising all independent regional states, including key Consas targets, into the Southern African Development Coordination Conference (SADCC), formed in 1980, which later evolved into SADC. SADCC's initial programme prioritised 'reducing the dependency (of its members) particularly but not only on the Republic of South Africa'.[8] In this context, total strategy in the southern African region, like its home-based component, fell back to inverting the formula and becoming 80 per cent military action. Cross-border raids and assassinations were carried out against suspected residences or bases of the liberation movement, with increasing indifference to the harm caused to innocent civilians and bystanders. The Reagan administration's doctrine of supporting right-wing 'contra movements' to wage guerrilla war on left-wing governments in Nicaragua and elsewhere in Latin America was imported and applied in what became known as 'destabilisation'.

In Angola, this meant the South African Defence Force (SADF) supporting and equipping Unita in its quest to establish a 'zone of control' in southern Angola. By the mid-1980s, this had come also to include regular seasonal incursions into southern Angola by SADF special forces and even regular troops and conscripts.

In the case of Mozambique, the chosen vehicle was Renamo, which initially had been supported and equipped by Rhodesian special forces. After Zimbabwean independence, many Renamo members, including its titular leader, Afonso Dhlakama, moved to South Africa, where they fell under the wing of SADF Military Intelligence. A project code-named Operation Mila saw the SADF massively upgrading Renamo's capabilities and unleashing them as what were widely known in Mozambique as 'armed bandits'.[9] The Renamo assault caused widespread destruction across the rural infrastructure of much of the country. So successful indeed did the SADF consider this project that it later became a model for sponsoring 'black on black' violence inside South Africa itself.[10]

Destabilisation also came to include an economic component. Railway lines and other communications networks, particularly those prioritised by SADCC, became targets both in cross-border raids and in actions by contra groups. There was even a complete economic blockade of Lesotho in 1986, ostensibly in retaliation for the support given to the ANC by Prime Minister Leabua Jonathan. That blockade prompted a military coup in January 1986, which installed a more compliant military regime.[11]

Apartheid destabilisation cost the region an estimated US$10 billion between 1980 and 1985, an amount greater than all the foreign aid received and equivalent to one-third of its combined export earnings. More than 100 000 people lost their lives.[12] These bald figures, however, miss the harsh truth that many of the actions by contra groups deliberately targeted ordinary populations. The modus operandi of Renamo, for example, was to destroy schools and clinics in any village it came to (on the grounds that these were symbols of government authority). Press-ganging of young boys into its ranks was also common. So blatant were its war crimes that even an official of the Reagan administration accused the group of responsibility for 'one of the most brutal holocausts against ordinary human beings at any time since the Second World War'.[13]

This assault included even the assassination of a head of state, President Samora Machel of Mozambique. Machel had in fact attempted to spare his country from this assault by signing, in March 1984, a formal non-aggression pact with the apartheid regime – the Nkomati Accord. Machel's death in October 1986 followed the presentation by his government of irrefutable evidence of the apartheid regime's violation of the Nkomati Accord (see Chapter 3), and more immediately the mobilisation by Machel of pressure on Malawi to clamp down on the use of its territory by the SADF and Renamo. More precisely, Samora Machel died in a plane crash at Mbuzini in South Africa while returning from a special summit of the Frontline States on this question. The South African official inquiry blamed pilot error. But there were several reports over the years alleging that the SADF had used a 'false beam' device to lure Machel's plane off course. I was a researcher in Maputo at the time and carefully monitored the commentary being made by apartheid officials in the period leading up to the crash. This was full of threats and statements to the effect that Machel himself had become an obstacle to restoring relations along the lines desired by the apartheid regime and needed to be removed. Perhaps there never will be final closure on this question. But I certainly am one who remains extremely sceptical of suggestions from the standpoint of the apartheid authorities that Samora Machel's extremely timely removal was a mere 'accident'.[14]

By the end of the 1980s the wastelands of the struggle for South

Africa were not in South Africa itself but in the region around it – southern Africa. But it was also in southern Africa that apartheid finally encountered its own Stalingrad. In 1987–1988 the SADF made its regular seasonal incursion into southern Angola. As usual they were met by contingents of the Forças Armadas Populares da Libertação de Angola (Fapla, the Angolan armed forces). On this occasion a particular Fapla division found itself some distance from its supply lines, and this was seen as creating an opportunity for the SADF significantly to enlarge Unita's area of control. Analyses at the time suggested that the SADF/Unita strategists saw this as potentially creating enough of a territorial hold to demand negotiations for a power-sharing government. A 'linkage doctrine' supported by key Western powers held that there could be no advance in negotiations for Namibian independence without simultaneously dealing with the Angolan question.

The SADF piled in forces to take on the isolated Fapla division. This included deploying its advanced G5 and G6 artillery, its best fighter jets and ground troops that included not just special forces but also white conscripts. The SADF force would probably have out-matched available Fapla forces, but in a remarkable display both of international solidarity and strategic savvy, Cuba massively increased its forces, bringing in also new technology, including Soviet-made missile radar systems. The SADF force found itself tied down near the town of Cuito Cuanavale. Moreover, for the first time ever in its incursions in southern Africa, the SADF lost air supremacy, lacking any countermeasure to the missile radar system.[15] The prospect of being overrun loomed. At the same time, the combined Cuban-Fapla force began advancing towards SADF bases in northern Namibia. This raised the spectre of PW Botha's having to face the political challenge of explaining the arrival of body bags containing not just Unita and special forces but significant numbers of white conscripts as well.

Cuito Cuanavale was a turning point. Cuban leader Fidel Castro declared: 'The history of Africa will be written as before and after Cuito Cuanavale.'[16] Yet, in a debate in the National Assembly on the 20th anniversary of the battle of Cuito Cuanavale in 2007, voices from the old order repeated the claim that in fact it was the SADF that 'won' at Cuito Cuanavale.[17] This rested on a very narrow interpretation that the SADF's objectives were to halt the southward advance into Namibia of Cuban and Angolan forces. From a broader strategic perspective, PW Botha found himself obliged to sue for peace on terms other than his own. Indeed, the terms presented to him effectively turned the linkage doctrine on its head. To negotiate an orderly withdrawal of its forces, including significant quantities of its most advanced materiel, the Botha regime was required to negotiate independence for Namibia.

Namibia became independent on 20 March 1990 and from that point the path to South Africa's own transition, while still rocky in parts, was never in doubt. Cuito Cuanavale was indeed apartheid's Stalingrad. However, while the road from Stalingrad to Berlin saw large swathes of both the Soviet Union and Germany laid waste, in southern Africa the wastelands were confined to the region only.

3

Mozambican socialism

I arrived in Mozambique in 1979, four years after its independence. Frelimo, at its third congress a year earlier, had proclaimed itself a Marxist-Leninist party pursuing a programme of socialist transition in Mozambique. In 1979, local Frelimo party structures were mobilising neighbourhood communities for street-cleaning activities on Sunday mornings. Household groceries were obtained by joining a neighbourhood cooperative, which offered everyone defined amounts of basic goods at low prices. University students were mobilised to assist in harvesting rice. It was, in short, a time when popular mobilisation and enthusiasm for revolutionary change were strongly evident.

My access card to the Centro de Estudos Africanos (CEA), Maputo, where I worked for 11 years from 1979 to 1990.

For the next 11 years, I worked at the Centro de Estudos Africanos at Eduardo Mondlane University (Universidade Eduardo Mondlane,

UEM). Mozambique's only university at the time was named after the founding president of Frelimo, who had been assassinated in Dar es Salaam in 1969. The CEA was led by two remarkable personalities, both of whom suffered violent deaths at the hands of the apartheid regime.

The director was Aquino de Bragança. Originally from Goa, Bragança was a founder member of the Confêrencia das Organizações Nacionalistas das Colónias Portuguesas (CONCP), the organisation of resistance to Portuguese colonialism that predated the formation of country-specific liberation movements such as Frelimo and the MPLA. Bragança was widely respected in Frelimo and was a confidant of, and adviser to, President Samora Machel. It was widely assumed that he could have secured a senior political position, but he chose instead to devote himself to research and scholarship. He died in the Mbuzini plane crash with Machel on 18 October 1986.

The director of research at the CEA was Ruth First, who was well known as a journalist, author and leading member of both the ANC and SACP of the same generation as Nelson Mandela and Oliver Tambo. She was killed in her office at the CEA on 17 August 1982 when she opened a letter bomb. Ruth had just organised a conference on research support for SADCC and was in her office with some of the visiting participants when the letter bomb exploded. One of those was Pallo Jordan, who was slightly injured in the blast. I was deployed by the ANC to accompany President Machel when he inspected the scene that evening. I had never before encountered the effects of a letter bomb. The image of blood and flesh splattered all over cracked walls and the ceiling is something I will never forget.

Years later, the notorious Craig Williamson received amnesty from the Truth and Reconciliation Commission (TRC) for this act.[1] Those of us around at the time still believe that the TRC erred in this case. Williamson claimed the bomb had been meant for Joe Slovo or 'the Slovos'. We never believed that Ruth opened Joe's mail, which also never came to her office at the CEA. Besides, Ruth at the time

Above: The staff of the CEA in the late 1980s (after the deaths of Aquino de Bragança and Ruth First). I am standing on the left.

Left: With Sidwell Medupe at the memorial to Aquino de Bragança and Ruth First outside the CEA, Maputo 2018.

was fully focused on her research work and was not involved in ANC underground work. She was convinced that the struggle to build socialism in Mozambique and the struggle for liberation in South Africa were inextricably interlinked. Many an ANC comrade passing through Maputo found it hard to understand Ruth's focus on issues of Mozambique. Killing her would have been akin to attacking National Party sympathisers working at universities in South Africa – something the ANC never did.

Both Aquino de Bragança and Ruth First championed the view that research aimed at providing 'critical support' could contribute significantly to the advance of national liberation in southern Africa in general, and to the building of socialism in Mozambique in particular. In fact, the conference Ruth had organised on the eve of her death grappled precisely with that question. Mozambique attracted a variety of Marxists, communists and left-wingers of all sorts. They included lecturers from Eastern Europe (the German Democratic Republic and Soviet Union in particular) deployed on state-to-state assistance programmes. Several of these taught formal courses on Marxism-Leninism that were compulsory for all students at UEM. These largely involved packaged summaries of some of the major philosophical propositions of the Marxist-Leninist classics plus lists of the 'achievements' of the Eastern European socialist countries.

These courses generated a considerable backlash among students. There was a joke that did the rounds at the medical school: you go to the Marxism-Leninism class the first time and get an injection. The second time you get another injection. By the third time you are totally immune to Marxism-Leninism. The CEA sought to promote a more creative approach, seeing Marxism as a tool of analysis to grapple with the concrete realities of Mozambique's attempted socialist transition. The central *raison d'être* was that there was a need for research that provided critical support to the Frelimo government's programmes and policies. The element of 'support' referred to the definition of the project and programme by the liberation movement, which was not in dispute. But the examination of concrete practice needed to be critical to arm and empower the party and government with insights to improve implementation. The CEA sought to establish space for this approach, and much of the seminar on research support for the then incipient SADCC grappled with this issue.

Mozambican socialism was in fact a very fragile project embarked upon in one of the most underdeveloped countries in the world. As indicated in Chapter 2, Portuguese colonialism had only a limited hold over the economies of its colonies. One of the first CEA projects established that the effective outsourcing of much of the south as a labour reserve for the South African Chamber of Mines had created an enormous dependency, among households living in the area, on remittances of mine wages. The sharp cutbacks in recruitment imposed by South Africa after Mozambican independence had resulted in very serious income challenges.[2] Outside of the labour-reserve south, only in the central part of the country was there Portuguese-owned capitalist production of any significance. This primarily consisted of agricultural plantations drawing migrant labour from surrounding peasant populations through measures that included forced labour. The northern part of the country was dominated by peasant household production. This was not, however, just subsistence production. Peasant producers were forced by directives of colonial administrators to grow cash crops, foremost among them cotton.[3] Cotton growing required peasant families to devote considerable time and effort to cultivation of the crop – more than required in food production. But the prices paid under the centralised procurement regime were low. Cotton growing was, therefore, underpinned by enforced compulsory cultivation. This specified that a defined portion of a household's land had to be used for cotton production, while inspectors were deployed to ensure that households carried out the various tasks required to bring the crop to harvest. I recall, during a CEA project in Nampula province in 1979, reading documents produced by colonial administrators only a decade earlier, all including a section on the 'attitude of the natives' in carrying out these tasks.[4] At some stage, this compulsion was expedited through beatings applied with a device called a *palmatória* – a disc with holes in it, attached to a handle, that magnified pain by creating suction that drew up the skin with each application. The cotton was ginned (removing the weighty cotton seed) in Mozambique before being exported to Portugal. Only towards the end of the colonial period did a few textile mills appear in a country that was a significant cotton producer. Industry generally

33

was very limited and confined to the main cities, Maputo and Beira.

Decolonisation came to Mozambique without any real plan or timetable. Portugal, the weakest of the colonial powers, was also the last to decolonise. The fascist regime of Marcelo Caetano was determined to hold on to its colonies through military force, relying on Portugal's membership of NATO to ensure access to military supplies. But by the start of the 1970s, it was clear that Portugal's colonial wars were not going well. A major operation called 'Gordian Knot', conducted between July 1970 and January 1971, failed to prevent Frelimo forces from infiltrating from Tanzania. This and other setbacks fuelled dissatisfaction among young military conscripts, who eventually supported the overthrow of the Caetano regime by a movement led by young officers on 25 April 1974. On 7 September, the new Portuguese revolutionary junta reached an agreement with Frelimo, called the Lusaka Accords. This provided for independence on 25 June 1975, with a joint administration running the country in the interim. A few days after the Lusaka Accords, settlers in Maputo attempted a counter-coup and called on apartheid South Africa to intervene. According to the narrative in security circles in Maputo, then Prime Minister Vorster was inclined to accede and began assembling an intervention force, but was dissuaded by then Defence Minister PW Botha and the military, who argued than any such operation was bound to fail. After that, settlers began leaving Mozambique en masse, often just abandoning their property and committing acts of sabotage.

Like many liberation movements of the time, Frelimo developed a strong socialist inclination. This was based in the first instance on a recognition that the state would of necessity be obliged to play a leading role in any serious process of transformation of the inherited conditions of underdevelopment. It was also reinforced by the experience of the struggle against colonialism – including the fact that material support for the war of liberation came from the socialist bloc countries, while its adversaries were armed by NATO. But Frelimo came to power in 1975 without a fully worked-out programme of socialist transition and was obliged to engage in much on-the-job learning.

There is a boulevard in Maputo called 24th of July Avenue. The name refers to the date on which, in 1975, the nationalisation of colonial property was announced. Apart from the banks, most other nationalisations were in fact defensive. The abandonment of enterprises by fleeing settlers and associated sabotage left the Frelimo government with the responsibility to manage and run not just banks and other 'commanding heights' of the economy but also rental property, restaurants, small shops and even hairdressers. This put major pressure on its available resource capacity and also required the recruitment of large numbers of foreign *cooperantes* from around the world.

The CEA's research projects during the tenure of Ruth First took the form of collective research field trips by members of the Centre's staff, as well as by students on the postgraduate development studies programme it ran. The main conclusions of CEA research had a remarkable echo in later debates in South Africa on the Reconstruction and Development Programme (RDP). Most of the early socialistic interventions in the countryside, where the vast majority of the people lived, were of a socio-political nature, with transformation of the productive base falling far behind. Frelimo focused initially on building *aldeias comunais* (communal villages). These brought scattered peasant households into an organised village where infrastructure, such as schools and clinics, was also provided. The building of cooperative production was, however, not emphasised, because of a view that state farms represented an inherently 'higher form of socialism'. Most of the state farms were established on farms taken over as settlers abandoned them. They included both plantations and smaller, former family-owned settler capitalist enterprises, several of which were amalgamated into larger units. Most of the state farms were run by technicians from the Eastern European socialist countries (mainly the German Democratic Republic and Bulgaria). Although they were state-owned and -run, CEA research[5] argued that they represented very little transformation of the relations of production.

There was a considerable amount of triumphalism about the state farms. One of our colleagues in the CEA, Marc Wuyts, found himself severely criticised in the university for injecting a tone of realism into statistical understanding. In remarkable similarity to the later neoliberal fetishisation of GDP growth rates, state-farm triumphalism involved trumpeting throughout the media that there had been an x per cent increase in output compared to the year before. The controversy around Wuyts emerged because he pointed out that growth rates depended on the base from which they were calculated. If production halved, you had a contraction of 50 per cent. If this was followed by a restoration of half that amount you had growth of 50 per cent, while restoring the full amount required growth of 100 per cent. None of the state farms ever achieved the highest levels of production of the colonial period, while the overall gross domestic product (GDP) remained below that recorded in 1973. The CEA supported a stronger emphasis on building cooperatives both in the southern labour-reserve area and elsewhere. The CEA saw this both as creating immediate income-generating opportunities and as the best available route to socialise the relations of production in the countryside.

With regard to industries and the urban working class, as indicated earlier, these were always small and underdeveloped in a country with an overwhelmingly poor peasant majority. In the mid-1980s, I delivered a paper at a Ruth First Memorial Lecture chaired by Jacob Zuma, then ANC Chief Representative in Mozambique. That paper was later published under the title, 'Nationalisation, Socialisation and the Freedom Charter'.[6] The main argument was that socialisation was a much broader concept than nationalisation. Nationalisation was a change in legal property relations, or, more precisely, the transfer of legal ownership to a state. It could occur under a variety of forms of state with diverse objectives. Socialisation, on the other hand, implied the collective reappropriation of control over the means of production by the producers. More precisely it meant the reappropriation of the powers of economic ownership (powers to decide on the use of surplus value produced), as well as the powers of possession (powers in relation to the organisation of actual labour processes). Drawing on CEA research at the Texlom textile factory in Maputo, I argued that through their experience of struggle with the former colonial management, workers at Texlom had achieved a degree of collective organisation in the work-place that enabled them to exercise a greater level of real participation in management decisions. This potentially allowed them to make more progress towards socialisation than was the case in other enterprises where nationalisation had simply seen the instalment of a ministry-appointed management team. Alas, by the time I left Mozambique, Texlom had ceased to exist as any kind of enterprise.

While it had weaknesses, Mozambican socialism also had real achievements. These included a school system much better after only a few years than its colonial predecessor. The health system had a broad reach and a strong emphasis on primary health care. The com-munal villages brought real social advances and better service delivery to thousands of rural citizens, who were also decisively liberated from forced labour and forced cultivation. Whatever its weaknesses, Mozambican socialism did not wither away because of these. The truth is that the socialist experiment in Mozambique never had a chance to develop its potential. It was overwhelmed by apartheid destabilisation. Communal villages, clinics, schools, cooperatives and state farms were all prime targets in the apartheid-directed Renamo assault. Towards the end of this period, Frelimo made a bid to join the Council of Mutual Economic Assistance (CMEA, also known as Comecon). This was a grouping mainly of Eastern European socialist countries, but also included Cuba, which received guaranteed, higher-than-world-market prices for its sugar exports. At the time, the Soviet Union characterised Mozambique, along with other socialis-tic African countries, as a country of 'socialist orientation'. Frelimo argued for a higher level of recognition, as a 'new socialist country', as the basis for its admission to the CMEA. To no avail. Perhaps because the Soviet Union was unwilling – even before Mikhail Gorbachev took over – to contemplate a major increase in support for African countries, Frelimo never succeeded in this endeavour.

One of Mozambican socialism's last gasps was also its lowest point. In 1983, amid a significant influx into towns of war refugees from the countryside, the Frelimo government organised 'Operation Production'[7]. Anyone present in towns without a work card was rounded up and deported to rural areas that were allegedly short of labour. Predictably, this failed to restore rural production, and many individuals suffered great injustice in the process. Thereafter Frelimo decided it could no longer afford to fight on many fronts and that it needed to act to isolate the apartheid assault from actual or potential backing by Western powers.

One move in this regard involved joining the International Monetary Fund (IMF) and negotiating a structural adjustment facility with it. The Mozambican government decided to draw up its own IMF-type programme, and, when the IMF agreed to it, presented it at home as a victory for its diplomacy. In fact, several IMF staffers said privately that the Programa de Reabilitação Económica (Economic Rehabilitation Programme, PRE) was a lot tougher than a programme they would have been willing to agree to. The PRE resulted in a rapid devaluation of the local currency, the metical, which had for many years been pegged at an official rate of 40 to the US dollar. There were also budget cuts and widespread privatisation.

After this, and amid the continuing costly war of destabilisation, the government of President Machel finally decided that it needed to reach a security agreement with the apartheid regime. Negotiations began in secret in 1983 and culminated in the signing of the Nkomati Accord at a high-profile ceremony in March 1984. The accord was essentially a non-aggression pact, in terms of which both parties undertook to refrain from hostile actions against one another, including not providing support to 'irregular forces or armed bands'.[8] The

Frelimo government saw itself as having talked to the 'organ grinder' rather than the 'monkey', and calculated that if it could oblige the Botha regime to desist from supporting Renamo, the war of destabilisation would quickly wind down. To demonstrate its commitment, the Frelimo government moved with speed and thoroughness in expelling all members of the ANC, except for ten members of a representative office and persons like me who were contracted to a Mozambican entity.

Nkomati certainly had a disruptive effect on ANC underground operations for some time. Within a few weeks of the signature of the agreement, the bulk of the ANC membership resident in Maputo were obliged to leave the country for Lusaka, Zambia, on chartered aircraft. I was, at the time, a member of the ANC's Regional Political Committee and was asked by the Chief Representative to assist him and a Mozambican official in recording the departure of named persons. I recall one of them calling out 'Ghebuza' (the *nom de guerre* of Siphiwe Nyanda) only to find someone else boarding the plane. Several of the senior comrades, including Ghebuza, moved clandestinely to Swaziland, where the regime, in collaboration with the Swazi police, tracked a number of them down.

Despite the Nkomati Accord, the war of destabilisation in Mozambique continued unabated, and in fact spread to parts of the country previously less affected. In August or September 1985 – a little more than a year after the signature of what was supposed to be a formal and binding agreement – Frelimo government forces captured a Renamo base at Gorongosa in Sofala province and discovered there a diary kept by Joaquim Vaz, the secretary to Renamo leader Afonso Dhlakama. The diary recorded instances of continued shipments by the apartheid regime of arms and materiel, as well as high-level clandestine visits to the base by senior military and political figures – including the Botha regime's Deputy Foreign Minister, Louis Nel. At the press conference where these diaries were made public, Mozambican Security Minister Sérgio Vieira said that they recorded more than violations of the Nkomati Accord. They pointed to a decision 'taken at the moment of signing the agreement, not to observe it, but to maintain a climate of instability and war in the area'.[9]

One of those who were allowed to remain in Mozambique after Nkomati was the then aged and ailing General Secretary of the SACP, Moses Mabhida. He died in Maputo in March 1986, a few months after the discovery of the Vaz diaries. The Frelimo government accorded him what was virtually a state funeral. ANC President Oliver Tambo and the incoming SACP General Secretary, Joe Slovo, both attended. A saying doing the rounds at the time was that there were two burials that day – one of Moses Mabhida, the other of the Nkomati Accord.

The death of Ruth First in 1982 coincided with the end of the period when research field trips to rural areas were still possible. The security situation quite simply made these no longer feasible. Besides, the issue of the day had become the war of destabilisation, with understanding the machinations of the apartheid regime now a priority. Within the CEA, I was appointed to head a unit focusing on this issue. Our team included, at various times, Dan O'Meara, a major analyst of the National Party, Sipho Dlamini, the *nom de guerre* of ANC deployee Attie Tshabalala, Thomas Ohlson from Sweden (who produced, in my view, one of the best analyses of the military dimensions of the battle of Cuito Cuanavale[10]) and Gottfried Welmer from West Germany. Among our publications was the two-volume reference work *The Struggle for South Africa*[11] and regular 'dossiers' on developments in the region. Our work involved analysing trends in the struggle for South Africa and their implications for both Mozambique and the ANC. One time I recall our deciding, on the basis of commentary and threats from members of the apartheid regime, that a raid was imminent. We warned our bosses in both Mozambique and the ANC. Precautions were duly instituted. We were both right and wrong. Right because there was a raid within days. Wrong because it struck Maseru, not Maputo.

During the battle of Cuito Cuanavale, I was invited to several discussions with the Cuban ambassador. He wanted to know whether the apartheid regime could be trusted in negotiations. The view I expressed in a number of papers, which I was told were read at the highest levels in Havana, was that it would be objective conditions on the ground that would oblige the apartheid regime to negotiate, and that it would be prudent to be wary of subjective expressions by members of a regime whose track record was one of backtracking and betrayal, not least over the Nkomati Accord. At about this time I also became a commentator on developments in South Africa on Mozambican television

Towards the end of my time at the CEA, we began thinking about how the southern African region might be reconstructed after the end of apartheid. Our centre developed a joint research project with the Fernand Braudel Center for the Study of Economies, Historical Systems, and Civilizations at the State University of New York at Binghamton. The Braudel Center was headed by a major world systems theorist, Immanuel Wallerstein. Our initial thinking was published in a volume entitled *How Fast the Wind: Southern Africa 1975–2000.*[12]

After the unbanning of the ANC and SACP in February 1990, those of us in exile began to think about going home. In July 1990 Nelson Mandela visited Maputo. He was accorded the honours normally reserved for a head of state, even though he was at that point not even president of the ANC. The exile community held a small birthday commemoration for him on the morning he left (18 July). Mandela told the exile community that he was working to ensure our return. Around this time, I handed in my three months' notice to the CEA, and one evening there was a small party at our house. A few members of ANC security called round. I thought they were coming to join us, but they asked to talk to me privately. They told me they had information that I was next on the apartheid regime's assassination list. The February unbanning had

41

*With the ANC community of Maputo, welcoming Nelson Mandela
at an official ceremony in July 1990.*

*Bidding Madiba farewell: my daughter Ellen (then five) and son Joe (then eight)
are behind the first flag on the left. I am standing on the right – minus beard in an
attempt to look less recognisable to the CCB.*

not, of course, ended extra-judicial murders by the regime's agents, and there were several incidents inside the country. In April 1990 some of us were in Harare for an economic policy meeting. One evening we heard a loud boom from our hotel, and found out later that it was the letter bomb sent to Father Michael Lapsley, who lost both his hands and an eye.

Strange as it may seem, my first reaction was to be grateful for the warning. All of us in the ANC community knew in a general way that we could be a target at any time and had responded to earlier alerts by sleeping away from home and increasing vigilance. By 1988–1989 we had also begun to hear that apartheid operatives had calculated that if they could eliminate 3 000 ANC members inside and outside the country, their 'ANC problem' would disappear. The stepped-up wave of assassinations in that period seemed to be an attempt to act on this proposition. For about three weeks after receiving my warning, I made sure that everywhere I went I took a bag containing the Scorpion submachine pistol and 29 rounds of ammunition given to me by the ANC for personal protection.

Then, finally, the newspaper *Vrye Weekblad* published the story.[13] They had obtained access to an authentic Civil Cooperation Bureau (CCB) death dossier, and for some reason it was the one compiled on me. The CCB was a notorious apartheid hit squad responsible for numerous assassinations both in South Africa and outside. The dossier gave me a 'subject number' of S1/8362, and contained a biography, some of it correct and some not, together with a justification for targeting me. The latter included my commentaries on Mozambican TV along with work it identified, partly rightly and partly wrongly, as having been carried out for the ANC. Three methods of 'eliminating the subject' were then identified, any of which could have succeeded but two of which would also have cost the lives of my minor children. I sometimes joked thereafter that I was a beneficiary of corruption in the state. 'What did you do?' was the general retort. The answer was I did nothing. But the CCB

The dossier compiled on me by the CCB included photos of my Volkswagen Beetle, and of my family and home in Maputo. This photo from the dossier appeared in Jacques Pauw's book In the Heart of the Whore.

dossier recorded that there was a dispute over funds between the Maputo/Swaziland unit and head office, which led to the suspension of the former's projects. Corruption within the CCB, it seems, probably saved my life. Finding out that the threat was historical rather than current was a great relief, and within months I was back in South Africa after 19 years in exile.

4

The changing global context

The changing global context had a major impact both on the transition from apartheid to a democratic constitutional order and on the economic policy choices made thereafter. There were, in fact, two separate but related processes that shaped the context for developments in the 1990s. The first was the collapse of the Soviet Union and Eastern European socialism, and the second was the processes described as 'globalisation'.

The collapse of the Soviet Union in 1991 was preceded by the election of Mikhail Gorbachev as General Secretary of the Communist Party of the Soviet Union (CPSU) in 1985. Gorbachev was well known for developing two new concepts as integral parts of his reform programme: glasnost (openness) and perestroika (restructuring).[1] Many socialists and communists around the world initially welcomed Gorbachev's policies as potentially breathing fresh life into Soviet socialism. However, after a few years it became apparent that the Soviet Union was losing out in a number of areas of competition with the West and that Gorbachev's programmes, while opening up debate, actually had no real answers to the challenges facing the Union of Soviet Socialist Republics (USSR). Among other things it was clear that the Soviet Union was potentially vulnerable to a new arms race, particularly one involving the high-tech, space-based weapons the Reagan administration seemed determined to deploy. Underlying this, as Manuel Castells later argued,[2] was the fact that the Soviet Union was far behind in the development of information and communications technology (ICT). I visited Moscow's Museum of Economic Achievements on several occasions in the 1980s and always left amazed at the Soviet Union's prowess in heavy engineering and rocket technology. But Soviet computers, even to the non-specialist eye, were large and clumsy compared to Western alternatives. Even Soviet televisions were set in large thick boxes. As Castells argued, the Soviet Union had failed to master the technologies of miniaturisation, as well as failing to develop comparable ICT.

Among other things, the policies of glasnost and perestroika sought to replace outright confrontation or competition with the West with new initiatives. These were to include applying new thinking aimed at finding political solutions to long-standing regional conflicts, including exploring new ideas and approaches to the conflicts in South and southern Africa. Immediately and directly, it meant that the Soviet Union was no longer willing, unlike Cuba, to risk serious confrontation with the West over issues in southern Africa. Dr Victor Goncharov, Deputy Director of the Institute of African Studies of the USSR Academy of Sciences, told a conference in Harare in 1987 that seeing the struggle in South Africa as a proxy for Cold War conflict between the United States and the USSR was a myth perpetuated by the apartheid regime. The Soviet Union, in fact, had 'minimal interests' in southern Africa, and while it would continue to support the 'forces of national liberation', it would henceforth encourage a negotiated settlement that would require 'real compromise'.[3]

In this climate, some researchers at the Institute of African Studies in Moscow began to go even further, to the point of questioning the role and significance of the ANC and SACP in bringing about 'change' in South Africa. While old friends and comrades, such as Vladimir Shubin of the CPSU and Slava Tetiokin of the Friendship Association, remained staunch in recognising the centrality of the national liberation movement, we soon encountered a new generation of researchers who were unpacking everything and showing a distinct inclination to fundamentally challenge every previously established position. This included an inclination, at least implicitly, to see the ANC as out of touch with reality on the ground in South Africa and no longer a major factor. For some of those with this inclination, 'change' was rather seen as more likely to emerge from the interactions of '*verligtes*' (those with enlightened views) in the regime with 'reformist groupings' within the black population.

I once attended a seminar in Moscow, together with Pallo Jordan, organised by this generation of researchers. A week earlier, the Institute of African Studies had received their first visit from someone connected with the apartheid regime – Philip Nel, director of the Institute for Soviet Studies at the University of Stellenbosch. Nel had apparently boasted to his hosts that he had ties to the regime's National Intelligence Service (NIS) and presented them with some version of the thesis outlined above. We encountered a number of the young researchers at the Institute, still wide-eyed and clearly believing that they had better first-hand information about the situation in South Africa than we did and, more importantly, being inclined to believe in the ANC's marginality.

A few months earlier, in December 1986, Albie Sachs, Alpheus Manghezi and I travelled to Kazakhstan on behalf of the ANC. We were invited to Kazakhstan because it was there that the first explicitly ethnic protest had occurred in the Soviet Union. Kazakhs were at the time the largest component of the population of the republic, but they were not the majority. Other nationalities – Russians, Germans and others – together made up a larger number. During our visit, we were told frankly that ethnic Kazakhs were underrepresented in all areas of economic and social life. Only in the Communist Party structures were they numerically dominant. When Gorbachev removed the Kazakh party secretary after allegations of corruption, he installed an ethnic Russian in his place. This sparked ethnic mobilisation and protest. The message conveyed to us, perhaps surprisingly (given that you could read into this example a strong case for 'affirmative action'), was that the ANC needed to realise that racial and ethnic identity mattered, and that we needed to find a model that would accommodate the demands of ethnic minorities. Some of the young researchers at the Institute were indeed flirting with ideas that were remarkably close to the notions of 'consociational democracy' (racial bloc representation) then in vogue in conservative circles in South Africa. Interestingly, hardly any of those promoting these ideas stayed in Russia after the collapse of the Soviet Union.

The weaknesses of perestroika became evident within a few years. Far from strengthening socialism or communism, the lack of a strategy to take the socialist project forward meant that it unleashed forces whose aim in the end was to undo socialism. In August 1991 a messy attempted coup against Gorbachev was resisted by the then leader of the Russian Federation, Boris Yeltsin. Gorbachev was restored to power but only briefly. At the end of the year he agreed formally to dissolve the USSR, which within weeks joined other Eastern European socialist countries in becoming a 'former' socialist country, and indeed, in its case, also a former union of republics.

Joe Slovo, then General Secretary of the SACP, argued, in an article entitled 'Has Socialism Failed?',[4] that what had failed in Eastern Europe was not socialism per se but the 'socialism' of the one-party state, and of party elites distancing themselves from the people. But from the right, many more triumphalist voices emerged. Francis Fukuyama coined the phrase 'the end of history' to describe the failure of Soviet-style socialism and the triumph of liberal capitalism.[5] Fukuyama meant this in a Hegelian sense of the term. The 'history' that had ended was the clash between systemic alternatives, and liberal capitalism had emerged as the highest form of civilisation. Fukuyama visited South Africa just before 1994, one of the never-ending stream of voices of capitalist triumphalism to do so.

The end of the Cold War had multiple effects on the transition in South and southern Africa. FW de Klerk specifically cited it as a reason why he had been willing to unban the liberation organisations, including the SACP, and to release Nelson Mandela from prison. But it also meant, at least until the rise of China and the formation of groups such as BRICS (Brazil, Russia, India, China, South Africa), that developing countries, including South Africa, had no alternative bloc they could relate to in structuring trade and investment relations. This added to the sense that 'there is no alternative' (TINA), actively promoted as what was called 'globalisation' began to shape the world economy.

The United Nations Development Programme (UNDP) argued in its 1997 *Human Development Report* that the term 'globalisation' was in reality 'both a description and a prescription'.[6] As a description, the term referred to a series of interconnected, profound changes taking place in the world economy from the mid-1980s onwards. These included:[7]

- the rise to dominance of transnational capital and the creation of a system of economic activities in which state territories and frontiers were no longer the basic framework for economic activity, but were often complicating factors;
- the rise, facilitated by the emergence of ICT, of what Manuel Castells[8] called 'globally networked' capitalism – allowing the organisation and coordination of production, finance and distribution on an increasingly global scale;
- financialisation, in which financial sectors and new financial 'products' (derivatives, securities and futures) mushroomed in ICT-driven trading across national borders.

These objective developments in the modus operandi of globalised capital were accompanied by what the UNDP called a 'prescription':

The prescription is to liberalise national and global markets in the belief that free flows of trade, finance and information will produce the best outcome and growth for human welfare. All this is presented with an air of inevitability and overwhelming conviction. Not since the heyday of free trade in the 19th century has economic theory elicited such certainty.[9]

Governments around the world were persuaded to respond to these changes by allowing the 'free movement' of capital and goods (but notably not of labour) across national borders. Implementing only 'light touch' regulation of new products and processes, particularly those linked to financialisation, was also part of a broader set of recommendations for states to withdraw from 'distorting markets'. This doctrine, known as neoliberalism, or by its adherents as the 'Washington Consensus', was pushed by rules and conditionalities imposed by organisations such as the IMF, World Bank and World Trade Organization (WTO).

Both of these processes impacted significantly on South Africa's transition. As indicated above, Gorbachev's perestroika policies reinforced the momentum towards negotiations, while the later collapse of Eastern European socialist regimes, and eventually of the Soviet Union itself, persuaded FW de Klerk to go further than he might otherwise have done in unbanning proscribed organisations and releasing political prisoners. At the same time, the onset of globalisation, accompanied by a neoliberal policy prescription promoted 'with an air of inevitability and overwhelming conviction', impacted significantly on policy debates both in the period of transition and after the installation of South Africa's first democratically elected administration.

5

Economic policy in the transition to democracy

The ANC's serious engagement on economic policy development began in exile only in the 1980s with the revival of the Economic Policy Committee, headed by Max Sisulu, who later became Speaker of the National Assembly. Sisulu invited a number of ANC members seen to have some economics background to meetings aimed at generating economic policy for a future ANC government. Vella Pillay, who was based in London, worked for a Chinese bank and later coordinated the Macro-Economic Research Group (MERG), was a prominent member of this team. Tito Mboweni, who later became Reserve Bank Governor and Finance Minister, joined the EPC as a nominee of the Political Committee. I was also one of the regular participants in EPC work. The EPC was overseen by NEC member Sindiso Mfenyana, later Secretary to Parliament.

At the start, the EPC grappled with a critical question: how to restructure the economy of a post-apartheid South Africa in such a way that it would be able to deliver redress to the oppressed majority, and to address backlogs in the delivery of a range of public services. The focus in such early formulations could be described as 'redistribution'. They emerged also in a context where the Freedom Charter was recognised as the overarching policy vision for a National Democratic Revolution in South Africa. Among other things, the Freedom Charter called for the transfer of mines and monopoly industry to the ownership of the people as a whole. While there was some debate on the meaning of this, the general assumption was that there would be a strengthening of state involvement in a 'mixed economy'.

Towards the end of our time in exile, the EPC was drawn into a number of engagements with (white) business groupings then travelling to meet the ANC in exile. These delegations tended to argue in favour of policies that prioritised raising GDP growth, arguing that this was essential to obtain the resources necessary for redistribution. Based on these conflicting propositions, the economic policy debate became focused on the relationship between redistribution and growth.

Inside the country, meanwhile, the Congress of South African Trade Unions (Cosatu) commissioned a team of economists, in what was called its Industrial Trends Group, to produce an 'industrial strategy' proposal.[1] The Industrial Strategy Project (ISP) critiqued the performance of the 'inward industrialisation' approach of the apartheid regime and called instead for a more export-orientated approach along the lines of the South Korean model. It also noted that most initiatives by the apartheid regime had supported heavy and capital-intensive sub-sectors. The ISP called instead for a greater focus on more labour-intensive downstream activities. It recommended that as far as possible an industrial strategy work 'with' rather than 'against' markets and that policy emphasise raising productivity. Among the directions highlighted for future industrialisation were mineral beneficiation (adding more value to mineral products before export) and creating more opportunities for empowerment.

It was in this context that the ideas of neoliberalism or the Washington Consensus began to be inserted, particularly in the period between the unbanning of proscribed organisations in 1990 and the 1994 democratic elections. The period, in fact, saw a major exercise in 'opinion forming' by proponents of neoliberalism. The World Bank and IMF both started engaging individuals perceived as actual or potential ANC advisers. One conduit for this was Geoff Lamb, who had been detained as an SACP activist in the 1960s but by the 1990s was working for the World Bank. He re-established connections with influential leaders in the movement and used these to identify cadres to be taken to the Bank for 'training'. The years between 1990 and 1994 saw many conferences and seminars on economic policy options for South Africa after apartheid, many of them attended by 'international experts' peddling neoliberal views. Several of the biggest names of the Washington Consensus visited South Africa and participated in these events. They included John Williamson, who coined the phrase 'Washington Consensus', Francis Fukuyama and practically every conceivable international expert. The advice proffered was unidirectional: macroeconomic policy reform was the 'royal road' to economic growth and prosperity. This required prioritising the cutting of the budget deficit to less than three per cent of GDP, cutting inflation to single-digit levels and instituting widespread tariff liberalisation (to integrate South Africa into the globalising world economy). In addition, the Reserve Bank needed to be independent and focus laser-like on holding down inflation, the state needed to withdraw from market- and price-distorting interventions, and privatisation rather than nationalisation needed to shape policy. A sign of the times was that one of the very few international engagements that went sour on ANC president Nelson Mandela was his input at the World Economic Forum in Davos in 1992. In his presentation, Mandela announced that the Freedom Charter would be the basis of the economic policy of an ANC government and that this required 'transferring to the ownership of the people as a whole' the banks, mines and monopoly industry.

One outcome of this neoliberal opinion forming was that macroeconomic policy came to be seen as the fundamental focus of future policy and a major lacuna in existing policy positions. Economic modelling accordingly became a preoccupation, particularly as the state had its own Normative Economic Model, often cited to call for budget deficit reductions as a priority. Eventually, the ANC marshalled its forces behind the MERG project. Virtually every ANC-aligned economist worked alongside a team of supportive international economists on the MERG, whose director was Vella Pillay.

The name MERG reflected a reality. In the dominant discourse of the time, the 'real issues' of economic policy were held to be matters of macroeconomic management and/or reform, not issues of empowerment, redistribution or even industrial policy (then held by neoliberalism to be anathema). But the name did not reflect the full scope of the report it published in 1993.[2] The MERG report, *Making Democracy Work: A Framework for Macroeconomic Policy in South Africa*, made many recommendations of a sectoral and institutional nature – including recommending an industrial policy, as well as developing a model and proposed trajectory for economic development.

The MERG spoke of different phases of growth. The first would be driven by consumption and redistribution, which MERG argued could achieve five per cent growth in a few years. This would then be followed by an investment-driven growth phase. The MERG also proposed that private shareholding in the SARB be ended, and that a fully state-owned Reserve Bank should derive its mandate from an elected government. It proposed a 'managed float' or 'crawling peg' system of exchange rate management. This would involve the central bank setting the exchange rate but doing this in such a way that it was informed by the direction of defined variables, such as inflation, and also targeted a competitive exchange rate to support industrial policy. It argued in favour of a relatively flexible approach to fiscal policy, and that the state should become an active player in a mixed economy. Several of these ideas were notably outside the parameters of the Washington Consensus. For example, the MERG did not embrace the idea that central banks had to be 'independent' bodies pursuing narrow inflation-targeting policies. The idea that exchange rates should be market-determined, that fiscal policy should prioritise ensuring that deficits remained below three per cent of GDP, and that privatisation should be widely implemented were also all key planks of the Washington Consensus that did not find an echo in the MERG.

I was tasked, together with my colleagues at the University of the Western Cape, with preparing an input on regional economic relations for the MERG. The main report itself included a very short section on this topic[3] but we prepared a longer document as part of the MERG work.[4] This essentially argued in favour of a democratic South Africa becoming part of organisations such as SADCC (as it then was) and adopting a developmental approach to regional integration.[5] As indicated earlier, I had also co-authored a study for SADCC on how that organisation should approach potential South African membership. These ideas were not very controversial within the ANC, which was clear throughout that a democratic South Africa would seek to affiliate to the then OAU and existing regional economic communities (RECs). However, towards the end of the transition period, I was deployed by the ANC to serve on a subcommittee of the Transitional Executive Council dealing with this matter. The Transitional Executive Council was a joint decision-making body dealing with strategic issues in the period just ahead of the 1994 elections. My counterpart from the National Party and the De Klerk government was Theo Alant, then Deputy Minister of Finance. In the course of this work, we encountered alternative proposals emanating from the outgoing regime. These suggested that South Africa should not seek early membership of RECs, but rather build on its leverage over SACU to underpin an essentially mercantilist negotiation with other bodies. In the end we managed to steer the subcommittee away from such notions.

The MERG report received a frosty reception from neoliberal quarters when it was eventually released. It was never presented to the NEC or any other structure of the ANC for adoption. Instead it was quietly shelved.

In 1992 the ANC adopted a document entitled 'Ready to Govern'.[6] This was a comprehensive indication of the incoming government's likely policy agenda, across the entire scope of government. It included a section on economic policy that focused largely on matters of redistribution and 'affirmative action' and was largely silent on macroeconomic policy issues.

On the eve of the transition, the ANC and its alliance partners adopted what became its flagship election programme, the RDP.[7] This was built on a number of pillars, which included meeting basic needs, developing human resources, building the economy and democratising the state and society. A central argument was that 'reconstruction' and 'development' were parts of an integrated process. This was contrasted with views that saw reconstruction and development as mutually incompatible, with each component being a deduction from the other. The RDP said that economic growth was, of course, desirable but argued that questions of sustainability and distribution of benefits were also critical. The key link between reconstruction and development was to be an infrastructure build programme, focusing on electricity roll-out, water, telecommunications, transport, health and education.

6

Political and social transformation, 1994–1999

The democratic breakthrough in South Africa was a remarkable process by any standard. The election held on 27 April 1994 saw millions of previously disenfranchised people queuing to cast their ballots. Despite threats of disruption and violence, the election passed off peacefully. A new non-racial Parliament was duly sworn in and one of its first tasks was to elect a new president. Nelson Mandela became South Africa's first black president elected through a non-racial electoral process. His inauguration was attended by a panoply of international dignitaries, who heard him solemnly declare, 'Never, never and never again' would South Africa be a racist pariah.[1]

I was rather surprised when my ANC branch nominated me for the National Assembly. I did not imagine that I would be placed on the list in an electable position. I was, in fact, the last ANC nominee on the Western Cape province-to-national list to make the cut and be elected as a Member of Parliament (MP) in 1994. Right behind me on that list was Bulelani Ngcuka, who was not elected and was instead deployed to the Senate (which became the National Council of Provinces in 1997) before becoming head of the National Prosecuting Authority (NPA). In the National Assembly, I was drawn into the portfolio committees on Finance, Foreign Affairs, and Trade and Industry.

The first two years saw the new Parliament doubling up as an elected Constitutional Assembly. The constitution-making process involved a high level of public participation and outreach, but it was also bound by the constitutional principles agreed before the election, as well as being influenced by the content of the negotiated

Interim Constitution. The big issues in the Constitution were the Bill of Rights and the balance between spheres of government – national, provincial and local.

The Bill of Rights provided substantive equality for all citizens and proscribed unfair discrimination based on race, gender and other similar grounds. It entrenched 'second generation' rights, such as the rights of communities to participate in development, as well as more conventional 'first generation' individual rights. The Constitution was justiciable, meaning that citizens or communities were empowered to approach the courts to require public authorities to show that they were making 'reasonable' efforts to develop programmes to address their needs. Workers were constitutionally guaranteed the right to organise and engage in collective bargaining. The 'right to life' clause was entrenched in a Table of Non-Derogable Rights that were unalterable unless approved by a special majority in Parliament and authorised by the Constitutional Court.[2] This clause effectively proscribed the death penalty. The so-called property clause, required as one of the constitutional principles, was hard fought in the Constitutional Assembly. The final text provided that property could only be expropriated through a law of general application and on payment of 'just and equitable' compensation. The assessment of what was just and equitable would take account of a number of factors weighed together, including market value, how the property was acquired and the extent of any improvements. An overriding provision said that nothing could be interpreted as preventing government from addressing redress and land reform.

With regard to provisions on the functions of the different spheres of government, the ambition by the National Party, Inkatha Freedom Party (IFP) and other smaller parties was for a higher degree of quasi-federalism than that favoured by the ANC. This was because these parties saw greater prospects for themselves in participating in government at sub-national rather than national level. In the

Constitutional Assembly, they pushed for relatively strong provincial governments and wider exclusive powers for provinces than was favoured by the ANC, which preferred stronger national and local government. A separate independent commission had established that there would be nine provinces. The eventual constitutional outcome was that they would each have their own elected legislatures and an executive headed by a leader with the title of premier rather than prime minister. Provinces had exclusive legislative competence in a few areas and concurrent legislative competence (with national government) in others. They had limited powers to raise their own revenue, but along with municipalities were constitutionally guaranteed an 'equitable share' of revenue raised nationally. A National Council of Provinces elected by provincial legislatures was established as a second chamber of Parliament, and all three spheres were required to follow principles of cooperative governance as defined in Chapter 3 of the Constitution – meaning respecting each other's constitutional status while cooperating with each other in mutual trust.

Within the Constitutional Assembly, I was deployed to chair a subcommittee that dealt with provisions on budgeting and economic institutions.[3] The most challenging issue in this subcommittee were the provisions on the SARB.[4] A constitutional principle required that the Bank be independent. Our subcommittee explored options of providing it with operational independence within a policy framework set by the government, along the lines proposed by the MERG. This provoked a massive backlash from proponents of the prevailing neoliberal orthodoxy, which at the time favoured central banks' having a high level of both goal and operational independence. Anecdotes about how the SARB had been prevailed upon by the apartheid regime to lower interest rates just before elections were cited to support this position. I recall being asked by a journalist to comment on a staunch defence of such a position by the then Reserve Bank Governor, Chris Stals, who was also the last Governor appointed by the apartheid regime. I made some throwaway comment to the effect that Mandy Rice-Davies' famous remark, 'Well he would, wouldn't he?' came to mind. To my surprise this became the story in some of the newspapers, leading one to comment that actually the matter of Reserve Bank independence was a matter of relativity. If someone like Stals was in charge you would want the Bank to be as independent as possible, but if a decision were ever taken to appoint as Governor someone like Rob Davies, you would want to ensure that the Bank was under firm Treasury control.

Sensing little appetite for a major fight on this issue, we eventually settled on a compromise formulation that required the Bank to act 'in the interest of balanced and sustainable economic growth' and engage in regular 'consultation' with the Finance Minister as it preserved its operational independence to defend 'the value of the currency'.[5] I remain convinced that this constitutional formulation provides sufficient space for the SARB to pursue a developmental monetary policy. This view was reinforced in 2005, when I had the opportunity to visit New Zealand on a study tour by the National Assembly's Finance Portfolio Committee. The New Zealand central bank had a legislative mandate to act in the interests of promoting full employment, but at the time argued that high inflation was bad for employment, which in practice led it to pursue narrow inflation targeting. From this experience, I concluded that the central issue was not the constitutional provision but the ongoing mandating process arising from the consultation with the Minister of Finance. It was this that led to the setting of the three to six per cent inflation target upon which, in its early years, the SARB maintained its focus, regardless of all other factors. This approach was graphically exemplified by Stals's response to a question posed by an MP during a meeting of the Finance Portfolio Committee. When asked what he thought of the RDP, Stals responded by saying he was like the fellow who went on holiday to Durban. When someone asked him, 'Aren't you worried about the sharks in the sea?', he replied, 'I have a deal with the sharks. I don't go into the sea. They don't come into the bar.'

The Constitution was finally approved in 1996, with the support of most parties represented in Parliament. It was widely hailed as a ground-breaking advance in constitutional jurisprudence second to none in the world. Democratic South Africa under the presidency of Nelson Mandela was much courted internationally. State visitors included the President of the United States, Queen Elizabeth II, many European Union (EU) heads of state and government, the Prime Minister of India and many leaders from the African continent. Democratic South Africa joined the OAU (later the African Union, AU), SADC, the Commonwealth, the African, Caribbean and Pacific (ACP) Group of States and a host of other international organisations.

What took a little longer was normalisation of relations with the People's Republic of China. Apartheid South Africa had recognised the Kuomintang regime on Taiwan as the 'government of China'. In the run-up to the 1994 elections and for some years thereafter there was still a Taiwanese embassy in South Africa. It undertook a major lobbying effort to persuade the ANC to allow it to retain that status, promising all sorts of economic cooperation in return. Had they succeeded, they would have achieved a major diplomatic victory over Beijing. President Mandela wanted to establish diplomatic relations with the People's Republic, but wanted also to maintain official ties with Taiwan – particularly as Taiwan had donated money to the ANC to support the 1994 election campaign. At the time, South Africa's trade and investment relations were roughly divided evenly between what some called the three Chinas (People's Republic, Taiwan and Hong Kong), and that was also cited to support this proposition. I was a backbench MP serving on the Foreign Affairs Portfolio Committee at the time, vocal in support of recognising Beijing and aware that the 'one China policy' was a deeply entrenched matter of principle to the People's Republic of China and something they would not compromise on. I was invited with a few other members of the committee to a discussion with President Mandela at his official residence in Cape Town. I had never been to a presidential residence before, and was even more bowled over when it was President Mandela himself who poured our tea. The President told us he would send an exploratory mission to identify options. When it returned advising that Beijing was firm on the 'one China policy', diplomatic relations were finally established in 1996.

The removal of legal racial discrimination and application of affirmative action led to quite rapid changes in the demography of government departments and agencies. Black South Africans began to take leadership positions denied to them in the past, not at a pace proportional to the overall national demographics but at least sufficient to establish that a new reality had become implanted in the country. Capable black persons began to shine in an ever-increasing number of activities. On the surface, the social order of racial separation put in place by apartheid evaporated remarkably quickly. Words such as 'miracle' became attached to descriptions of the transition and South Africa started to be called the 'rainbow nation'.

Underneath this, however, was a dialectic of continuity and fairly profound change in class structure and class relations. Within capital, white-owned monopolies and oligopolies continued to own and control the vast majority of the means of production, but they nevertheless underwent important changes. Apartheid had left a legacy of a high level of concentration and centralisation of capital. Not only were large parts of each sector controlled by very few firms (exhibiting exceptionally high levels of monopolistic control by international standards) but large domestic conglomerates had sprung up, operating across multiple sectors. Companies that began their operations in mining had acquired banking, manufacturing and service interests. Banks had acquired mines, manufacturing interests, and so on. This was partly a consequence of sanctions and economic isolation, which prevented these companies from expanding internationally and drove them therefore to pursue instead conglomeration inside South Africa. Anglo American stood at the head of the biggest conglomerate, but others were headed by companies such as South African Mutual (Old Mutual), Barlow Rand and Sanlam. Even other large companies, such as South African Breweries, were part of one or other of these conglomerates (in this case the Anglo stable).

As we shall see in Chapter 7, the period after 1994 saw these conglomerates rapidly restructuring themselves to focus on a 'core business' and disposing of other components of their portfolio. This was very much in line with the conventional wisdom of the time. Several then went further to take advantage of the new opportunities created by the ending of the country's pariah status by internationalising their operations. Eventually, a few decided to take the next step of attempting to turn themselves into transnational corporations with headquarters located in financial centres offshore. This was achieved by persuading financial regulators to permit offshore share listings, 'justifying' this as a move to enable them to raise capital more cheaply, including to support their operations in South Africa.

Also within the bourgeoisie, this period saw the emergence of a small but influential stratum of black capitalists. Until the passage of an Act in 2003, black economic empowerment (BEE) was more of a general policy thrust than an actual government programme. Companies were urged to embrace empowerment and often lauded if they could argue that they had done so. BEE conceived as in any way 'broad-based' proceeded painfully slowly. Employment equity reports showed that leadership positions in the economy as a whole, and particularly in the private sector, remained overwhelmingly a white male preserve. But the period did see several high-profile 'BEE deals', which usually involved lending money for the purchase of shares at a discounted price to a small number of individuals, who were then expected to be the empowerment face of the enterprise concerned. The small emergent black capitalist class, supported by a slightly larger number of middle-class professionals, became an increasingly influential voice, generally calling for more support by way of making available state tenders and resources, as well as for a short time also favouring privatisation of state assets. Few within this stratum acquired much by way of sector-specific acumen, usually being business generalists. At the extreme, some became what were later known as 'tenderpreneurs', seeking nothing more than access to a government tender, which once obtained would be outsourced to usually a white company to carry out the work after charging a premium price.

On the side of the masses, workers in employment received stronger rights to organise and engage in collective bargaining under the Constitution and the Labour Relations Act 66 of 1995 (and as amended). But this did not translate into either higher average real wages or a larger proportional share of wages in national income. This was largely the result of the import of global trends associated with capital restructuring. The focus on restructuring around 'core business' led to the outsourcing and casualisation of many jobs, not just in profit-making firms but also in institutions such as hospitals and universities. At the same time, rapid tariff liberalisation undermined the stability of employment in a number of sectors, affecting the bargaining environment and the ability of unions to raise wages.

Among the large unemployed surplus population, jobs were never created on a scale to significantly reduce the high level of unemployment. The delivery of new social security services, on an impressive scale, did at least mitigate some of the extreme effects of poverty on unemployed families. The final end of influx control also spawned significant urbanisation, meaning that the impoverished unemployed were now increasingly found in informal settlements around towns as well as in rural 'homelands'.

7

Economic policy in the first administration: From the RDP to GEAR

The first democratically elected government took office in 1994 with a commitment to implement the RDP. There was an enormous backlog in delivery of basic services to the majority of the population. Under apartheid these had either been virtually non-existent or provided on a racially discriminatory basis. The housing backlog was identified at 3 million units and 12 million people did not have access to clean drinking water, while 21 million did not have adequate sanitation and only 36 per cent of households were linked to the electricity grid.[1] Health services were provided differentially to the racial groups defined by apartheid. Education was likewise racially skewed, with a hugely inferior quality made available to black people in general, and to Africans in particular. The state pension and social security grants were similarly differentiated by racial category. The RDP envisaged a massive programme of delivery on all these service areas as top priority. The ANC-led Government of National Unity recognised that it had inherited a large budget deficit, meaning resource mobilisation was a challenge. One part of the answer to this was to promote a major reprioritisation of expenditure programmes. This began by requiring all departments to surrender a rising percentage of their budgets, starting with 2.5 per cent and increasing by a similar percentage each year, to an office operating under the Minister without Portfolio in the Presidency responsible for the RDP, Jay Naidoo. Naidoo's office then received bids from departments for allocation to RDP-aligned programmes. Another element was the development of a fairly successful programme of tax administration reform that brought in increasing amounts of tax revenue.

Whatever the official characterisation, there was a strong element of 'growth through redistribution' in the RDP thinking. The delivery of RDP houses (low-cost houses provided free to low-income people) was, for example, viewed as a way of providing poor people with an asset that could both stimulate demand for household consumer durables and create possibilities for raising loan capital to support small business development. Other programmes included a Small Business Strategy, resulting in the establishment of institutions to provide both financial and non-financial support to small, medium and micro enterprises (SMMEs).[2] An articulated policy direction, but not yet an explicitly designed programme, sought to promote BEE. This involved government generally indicating its support and encouragement for the private sector to promote BEE schemes. Most BEE deals at this time involved creating 'special purpose vehicles' to provide loan finance to selected individuals, enabling them to buy shares at discount prices in established firms.

During the first years of the new administration there were, in fact, quite significant advances in the delivery of basic services. Between 1994 and 1999, 721 813 RDP houses were built and delivered free of charge to poor households[3] and 2.5 million households were connected to the electricity grid – taking the percentage of households with access to electricity from 36 to 66 per cent[4] – while the number of households with access to piped water increased from 8.6 million to 10.8 million.[5] Despite these achievements, poverty, inequality and unemployment remained deeply entrenched,[6] as the impact of these measures on economic development fell far short of what may have been hoped for. Many recipients of RDP houses, for example, were unemployed and little able to use their new asset as a tool of economic self-upliftment. Besides, financial institutions showed little inclination to accept RDP houses (in what were still identified as 'red-lined' areas) as collateral for small business loans – despite being offered extensive government guarantees. Those that did get some income from their new asset did so through renting it out while they themselves continued to live in informal housing. Any rent money was most often used to support basic household consumption. The harsh realities of economic power, coupled with racially skewed unemployment and poverty, rendered remote the romantic ideas of Peruvian economist Hernando de Soto,[7] about how the distribution of assets to the poor could unleash a wave of entrepreneurial activity, in the concrete conditions of South Africa.

The negotiated political compromises of the transition were clearly intended to constrain, among other things, economic policy decisions. More than that, and in the face of considerable external pressure, the ANC decided that it would be prudent to allow the first Finance Minister appointed under the GNU to be the nominee of the National Party. The appointment of Derek Keys, who had also been Finance Minister in the outgoing De Klerk administration, was clearly intended to send a message of continuity to the markets. Even after Keys' early departure in 1995, he was replaced by a non-party technocrat, Chris Liebenberg, a former Nedbank CEO. Only in 1996, with Liebenberg's departure and the appointment of Trevor Manuel, was a Finance Minister drawn from the ranks of the majority party.

All of this pointed to the extreme sensitivity within the GNU to 'market sentiment'. Democratic South Africa in fact inherited one positive thing from the apartheid regime: there was no outstanding IMF or World Bank loan[8] that could be used to subject democratic South Africa to the type of conditionalities that had driven one developing country after another to adopt devastating structural adjustment programmes. As indicated in Chapter 5, the transitional period had seen a major effort at neoliberal opinion forming, involving conferences, training programmes offered to selected liberation-movement-aligned cadres, etc. But the real question for those forces, both domestic and international, seeking to promote neoliberal conformity was how to ensure that the South African government, once installed, would conform to the Washington Consensus. The mechanism that eventually emerged can be described as the 'market message'. What were perceived as negative movements in stock exchange prices, or more importantly in currency markets, were accompanied by a stream of commentary suggesting that the underlying causes were that government had lost the confidence of the markets and needed to act to rebuild it. Shortly after his appointment, Trevor Manuel made a passing remark about 'amorphous markets'. The pushback against this was intense, and Manuel became the subject of a howl of protest and ridicule, and was told that remarks like this would undermine his being taken seriously as Finance Minister. Manuel never repeated any such remark ever again.

The GNU had in fact inherited a sizeable, but not unsustainable, fiscal deficit. This had increased sharply in the last years of apartheid rule to reach a high point of 9.2 per cent of GDP by 1994.[9] The GNU set out with a programme progressively to cut the deficit by half a per cent a year, while simultaneously seeking to reprioritise spending using the mechanism of a compulsory surrender of defined percentages of budgets to the RDP office, as described above. By 1996 the pressure to go further had become intense. In March 1995 the GNU ended the pegged dual currency system (commercial rand and financial rand) in favour of a single floating exchange rate. The subsequent period saw a wave of depreciation episodes, with several devaluations occurring in 1996. Each of these events was accompanied by a market message arguing that the underlying reason was that markets did not have 'confidence' in the government. Commentator after commentator opined that this was because the ANC-led government lacked a 'credible' macroeconomic policy. At about the same time, the South African Foundation, which had been formed in the apartheid period to campaign against sanctions, was restructured to become a voice of big business. One of the Foundation's outputs at the time, entitled *Growth for All*, called for a tighter macroeconomic policy based on the canons of the Washington Consensus.[10] More specifically, it called for the deficit to be slashed to two per cent, for a substantial increase in value-added tax (VAT) with a cut in direct taxes, the introduction of a 'two-tier labour market' with lesser rights (particularly on matters of hiring and firing) for lower-paid, lower-skilled workers, and a 'brisk privatisation programme'.[11]

Underpinning all of this was the narrative of the Washington Consensus, which held that governments everywhere and at all times should focus on 'getting macro fundamentals right'. The influential commentator Thomas Friedman, much read at the time, argued that donning the 'golden straitjacket'[12] of neoliberal reform offered all countries and peoples a pathway to the riches offered by the hyper-globalising world (the world of the Lexus luxury car). Rejecting this would consign them to lower-value activities (the world of the olive tree). Key elements of the golden straitjacket would be macro-economic reforms that reduced budget deficits to below three per cent of GDP through expenditure cuts, and the aggressive use of interest rate policy to drive inflation down to single-digit levels. All of this was to be accompanied by a policy framework prioritising the 'de-s', among them deregulation and denationalisation, or privatisation of state assets. Absent from this type of framework was any real micro or sectoral policy, on the grounds that the role of government was simply to step aside and leave it to the market to 'get prices right'. Nobel economics laureate Joseph Stiglitz, in a trenchant critique, described this approach as a recipe for 'decommissioning' important policy tools and instead applying a simplistic 'ready reckoner' of predetermined targets for key macroeconomic variables without any substantial appreciation of underlying fundamentals of the real economies of individual countries.[13]

The above shaped the context within which, in 1996, the government adopted its Growth, Employment and Redistribution (GEAR) policy.[14] GEAR was prepared in great secrecy by a team assembled by the Finance Ministry. Trevor Manuel's biographer says that the name was chosen after the programme was developed, on the recommendation of the then Deputy Finance Minister, Gill Marcus.[15] The name belied its content. GEAR's essence was a series of macroeconomic adjustments, the main one being a commitment to cutting the budget deficit by one per cent each year (rather than the half a per cent per annum implemented up to then). Other 'contributions' included a commitment by the DTI to effect tariff reductions at a pace faster than required by the 1994 Marrakesh Agreement (which, because the apartheid regime had proclaimed for decades that the country was 'developed', were indeed tougher than those applicable to most comparable developing countries). Although presented as a plan to achieve six per cent growth and create 400 000 jobs, there was in fact no endogenous relationship between these outcomes and the macro adjustments that were the main content of the programme. I was invited to a briefing about a week before the public launch of GEAR and heard it explained by a Treasury official as a 'confidence trick'.

The model on which the growth and job outcomes were predicated presumed a significant exogenous rise in foreign direct investment (FDI). In other words, it was based on an assumption that foreign investors would 'like' the macro policy reforms and respond by pumping in significantly increased amounts of FDI – sufficient to achieve the growth and jobs targets. None of this, in fact, materialised. Gross fixed capital formation in the private sector hovered at around ten per cent of GDP between 1996 and 2003, while South Africa lagged behind several other African countries as a recipient of FDI. In the world of financialisation and 'increasing shareholder value', a large part of what did arrive was directed at supporting mergers and acquisitions.[16] The recovery in gross fixed capital formation recorded between 2000 and 2008 was, in fact, largely driven by the public sector, with a significant part being preparations for the 2010 FIFA World Cup.[17] GEAR, in short, appeared to confirm the experience of many other developing countries. Private capitalist investors, foreign or domestic, respond to perceived concrete profit-making opportunities in the real economy and not to macro-economic policy frameworks (even if they like them).

GEAR became a major point of contention within the ANC-SACP-Cosatu tripartite alliance, as well as a lodestone around which the different contending forces in the struggle over the direction of the NDR would mobilise for years to come. One of the immediate reasons for early discomfort was the way GEAR was developed, without prior consultation within any of the political structures of the alliance. When it was finally publicly released, all formations were taken by surprise. This included the ANC, which had shortly before issued a stinging rebuke of the South African Foundation's *Growth for All*.[18] The way GEAR was developed was, in fact, very much in line with the recommendations of proponents of the Washington Consensus at the time. 'Reform' was held to be a process that was susceptible to being blown off course by 'populist' pressures. The recommended role of 'reformist leadership' was thus not to consult with constituencies in advance, but rather to develop policy in narrow technocratic circles and then 'sell' it to the broader public.[19] GEAR's development had all of the hallmarks of this approach.

GEAR shaped government economic policies at least until the early 2000s. One immediate casualty was the closure of the RDP office. Reprioritisation, it was said, would from henceforth occur within the budget process and Jay Naidoo was redeployed to the Posts and Telecommunications Ministry. Although it was said that the RDP continued to remain 'in force', in practice it was GEAR that became the flagship programme, as the Finance Ministry progressively assumed hegemony over economic policy. Among other things, this transition meant abstaining from the development of any kind of overt industrial policy. Industrial policy was, of course, anathema to the Washington Consensus on the grounds that it involved governments 'distorting' market outcomes. The main thrust of programmes in the manufacturing sector instead became to use tariff reductions as a means of driving manufacturing companies to raise competitiveness.

The International Trade Administration Commission (ITAC), the body responsible for tariff setting, operated until 2009 on a tacit mandate that it could consider proposals to lower tariffs but never make any recommendation to raise tariffs, even if there was legal policy space to do so under South Africa's commitments to the World Trade Organization (WTO). Companies or industries seeking tariff support, or opposing tariff reductions, were demonised as 'rent-seekers' out of touch with a changing global reality.

A partial exception to this was in the motor industry. A significant local motor manufacturing industry had developed, driven by the apartheid regime's 'inward industrialisation' strategy. Under this, tariffs were raised to levels well over 100 per cent, with firms required to meet progressively increased levels of local content to qualify for this tariff protection. The industry that developed was orientated to the local market, and based on short production lines delivering multiple models to the local market at high cost. In 1993 President Mandela (not then President of the Republic) managed to secure a limited carve-out for the motor industry from the harsh tariff-cutting obligations applicable under the Marrakesh Agreement (which established the WTO), as well as for clothing and textiles. For good reason. The motor industry was one of the largest industrial sub-sectors, with strong forward and backward linkages to at least half a dozen other sub-sectors. The demise of the motor industry could indeed have had major implications.

In 1995 the GNU launched the Motor Industry Development Programme (MIDP). This was in fact a significant intervention. It sought, and managed to achieve, a significant change in production platforms. Rather than supporting the production at high cost of a large number of models destined exclusively for the domestic market, the MIDP sought to support production of a smaller number of models at a higher volume both for export and for the domestic market. The programme lowered the tariff rate to a still significant 25 per cent and provided substantial rebates and financial incentives against export performance. By 2013, when the MIDP was replaced by its successor, the Automotive Production and Development Programme (APDP), it had supported an increase in automotive production from 376 000 units in 1995 to 550 000 units in 2013, creating employment for 100 000 people, with a further 200 000 employed in the retail and repair sectors.[20]

In the case of clothing and textiles – the other sector benefiting from the policy space carved out by President Mandela – the story was much less positive. The programme developed for this sector was, like the motor programme, based on supporting export performance. But the circumstances in the clothing and textile sector were very different. While South African clothing products had achieved some level of export penetration, this was the era of the rise of China as a world-class producer and exporter of low-cost clothing and textiles.

From 1996, the phasing out of the Multi-Fibre Arrangement, which had governed world trade in textiles and garments since 1974, led to the decimation of domestic clothing production in one country after another as Chinese imports penetrated markets across the world. Defence against both legal and illegal import penetration into South Africa was weak. Applied tariffs were kept below the WTO bound rate, and efforts to combat illegal imports circumventing even those duties had little success. A study commissioned by the National Economic Development and Labour Council (Nedlac) found that there had been a discrepancy of 63 per cent in 2003 and 41 per cent in 2004 between the value of clothing exports to South Africa recorded by China and the amount recorded as imports by South African customs authorities, meaning that under-invoicing was rife.[21] The problem was exacerbated by the Duty Credit Certificate Scheme (DCCS) incentive that was developed at the time. Conceived as a way to reward export performance, the DCCS allowed firms to claim export credits that could be redeemed against duty-free imports. Although this was intended to encourage the acquisition of competitiveness-raising technology, most Duty Credit Certificates (DCCs) were in fact sold to clothing retailers, who used them instead to import finished products, adding to the challenge of surging imports. With the rise of small but significant clothing industries in other SACU countries (Lesotho and Eswatini) exporting to the USA under the African Growth and Opportunity Act (AGOA), these producers also earned DCCs, which they promptly redeemed by selling them to retailers in South Africa. For many years the industry was in free fall. Between 1996 and 2005, clothing and textile factories shed more than 85 000 jobs as total employment fell from 228 053 in March 1996 to 142 863 in March 2005.[22]

In agriculture, interventions over the first term of democratic government focused on tearing down the extensive support edifice that had been built up over the apartheid period for the benefit of exclusively white commercial farmers. This included withdrawing various subsidies and dismantling statutory control boards and marketing bodies, several of which had exercised regulatory powers, as well as channelling state funding to marketing and agro-processing cooperatives controlled by white commercial farmers. However, while tearing down the edifice of racially exclusive support commanded widespread approval as being consistent with the ethos of building a non-racial democracy, the fact is that it far outpaced any replacement with a genuine developmental programme for the sector. A cautious land restitution and land reform programme was launched, based de facto on 'willing buyer/willing seller' purchases by the state for transfer to beneficiaries, but by 2009 only around five per cent of arable land had been transferred to black beneficiaries.[23] Agricultural policy focused in a general way on offering some support to emerging small farmers and beneficiaries of land reform programmes, but again the impact was extremely modest.

As indicated earlier, GEAR shaped contestation on economic policy within the alliance for many years. On the one hand, the government and many in the ANC argued successively that GEAR was an essential underpinning of growth, and later that it was imperative to insulate the country against the disastrous consequences of potential over-indebtedness. On the other hand, the SACP and Cosatu consistently saw GEAR as inflicting unnecessary austerity. On reflection – I say this self-critically, having been one of the minor protagonists[24] – the entire debate was overdetermined by what could be called 'macro-economic fundamentalism'. By this I mean that perspectives on both sides of the debate were shaped by a priori positions on the extent to which keeping the budget deficit, debt-to-GDP ratio or inflation rate within the parameters of the prescripts of neoliberal orthodoxy were or were not priorities. What the SACP later called the '1996 class project' emphasised the need for macroeconomic discipline. Its antithesis, whether recognised or not, tended to be based on some form of vague neo-Keynesianism, arguing that deficit funding could be widened and this would be the path to higher levels of more inclusive growth. Largely missing from the debate at this time was any profound engagement with the constraints being imposed by the structural characteristics of the productive economy, the changes that were taking place in it and the kind of transformations that were therefore necessary at this level to move to a qualitatively different new growth path capable of addressing the triple challenges of unemployment, poverty and inequality. As we can see now, with the benefit of hindsight, the absence of such a perspective meant that most alternatives to GEAR posed at the time were unable to answer a fundamental question: what kind of macroeconomic policy (fiscal, monetary and trade policy) was required to support a shift onto such a new, qualitatively different developmental trajectory?

As indicated above, in the first and second terms of democratic government, significant progress was made on the delivery of basic services and rights. Housing, health care, electrification and water programmes were significant successes, and visibly changed the reality of South Africa permanently. But a fact now widely recognised is that these policy-driven political and social transformations far outpaced any corresponding transformations in the economic sphere.

This is not to say that the first phase of the NDR saw no structural changes in the South African political economy. The South African economy in fact underwent profound changes between 1994 and the mid-2000s, but these were driven largely by external factors – trends in the global economy. Some of these were changes common to many, if not all, economies at the time, trends driven by processes associated with globalisation and digitisation. These included the rise of financialisation. South Africa had a significant monopolised financial sector dating back to the early years of the emergence of the country as a mining economy. Globally integrated (at least to the City of London financial nexus) from the start, South Africa's emergent financial sector served primarily to channel foreign capital to support the emergence of South Africa as a semi-peripheral gold-mining economy. Over time, the financial sector became highly concentrated and centralised, maintaining strong links with foreign finance capital, even through the years of sanctions. The main changes in the South African financial sector were those associated with globalisation. The United Nations Conference on Trade and Development (UNCTAD) described these as follows:

> Banking stopped being boring during the financialised transition to a globalised world, and it also stopped serving the needs of the productive economy. The transformation of banking into a high-glamour, high-paid, globalised industry came with financial deregulation and a surge of cross-border capital flows. As a result of deregulation, retail banking activities blended with investment activities to create financial behemoths operating with an 'originate and distribute' business model whereby loans were securitised and a range of financial services boosted the rents they could earn. The resulting shift to packaging, repackaging

and trading existing assets created a system in which the bulk of transactions involved other financial institutions, predatory practices became acceptable and contagion effects were aggravated.[25]

Historian Robert Brenner[26] also identifies a major shift in the prevailing pattern of cross-border investments away from longer-term direct investments into short-term portfolio investments managed and traded by ICT-driven global networks. South African financial institutions, though perhaps less reckless than some of their peers in the developed world (thanks in part to better credit regulation,[27] discussed in the next chapter), were profoundly affected by these trends. Like their peers elsewhere, South African financial institutions progressively shifted from being creators of credit to support investment in the real economy to becoming investors and traders in 'financial products' based on an expansion of private debt for consumption purposes. The extensive financialisation of the South African economy was only partially reflected in the fact that the financial sector's share of GDP increased from 6.5 per cent in 1994 to 12 per cent in 2007 and almost 20 per cent by 2009.[28]

Another major trend was the impact of digitisation across all sectors. Digitisation had the profound effect of eliminating unskilled labour processes. Routine tasks in all sectors were progressively replaced by less labour-intensive ICT-driven processes. Transposed on the realities of the inherited South African political economy, its effects were significant. By the late 1970s, the South African gold-mining industry began to pass its peak,[29] and the period thereafter saw the progressive reduction in the employment of low-skilled, low-paid migrant workers it had depended on. This began with reductions in the number of workers recruited from outside the borders of South Africa, but by the early 1990s was also affecting South African workers. The 1987 mineworkers' strike added another dimension. Mining capital responded to the wage increases won in that strike (which in fact only raised the real wage for the first time to a level above that of 1889) with increased mechanisation.[30]

Meanwhile, processes of digitisation led to sharp contractions in demand for unskilled labour power elsewhere. By the mid-1990s study after study was reporting that any net job creation was in occupations requiring at least some post-school qualification.[31] These trends have continued unabated. Apartheid tried to keep the growing surplus population (that is, surplus to the needs of capital) hemmed into the so-called homelands through its notorious influx control laws. But even before the end of apartheid the regime found itself unable to thwart a growing movement of the marginalised population to squatter camps around cities and towns. The removal of apartheid influx controls accelerated the process of urbanisation of the marginalised population, creating the reality confronted today of growing informal settlements or squatter camps, as well as marginalised people in the former homelands subsisting not through any kind of productive activity but increasingly on social grants.

On top of these trends was another process more specific to South Africa. This was the offshoring of South African conglomerates. Anglo American, Old Mutual and South African Breweries were among the most prominent of large South African-based companies that applied for, and were granted, authorisation under exchange control regulations to list on overseas stock exchanges. This was presented and justified as a move to obtain investment funding more cheaply in order to, among other things, expand their operations in South Africa. With the benefit of hindsight, it is clear that the main content of this process was in fact to facilitate the transformation of these former South African-based conglomerates into transnational corporations. Various considerations, no doubt, underpinned this exercise, including the desire of conglomerates hemmed into the South African economy by sanctions against apartheid to benefit from global opportunities. Its effects, however, were also more profound.

Several of the former giants of South African capitalism, whose fortunes were inextricably linked to those of their home country throughout the apartheid period, became foreign investors, relating as such to the new democratic government in South Africa. Interestingly, several of these early movers established their offshore listings in the capital of the erstwhile colonial mother country, London. Not many were particularly successful in their quest to become transnational corporations. Anglo American shrank in significance as a global mining company, initially through its exposure to risky ventures in Brazil, and is now only the seventh-largest global miner.[32] Old Mutual found that its core business remained in South Africa, and in 2018 ended its London listing. South African Breweries, after several ventures resulting in its becoming at one stage the leader of the second-biggest brewery group in the world, was eventually taken over by multinational AB InBev to become just a part of another stable. More successful were some of the former Afrikaner conglomerates. They included media giant Naspers, which became a significant investor in China through its stake in Tencent, and Remgro/Rembrandt, whose luxury brand business (Richemont) is active more broadly across Europe.

The government's first Industrial Policy Action Plan (IPAP), launched in February 2010, argued that there were significant and worrying 'structural imbalances' in the growth path that South Africa had been on in the first decade and a half of democratic rule. This had been 'driven by unsustainable increases in credit extension and consumption, not sufficiently underpinned by growth in the production sectors of the economy'. Thus, while consumption-orientated sectors (such as financial intermediation, insurance and real estate; transport, storage and communication; and wholesale and retail trade, catering and accommodation) had grown by an average of 107 per cent between 1994 and 2008, or by 7.7 per cent annually, production sectors (agriculture; mining; manufacturing; electricity and water; and construction) had grown at half that rate – by 41 per cent between 1994 and 2008, or 2.9 per cent per annum.[33] The DTI later reported that in the 84 quarters between 1993 and December 2014, growth of five per cent or more was recorded in only 16 quarters. In those 16 quarters, that growth was driven by consumption sector growth and/or by the mineral commodity supercycle, which was over by 2012.[34] Eventually, and in the context of the onset of the 2008 financial crisis as well as after the ANC's 2007 Polokwane conference, the focus of economic policy began to shift towards the content of the growth path and to seek structural change therein.

8

Polokwane, crisis and the six I's

The ANC's 52nd National Conference, held at Polokwane in Limpopo province in December 2007, was a significant watershed event in the struggle over the direction of the NDR. In more recent times, and in the light of the state capture revelations, it has become fashionable to refer to the entire period after Polokwane as 'nine-plus lost years'.

My view is that while the main legacy of the Zuma presidency ended up being an extremely destructive demobilisation of state capacity through rampant looting, Polokwane and the years thereafter cannot be reduced in their entirety to this alone. Rather, this was a period characterised by contradiction and contestation with some advances as well as many setbacks. One of the most important advances came from the reversal of the previous policy of resistance to the roll-out of antiretroviral (ARV) treatment to the large numbers of human immunodeficiency virus (HIV) positive people in the country. By 2018, UNAIDS reported that 62 per cent of the 7.7 million infected people were on ARVs, cutting the deaths from acquired immune deficiency syndrome (Aids) by 50 per cent, from 140 000 in 2010 to 71 000 in 2018.[1]

There were also gains on the economic policy front – even if they later became overwhelmed by the effects of state capture. Besides, the notion of 'lost years' implies that all was fine in the preceding period, which is, in fact, far from the case. As indicated in the previous chapter, the economic policy framework that emerged in the immediate aftermath of the 1994 democratic breakthrough was strongly influenced by neoliberalism. Its domestic support base was what the SACP called the '1996 class project'. This was a loose alliance embracing BEE business beneficiaries and technocrats within the state and ANC convinced either of the merits or of the inevitability of neoliberalism.

President Thabo Mbeki presided over both the ANC and government for much of this time. Mbeki himself was a complex personality. A man of significant intellectual capacity and a convinced Pan Africanist, by the late 1980s he had come to the view that both South Africa and the wider continent had no alternative other than to adapt to the emerging norms of the age of hyper-globalisation. This was evident even in exile. At an ANC consultative meeting on constitutional models held in Lusaka, which I attended, Mbeki made an input citing Mikhail Gorbachev's perestroika-driven reforms of Soviet central planning. He argued even then that an ANC-led democratic government would have no option but to conform to Western norms – which led veteran Jack Simons to retort that Mbeki had presented a brilliant case for gloom! Mbeki was Deputy President at the time of the adoption of GEAR, but he was already the 'ideas and details man' in the presidency and a key driver of GEAR. Although Mbeki's stance on economic policy clearly located him within the dominant global paradigm, he was not a mere puppet or servant of Western interests. A consummate diplomat, Mbeki sought to position himself on the global stage as leader of a country 'punching above its weight'. On many of the key diplomatic and security issues of the time, South Africa under Mbeki took progressive positions. These included opposing the invasion of Iraq, supporting national self-determination for the Palestinian people and acting in solidarity with the progressive forces in Haiti, among others. He also remained throughout a strong proponent of Pan Africanism, displaying a strong commitment to the AU and regional bodies such as SADC.

Mbeki's world view and diplomacy, however, were also shaped in significant ways by his acceptance of the dominant economic paradigm. Perhaps the clearest example here was his pursuit of notions that South Africa could persuade Western leaders to commit large resources to 'partner' with the continent to promote African development. Considerable effort and resources were accordingly deployed, without real result, in trying to persuade bodies such as the G7 group of advanced developed countries to commit to a deal in which 'policy reforms' by African governments would be bargained against resource commitments to advance a New Partnership for Africa's Development (Nepad).

This world view was also evident in the approach to negotiating trade deals that emerged during Mbeki's leadership. The administration portrayed South Africa as an important trading nation standing at the crossroads between the developed and developing world, quite capable of accepting the obligations required of 'responsible' citizens and supporters of the multilateral trading system and not in need of the kinds of 'special and differential treatment' or 'less than full reciprocity' avidly pursued by comparable countries. The result was the emergence of trade agreements with clauses that later came to be recognised as significant barriers to the deployment of important and necessary policy tools.

Mbeki also, finally, had major blind spots. The main one was his approach to the HIV/Aids pandemic then devastating the country. Perhaps reacting initially to the hard sales pressures of global pharmaceutical companies pressing for potentially lucrative tenders, Mbeki embraced Aids denialism, with devastating consequences for many thousands of his compatriots who were denied effective access to ARV treatment through the public health sector until the end of his term of office.[2]

Even before he became President of the ANC in 1997, Mbeki had become visibly irritated with the interventions of Cosatu and the SACP – particularly on GEAR.[3] During his presidency, relations with the alliance partners became increasingly frosty as the ANC itself became less of a campaigning organisation and more of a narrow election machine. By the time of the ANC's midterm non-elective National General Council (NGC) conference, held halfway through his second term, Mbeki felt emboldened enough to propose a significant change in the culture and practices of the ANC. A document tabled ahead of the June 2005 NGC proposed 'modernising' the machinery of the party, including replacing the system of branch nominations for leadership positions with a process in which conferences endorsed 'slates' proposed by outgoing leaders. Other proposals would in effect have consolidated a transition of the ANC from a national liberation movement to a 'modern' social democratic-type electoral party. Significantly, these proposals were roundly rejected by delegates at the NGC.[4]

The NGC also delivered Mbeki another important defeat. On 14 June 2005 Mbeki dismissed Jacob Zuma from his position as Deputy President of the Republic following the conviction of Zuma's former associate Schabir Shaik for corruption and for making payments to Zuma. The NEC then called on Zuma to step aside as Deputy President of the ANC. Branch delegates to the NGC were, however, of another mind, and, in a dramatic defeat for Mbeki, resolved to prevent Zuma's being removed from office as ANC Deputy President.[5] The stage was set for a major clash.

The period between the NGC and the Polokwane conference saw the formation of a loose coalition around Zuma. It included the SACP and Cosatu, the ANC Youth League and an assortment of individuals who came to be known as the 'walking wounded'. These were people who had been removed from their positions after having crossed Mbeki. Many of those in this broad grouping saw Zuma neither as a messiah nor as someone without faults. Rather, he was seen as someone less dogmatic than Mbeki and someone, it was hoped, who would be more likely than Mbeki to engage constructively with alliance partners and support more progressive policies. Mbeki himself eventually agreed to accept nomination for a third term as ANC President, even though the constitutionally imposed term limit would have prevented his reappointment as President of the Republic. The presumption was that had Mbeki succeeded in being re-elected ANC

President, he would have handpicked the ANC's nominee for the presidency of the Republic. The other contender for ANC President at Polokwane was Jacob Zuma. The stakes could not have been higher, but in the end the result was an overwhelming victory for Zuma and his allies and a stunning defeat for Mbeki and his associates. Although Mbeki remained President of the Republic after Polokwane, within less than a year he was recalled by the ANC and replaced as head of state until the 2009 elections by Kgalema Motlanthe.

The Polokwane conference was also noteworthy for the adoption of a resolution on economic policy far more radical than anything that had been agreed to at earlier ANC conferences. Its central focus was on the need to create 'decent work' through, among other things, 'active industrial and trade policy'. Other elements included 'an active beneficiation strategy' (meaning adding value to mineral resources), more effective land reform and ensuring that macroeconomic policy became a tool for advancing the creation of decent work – a term deriving from International Labour Organization debates referring to respecting fundamental rights of people and providing acceptable conditions of work, safety and remuneration.[6]

The importance of this resolution, not much noticed at the time, was that it was beginning to articulate a position, spelt out more clearly at the 2012 Mangaung conference, that 'transform[ing] the structure of the economy through industrialisation'[7] was fundamental to the realisation of many of the other goals of economic transformation – decent jobs, greater inclusion, higher living standards and more real black economic empowerment. This, rather than the content or degree of success or otherwise of specific programmes, represents in my view the main advance of the Polokwane resolution.

The case for industrial policy as a central pillar of bringing about structural transformation in the productive base of the South African economy was compelling. First, it rested on the lessons of the experience of all countries that had made the transition from underdeveloped to developed, or from poor to rich. Heterodox economists and economic historians[8] had established the point that almost all countries that moved from being low-income societies to what we now call 'developed countries' passed through a stage of industrialisation. During this stage, all industrialisers without exception nurtured, supported and indeed protected their nascent or emerging industries. In respect of trade policy, they deployed tariff protection to support emerging industries as they developed and defended the policy space needed to support domestic industries against the calls by stronger economies to open markets. This was as true of the positions adopted by the US against the demands of Britain in the late 19th century as it was of positions taken by South Korea in the 1970s or by China in the 1980s. A saying common in the US in the 19th century, in response to calls from Britain for the US to adopt free trade, was, 'Don't do as the English tell you to do, do as the English did.'[9] Often, though, the defence of policy space went along with taking advantage of whatever market openings were available to support export growth. This was particularly evident in the case of South Korean and Taiwanese industrialisation, where the Cold War-inspired market access opportunities given by the US provided an important foothold for exports to the United States.

Poor countries stayed poor because they remained trapped in the much lower value-added production and export of some primary product or products – agricultural or mineral. Most of these countries were, at some stage in their history, colonised. Several were subject to colonial laws explicitly preventing their development of industries – particularly those that might have competed against industries in the mother country.[10]

The significance of industrialisation, whether by the long-industrialised 'core' countries or by those few countries that had more recently made this transition, reached beyond the fact that it inserted a higher value-added manufacturing sector into their economies. Manufacturing stimulated a host of related activities – from supplier input production and innovation to higher-value and more secure service sectors (financial services, transport logistics, design and management consulting, among others). All of this had an even broader, economy-wide impact in underpinning a generalised improvement in productivity that raised incomes across all sectors in industrialising economies. Norwegian economic historian Erik Reinert argues that the reason luggage handlers, bus drivers, hotel personnel, barbers and shop attendants in Peru are paid less than their counterparts in Norway has nothing to do with lesser abilities or the nature of the work they perform. Both do the same job, and indeed those in Peru probably work longer hours than those in Norway. The reason for their different incomes lies in the fact that industrialisation in Norway generated an overall increase in incomes in that country.[11]

Although anathema in neoliberal discourse, at least until the second decade of the 21st century, even the World Bank was obliged to concede that state-led industrial policies had been beneficial in the development of the East Asian 'Newly Industrialising Economies' (Taiwan, Hong Kong, Singapore and South Korea) during the 1970s, although it qualified this by saying that in these territories such policies had been driven by highly skilled technocrats capable of operating in harmony with market trends.[12]

South Africa's lacklustre economic performance, both in the late apartheid period and in the early post-1994 period, pointed to the urgent need for structural transformation and a shift to higher value-added production. The mineral base that had supported the country's growth since the end of the 19th century, gold mining in particular, was a finite and, from the late 1970s, increasingly wasting asset.[13] The growth of consumption-orientated service sectors, at twice the pace of all of the productive sectors combined, was an indication not that South Africa had moved onto a services-driven 'post-industrial' growth path, but rather that things were seriously wrong in the underlying productive sector base. The growth of service sectors such as wholesale and retail trade and financial services at a pace way beyond what was happening in the productive sectors was not sustainable in the longer run. Based, to an increasing extent, on debt-funded consumption of imported rather than locally produced products, this growth path was constrained both by the balance of trade and by the rising levels of indebtedness of consumers.

The Uruguay Round of multilateral trade negotiations, which led to the 1994 Marrakesh Agreement and the establishment of the WTO, had resulted in South Africa (claimed by its apartheid rulers to be a developed country) having to make industrial tariff cuts much steeper than those of comparable developing countries, coupled with further unilateral cuts imposed under GEAR. The manufacturing sector consequently underwent what is now widely recognised as excessive tariff liberalisation. This contributed to premature deindustrialisation, the extent of which was sharply highlighted in a presentation made in 2019 by development economist Ha-Joon Chang. In the early 1960s, Chang pointed out, South Africa had been 'literally the most industrialised nation outside of the "core" capitalist world', producing US$138 per capita manufacturing value added (MVA) – 61 per cent of that of Japan and 15 per cent of that of the US. Over time, it had regressed into becoming 'not a serious manufacturing nation' – with per capita MVA 18 per cent of that of the US but only 11 per cent of that of Japan's, 13 per cent of South Korea's (it once produced six times as much), 45 per cent of China's and 80 per cent of Brazil's.[14]

Within a few months of Polokwane, South Africa found itself battered by the onset of what was later dubbed the 'Great Recession' – the worst global economic crisis at any time since the Great Depression of the 1930s. In the first of successive waves of external shocks battering its economy, South Africa lost 1 million jobs (200 000 of them in manufacturing, even though the sector accounted for much less than 20 per cent of GDP). By the end of the first quarter of Zuma's presidency, the South African economy had chalked up its second quarter of contraction, meaning it was officially in recession.

The epicentre of the onset of the 2008 global economic crisis was of course far from South Africa, in the advanced developed economies.

Its major iconic events were the collapse of investment bankers Lehman Brothers and a host of other prominent financial institutions, up to then regarded as pinnacles of capitalist stability. The fact that the crisis began in the financial sector led to its being dubbed the 'global financial crisis', even though it was much more than that. In Volume III of *Capital*, Marx[15] showed that the anarchic nature of capitalism makes it impossible for the system to develop except in cycles of boom and bust. During boom periods, eventually the point is reached of overproduction of capital. This is also reflected in overproduction of commodities, as well as of capital existing in money form. Such overproduction is of course not in relation to social need. In that sense, in a world of poverty there is always underproduction. But, in relation to the possibilities of profitable investment of capital, a point is reached in the cycle where too much capital is created for it all to be profitably invested. When this point is reached, what unfolds is a competitive struggle to decide which capital is going to undergo the destruction necessary for the system to reconstitute itself for the next cycle of expansion.

The crisis that began in 2008, and whose after-effects were felt for many years thereafter, had all the hallmarks of a regular capitalist crisis. But it also had specific features that made its impact far more devastating. It occurred in a highly globalised and financialised capitalist world economy. Most analysts agree now, but did not then, that the prescripts of neoliberalism had led to too 'light touch' regulation by public authorities over trading in the new financial products appearing in the era of globalisation – particularly securities and derivatives.[16]

In the US, largely unregulated 'securitisation' fuelled a speculative boom of enormous proportions that eventually engulfed even the pillars of the financial establishment. This was most prominent in the creation of volumes of 'toxic' mortgage securities. Through securitisation, home loan providers could extend mortgages to clients without bothering too much whether or not recipients would be able to repay. By repackaging and on-selling securities that essentially provided buyers with rights to receive mortgage payments, the risk was simply transferred to the purchasers. Financial traders, private and public fund managers and individuals, across the world, including in many so-called world-class institutions, bought into what were dubbed US property securities (as well as other types of similar products) on a massive scale, while the growth of internet trading meant that transactions could take place across the globe at literally the press of a button. It was a huge pyramid scheme with some end-buyers of property securities probably unaware that they what they bought gave them no right to the underlying real estate. The ballooning financial economy created by derivative and securities trading no doubt delayed the onset of the underlying emerging crisis of overproduction of capital. The expanding bubble provided a cushion that allowed capitalist investors across the world to continue for some time to extract profits from financial products, even when these were not supported by underlying value in the real economy. But the very same factors also ensured that the inevitable crash, when it came, would be more intense and widespread than would otherwise have been the case.

The collapse of Lehman Brothers was accompanied by the failure of US mortgage lenders Fannie Mae and Freddie Mac and a host of other supposedly reputable institutions. These events revealed a situation in which many of the major pillars of the capitalist financial establishment across the world were in fact awash with toxic debt (debt with no chance of being repaid). The emperor was exposed with no clothes, and there was a very real possibility of a collapse of the entire financial system in several countries, with an actual collapse taking place in Iceland. Faced with this, the governments of the advanced capitalist world began ditching a number of erstwhile pillars of the Washington Consensus. Banks deemed 'too big to fail' were not allowed to go bankrupt (even though this was supposed to be the market's self-correcting mechanism). Instead they were bailed out with huge amounts of public funds, amid a tacit recognition that markets had actually got prices wrong. The impact of bailouts on budget numbers was also ignored amid the panic to 'save the financial system'. Ironically, the first major bailout in the US was approved while supposed free marketeer George W Bush was still President. Narrow inflation targeting and tight monetary policy – other erstwhile commandments of neoliberal economic management – were also partially and temporarily discarded in favour of neo-Keynesian 'quantitative easing' (the release of money in the hope of stimulating faltering growth). For a while even IMF staffers started writing self-critical papers discarding hitherto sacrosanct policy advice and in some cases advising countries to do exactly the opposite of what they had been insisting on only months before.

Globalisation meant that virtually no country was immune from the effects of the financial crisis. But its effects were uneven, impacting on different countries or groups of countries in different ways, and striking in successive waves. South Africa was, in fact, spared a systemic financial crisis, with its banks only having a fairly low exposure to toxic debt. Continued exchange control and – surprisingly to some – the National Credit Act (both nonorthodox regulatory measures) proved to be among the main bulwarks that prevented local financial institutions from indulging in the worst forms of recklessness seen elsewhere. Exchange control (which GEAR intended to wipe out, but which was still in force in a limited way) restricted the extent to which private and public institutions could invest in speculative products offshore. Unlike for example the United Kingdom (UK), where several local authorities lost large sums after investing in speculative products offered by Icelandic banks, no public institution in South Africa lost any significant sum. The National Credit Act had been enacted to protect largely low-income consumers from the predatory practices of loan sharks, known locally as *mashonisas*. It provided for the possibility that reckless loans could be rendered null and void. This became something of a deterrent to aggressive securitisation. For a while, the Act indeed became an object of a degree of international interest as former light-touch regulators scrambled to find alternatives.

But South Africa could not escape the broader impact of the global recession. As indicated above, the South African economy plunged into recession and lost a million jobs. The more than proportional job losses in manufacturing pointed to a very real risk of further significant deindustrialisation. The first response to the crisis was developed during the short presidency of Kgalema Motlanthe through social dialogue within Nedlac. The Crisis Response Programme identified expanding the infrastructure build programme as the main countercyclical response. Another important proposal was a partially subsidised 'training layoff' programme. The idea here was that employers contemplating layoffs could draw a subsidy to support a stipend to workers who would undergo training in preparation for their re-engagement as companies invested later on. Auto manufacturer BMW became one of the largest users of the scheme and the first auto original equipment manufacturer to invest after the recession. Surprisingly, the package encountered a degree of resistance from some in cabinet, largely on the grounds that a programme not drawn up by itself entailed commitments by government. But eventually it was agreed and some of its elements at least were implemented to good effect.

After his election as President of the Republic in May 2009, Jacob Zuma made a number of changes in the economic cluster within government. He established a new Economic Development Department and appointed the former General Secretary of the Southern African Clothing and Textile Workers' Union (Sactwu) and one of the main drivers of the Crisis Response Programme, Ebrahim Patel, to head it as minister. Long-serving Finance Minister Trevor Manuel became a Minister in the Presidency given responsibility for establishing a National Planning Commission and developing a National Development Plan (NDP). He was replaced as Finance Minister by the former Commissioner of the South African Revenue Service (SARS),

Pravin Gordhan. I had been a Deputy Minister in the DTI since 2005 and was promoted to Minister in the same department in a cabinet that included a number of other SACP Central Committee members, most prominently the General Secretary, Blade Nzimande, who became Minister of Higher Education and Training.

Within the DTI, we decided to seize the moment and take our work on industrial policy to the next level. Industrial policy also became the overarching focus shaping all other work in the department. In the first two or three years of the fourth administration (2009–2014), industrial policy had not yet been 'rehabilitated' in the eyes of orthodox economists, who caricatured it as ignorant and incapable governments' intervening to 'pick winners'.[17] We were, however, encouraged to pursue this work through engagements with several leading scholars – including Joseph Stiglitz, Ha-Joon Chang and Robert Wade – both at the start of the Zuma administration and, in fact, even before. Work on the development of what became the National Industrial Policy Framework (NIPF) had begun under the leadership of my predecessor, Mandisi Mpahlwa. When I was appointed Deputy Minister in 2005, I was charged with establishing a think tank to develop a strategy document, which eventually became the NIPF.[18] The NIPF argued the case for industrial policy and identified the domain of possible actions by government to support such a policy, but it was not yet an action plan. The NIPF's passage through the Mbeki cabinet was a tortuous one. Successive drafts were met with screeds of critical comment from a National Treasury demonstrating great scepticism about industrial policy. Even when some of these comments were accommodated in later drafts, further critiques emerged. The result was that it took more than 18 months before the NIPF was finally approved in 2007.

By 2009 we were ready to proceed with the next stage – turning the NIPF framework into a time-bound action plan. Sector specialists in the DTI had for many years been located in the division responsible for investment and trade promotion, on the grounds that the role of government industrial-sector specialists was fundamentally to seek out private-sector investors. During the tenure of Mandisi Mpahlwa, these specialists had been transferred to a large division in the department responsible for, among other things, small business development and broad-based black economic empowerment, as well as industrial policy. Soon after my appointment, we completed the work of separating out a stand-alone unit, the Industrial Development Division (IDD), and appointing a deputy director-general (DDG) to head it. The first IDD DDG was Nimrod Zalk, who had emerged as the main thinker and policy driver on industrial policy among DTI officials. Garth Strachan, a veteran of the liberation movement who had briefly served as Member of the Executive Council (MEC) for Finance in the Western Cape but later completed a master's degree in industrial policy, later joined the division and eventually took over as DDG.

Nimrod Zalk had established contacts with a number of leading analysts and practitioners of industrial policy in various parts of the world. Among other initiatives, Zalk and his team undertook an intensive study tour to Brazil, whose Banco Nacional de Desen-volvimento Económico e Social (National Bank of Economic and Social Development, BNDES) had been particularly helpful. The BNDES is roughly equivalent to the Industrial Development Cor-poration (IDC) and Development Bank of Southern Africa (DBSA) combined. It is the development finance institution responsible for funding most strategic infrastructure and industrial projects in Brazil. In late 2008, a BNDES team led by one of its executive directors, João Carlos Ferraz, visited South Africa and met with a broader group from the DTI, including me. The BNDES team told us that banks in Brazil, like those in South Africa, were focused on extending credit for consumption purposes rather than investment – at interest rates that were actually even higher than those in South Africa. The BNDES had assumed a pivotal position in industrial financing, being involved in many of the most important projects.

Through receiving a sizeable part of a job creation levy imposed on top of the equivalent of unemployment insurance, the BNDES was able to offer increasing amounts of finance for industrial projects at rates below those charged by South African development finance institutions. The BNDES team were remarkably frank about the way in which they and other public entities unashamedly promoted local manufacturing through, among others, placing obligations on recipients of its loans to procure Brazilian-made products.

Zalk was responsible for assembling the IDD sectoral team. A few months later, I had occasion to meet Robert Wade, a leading British academic analyst of industrial policy, particularly in South East Asia. When he said to me, 'I suppose you have a team of engineers developing your sectoral programmes,' I had to reply, 'Not exactly engineers, more like social scientists.' But then Ha-Joon Chang told us that, contrary to one of the main conclusions of the World Bank's well-known study, 'The East Asian Miracle', South Korea had not embarked on its industrial policy journey with a ready-made team of highly skilled technocrats but with something much more modest.

The first iteration of the Industrial Policy Action Plan was launched through a parliamentary ministerial statement in February 2010.[19] We decided, after some discussion, to structure the IPAP as a rolling action plan, whose main content would be a series of time-bound actions that would be carried out by different government departments and agencies in the financial year in question as well as in the next two outer years. Each financial year there would be a new iteration of the IPAP that would report on what had been done and not done and contain the new three-year rolling action plan. We also established regular IPAP meetings in which the executive authorities of all contributing entities would be invited to receive reports on progress. These disciplines around the IPAP were considered essential to turn it from yet another policy document gathering dust on shelves into an implemented action plan.

The first IPAP was replete with learnings from, and comparisons with, Brazil. These included the way in which the BNDES was able, through a regular injection of public money, to offer a growing volume of low-interest loans to support industrial development. This led to one important proposal in the first IPAP: that a study be undertaken to find ways to, (i) in the short term, leverage more funding off the balance sheet of the IDC while (ii) developing a longer-term funding model.

The IPAP established the point that the growth path that the South African economy had up to that point been on was one in which consumption-driven sectors such as wholesale and retail trade were growing at twice the pace of all of the production sectors. It also showed that private credit extension for consumption purposes had expanded massively while that for fixed investment had declined, to reach only 5.2 per cent of the total by 2008.[20]

One point raised in relation to this was that macroeconomic policy needed to be realigned to support the restructuring of the economy and to support a productive-sector-led growth path aiming progressively to move up the value chain. In other words, macroeconomic policy, instead of operating according to abstract norms established elsewhere, needed to be reconfigured to support real-economy imperatives under the concrete conditions existing in South Africa at a particular time.

A pressing issue at this time was the overvaluation of the rand. This was partly the result of the quantitative easing policies adopted by developed countries as an attempt to stimulate their still-sluggish economies. With virtually all available 'fiscal bullets' having been fired in the bailout of financial institutions, the only stimulatory tool left in their tool box was to loosen monetary policy. Interest rates across the developed world were lowered to virtually zero. The initial result was not quite what was intended. Instead of releasing funds to stimulate the developed economies, significant amounts of the short-term capital unleashed flowed into emerging markets still offering relatively higher interest rates. South Africa was not unique in experiencing this. Several other emerging economies in Latin America and Asia also saw inward flows of short-term capital pushing up the value of their currencies. In the case of South Africa, the IMF estimated that at one point this resulted in a 10 to 15 per cent overvaluation of the rand.[21] The effects on a nascent attempt at reindustrialisation were debilitating. Export products generally became more expensive, a double whammy on top of the depressed demand in 'traditional' developed-country export markets. Imports, meanwhile, became cheaper, leading to a flood of new imports, including products that had never before penetrated the South African market. This, as I will show later, became one of the most difficult and contentious issues.

Another key theme in the first iteration of the IPAP was that we needed to adopt a 'developmental approach' to trade policy, in which the needs of industrial development would shape our stances on tariff and trade policy issues. This amounted to a significant reversal of the mantra of neoliberalism, which held that trade liberalisation was the fundamental task of trade ministries and that the real economy simply had to adapt to this unalterable reality. Our 'developmental trade policy' was later elaborated in a trade policy document, developed under the leadership of Xavier Carim, the DDG responsible for the International Trade and Economic Development (ITED) division (discussed in Chapter 9). Localisation was a further theme. The fact that South Africa had not signed the WTO Optional Protocol on Transparency in Government Procurement meant that government retained the policy space to demand that public entities procure locally produced products in prescribed ways. The IPAP signalled, for the first time, government's willingness to use this tool to support industrial development.

Other transversal or cross-cutting themes included the need to draw in much more centrally the 'technical infrastructure' or SQAM (standards, quality assurance and metrology) institutions. This was borne of the recognition that defending borders against import penetration required much greater attention to 'locking out' substandard

97

products that were harmful to consumers, as well as constituting unfair competition to compliant South African-based manufacturers. 'Locking in' South African exports in foreign markets by winning recognition for South African written standards was the other side of the coin.

As far as sectoral work was concerned, the clothing and textile sector had for some time been in intensive care, haemorrhaging jobs on a massive scale.[22] By the beginning of the 21st century many were writing it off as a lost cause. Yet a study by Justin Barnes argued that there were still real possibilities not just to save but also modestly to grow the sector if we followed a new approach.[23] A major requirement here was to encourage local firms to invest in raising competitiveness with a view to capturing a larger share of the domestic market. Particular niches that competitive local firms could target included 'fast fashion' (developing a capability to respond to retailers' changing requirements within a period shorter than the four weeks it typically took to import new product). Specialist products such as sporting wear, workwear and industrial textiles also offered possibilities. A particular challenge was to reform the dysfunctional DCCS, which was applied not just nationally, but also throughout SACU. An early decision, which required much arm wrestling in SACU, was to replace the programme with a nationally operating Clothing and Textiles Competitiveness Programme. This had a number of sub-programmes, one of which allowed companies to earn credits based on value addition (rather than exports) and redeem these only against authorised competitiveness-raising investments.

In the motor industry, the transition from the MIDP to the APDP was already under way with the front-loading of one of its elements, the Automotive Investment Scheme. The main difference between the MIDP and the APDP was that the former provided incentive benefits in the form of rebates or grants against exports, whereas the latter did so against local production volumes. In part, this transition was made to insulate the programme against a potential, but disputable, WTO challenge dependent on the interpretation of rules against export subsidies. But, generally, the transition was well consulted and understood by the industry, which became among the first manufacturing sub-sectors to resume investments after the recession. The IPAP envisaged extending the APDP beyond its existing focus on passenger vehicles to include also medium and heavy commercial vehicles, as well as public transport vehicles (buses and minibus taxis). In addition, the IPAP envisaged work in metals fabrication and transport equipment, chemicals, advanced manufacturing (including aerospace), boatbuilding, agro-processing and film-making among other industries.

Meanwhile, Ebrahim Patel's newly established Department of Economic Development began work to develop a more comprehensive New Growth Path (NGP). Patel had been appointed without much real clarity on the role of his new department. Immediately, I saw the importance of working closely with someone like Patel, who had many strengths and talents as well as a generally progressive view of economic issues, demonstrated during his years in the trade union movement. I offered to house the new department on the DTI campus in Tshwane and was also happy to transfer responsibility for some of the agencies previously reporting to the DTI, in the hope that this would usher in a new way of working together in government beyond the silo mentality that so restricted the effectiveness of government work. One of those agencies was the IDC and another was Khula, which provided financial support to small enterprises. My own view was that Patel's department was well placed to play a strong coordinating role across government, and, if it had a number of development finance institutions (DFIs) reporting to it, could rationalise and make more effective developmental funding of a new growth path. I also hoped that this could lead to the transfer of some DFI reporting to National Treasury, including the DBSA and the Public Investment Corporation (PIC). The inclusion of these could have led to the creation of a powerful DFI along the lines of the BNDES. Alas, it was not to be.

By 2010, Patel and his team had drawn up the NGP.[24] This identified six job drivers: agriculture, infrastructure, manufacturing, the green economy, mining and tourism. The NGP also identified a number of issues where commitments from social partners through social dialogue processes could enhance efforts at job creation. Accords were in due course negotiated on issues such as education and training, the green economy and localisation (where all social partners agreed to work towards the aspirational target of 75 per cent procurement of locally produced products). More elusive was the 'grand bargain' outlined in the NGP that envisaged an incomes policy with differentiated levels of restraint in wages, salaries, bonuses and dividends traded against macroeconomic reforms (then seen as currency devaluation to a competitive level).

In the event, the Department of Economic Development never became the powerful coordinating entity some of us hoped it would be. The chairing of the economic cluster was assigned not to Patel but to the Minister of Rural Development and Land Reform, Gugile Nkwinti. Meanwhile, Trevor Manuel was assembling a team from outside government to prepare the National Development Plan, covering all related issues but also including the economy, adding another distinct locus of economic policy planning.

Patel did, however, come to play one very significant role. Following the conclusion in the mid-year cabinet lekgotla (conference) in 2011 that infrastructure planning left much to be desired, a Presidential Infrastructure Coordinating Commission (PICC) was established, to be chaired by the President. Patel became the leading light in the PICC Secretariat, which produced a highly professional plan to monitor hundreds of projects in 17 Strategic Integrated Projects (SIPs). By the end of the first term of the Zuma administration, more than R1 trillion had been spent on infrastructure projects in transport, energy, schools, hospitals and more – more than twice the level in any previous five-year term in the country's history.[25] Some of the credit for this was due to the much more effective infrastructure planning and coordination that took place in the PICC.

Another feature of the infrastructure programme was a strong emphasis on localisation. The DTI, Department of Economic Development and National Treasury had been able to agree on a process of 'designating' for purchase from local manufacturers certain percentages of products procured under the infrastructure build programme. By the end of the fourth term, designations in force covered bus bodies, clothing and textiles, footwear and leather (uniforms and workwear), power pylons, canned and processed vegetables, railway rolling stock, pharmaceuticals, office and school furniture, power and telecoms cables, solar water heaters and set-top boxes.[26] Cases of locally domiciled companies benefiting from these designations began to be cited. For example, while all the buses procured for the 2010 FIFA World Cup were fully imported, buses procured by municipalities for bus rapid transit programmes all had bodies manufactured in South Africa. In 2016 we launched the IPAP at the factory of a black industrialist who had taken over and was upgrading a forging company to produce wagon wheels for locomotive and wagon procurement (see Chapter 12), while General Electric (GE) took its first-ever decision to set up a loco-motive factory outside the US so that it could qualify for the same tender. While these developments indicated progress, we shall see later that many of these tenders became affected by state capture and corruption, with the building of local manufacturing capacity being a direct casualty.[27]

By the end of the fourth term the policy being pursued could be summed up in a phrase coined by Patel – 'six I's', for industrialisation, infrastructure, investment, innovation, inclusion and integration.

9

The trade policy challenges

As indicated in the previous chapter, early in the fourth term of democratic government the ITED team in the DTI, led by Xavier Carim, produced a document on trade policy titled the Trade Policy and Strategy Framework (TPSF). This was adopted by cabinet in July 2010, and an update focusing on changes since the onset of the Great Recession was adopted in November 2012.[1] The perspectives underpinning the TPSF were closely aligned with those on industrial policy. The TPSF explicitly argued for a 'strategic and calibrated' approach to setting tariffs that would be shaped by the needs of agricultural and industrial development. It argued that successful developing countries had followed such an approach to support the production and export of value-added products, in contrast to many others that had undergone excessive liberalisation and reverted to their static comparative advantage (as producers of raw materials).

The TPSF noted that South Africa's average applied tariff had declined from around 23 per cent in the early 1990s to 7.7 per cent in 2012, while 56.3 per cent of South Africa's 7 240 tariff lines were set at zero.[2] It indicated that tariffs would continue to be set through an evidence-based process on the recommendation of the ITAC. The same would apply to the use of 'trade remedies' such as anti-dumping duties. Both tariff adjustments and the use of trade remedies would, however, be subject to applicable WTO rules. The TPSF did not explicitly seek to direct any particular ITAC recommendation, but it did offer a 'general guideline':

> Tariffs on mature upstream input industries could be reduced
> or removed to lower the inputs costs for the downstream, more

labour-creating manufacturing. Tariffs on downstream industries, particularly those that are strategic from an employment or value-addition perspective, may be retained or raised to ensure long-term sustainability and job creation in the context of domestic production capabilities/potentialities and the degree of trade and production distortion on these products at global level.[3]

This ended the hitherto de facto tacit mandate of the ITAC – that 'reform' meant tariff reductions and that it could recommend the lowering but never the raising of tariffs. The TPSF further indicated that participation in trade negotiations would seek to improve market access, particularly for South African value-added products, while also preserving policy space to support industrial development, including a specific refence in the 2012 update to deploying export taxes.[4]

The TPSF shaped our approach to various ongoing or pending trade negotiations, The highest priority among these was the pursuit of 'developmental integration' on the African continent.[5]

Towards a developmental African Continental Free Trade Area

Regional integration had, of course, been identified as an objective from the time of the first wave of decolonisation of the African continent, with the adoption of the 1980 Lagos Plan of Action being a prominent example. Regional integration was, however, also conceptually a source of much confusion, contestation and muddle-headed external policy advice. In a short volume published in 2019, I suggested that 'practical' discussions in regional organisations often concealed a too-unselfconscious clash between contending paradigms.[6]

The first of these paradigms was a conventional trade integration perspective that saw integration as proceeding in linear succession up a 'ladder' of trade arrangements. These began with a *free trade area* (FTA, where parties remove duties on 'substantially all' products traded between them), followed by a *customs union* (where there is free trade in the union plus a common external tariff, or CET, in which parties apply the same tariff to third parties), and then proceed to a *common market* (where there is free movement of capital and labour, as well as of goods and services) before finally arriving at an *economic union* (where there is a high level of common regulation and policy setting).

In this paradigm, integration is driven by the adoption of formal trade arrangements, and more precisely by arrangements promoting trade liberalisation, particularly at the early stages. In neoclassical economic literature, economic integration was generally seen as beneficial if it created more trade between participating partners than it diverted away from extra-regional players. This was seen to be most likely where there was a high level of complementarity between the economies of cooperating partners. As this was seen to be most probable in developed-country regions, such as the EU, conventional neoclassical economists tended to be indifferent to regional integration in the developing world, where many efforts failed to translate institutional form into real-economy substance.

At least, that was the position of most neoclassical economists until the era of neoliberalism and the emergence of a variant of trade integration, styled 'open regionalism'.[7] Proponents of this approach began arguing that regional integration in the developing world could potentially be 'beneficial', but only if it 'assisted' in deepening the integration of the region concerned into the world economy at large through the reduction of overall tariff levels towards the world at large. This meant regional preferences would need to be accompanied by, or at the very least be a step towards, simultaneously lowering the region's average tariffs towards third parties. Theoretically, this was argued for through an assertion that any wide margin of preference to regional suppliers over those from the rest of the world would likely promote 'trade diversion' at the expense of 'trade creation'. Operationally, this would be achieved by insisting that regional arrangements reported to the WTO under Article 24 of the General Agreement on Tariffs and Trade (GATT) demonstrate that they had resulted in a net reduction in average tariff levels compared to those in force previously. With regard to customs unions, these would be seen as 'beneficial' if the CET led to cuts in tariffs towards the world at large.

An alternative paradigm that emerged in more heterodox literature was termed 'development integration'.[8] This argued that a narrow trade integration approach based on the ladder was Euro-centric and ignored the fact that in developing regions the major barriers to increasing intra-regional trade were not fundamentally tariff regimes but real-economy constraints. The latter included underdeveloped production structures and inadequate infrastructure. Put simply, if one underdeveloped country's trade profile is dominated by the export of some or other primary product (undergoing little processing in its domestic economy), it has little to trade with its neighbour whose specialisation is also as an exporter of the same or some other primary raw material. If the road and rail connections between the two are inadequate, this further impedes trade between them. From this, proponents of development integration argued that trade integration needed to be seen as only part of a broader integration strategy, which would also need to include cooperation to overcome infrastructure backlogs and explicitly promote economic diversification, including industrial development. Unlike the conventional trade integration ladder, development integration thus envisaged cooperation and coordination at an early stage. The specific trade integration pillar, moreover, would need to be calibrated to the concrete conditions of the real economies of cooperating partners and not driven by a priori or ideological considerations.

In an excellent paper specifically advocating the adoption of a 'developmental regionalism' in the construction of the African

Continental Free Trade Area (AfCFTA), Faizel Ismail[9] outlines four pillars that would need to underpin such an approach:

- asymmetrical trade integration to cater for the uneven development of the countries of the continent;
- structural transformation and transformative industrialisation, including the creation of regional value chains to build a robust regional market to unlock the continent's manufacturing potential;
- cooperation on cross-border infrastructure investment (and trade facilitation);
- cooperation to promote democracy, good governance and peace and security.

South Africa is a member of the AU, SADC and SACU. During my term as Deputy Minister under Mandisi Mpahlwa, I was deployed to meetings of all three bodies. Here one confronted positions shaped by all three of the paradigms outlined above, though often without proponents being aware of, to paraphrase Keynes, which 'defunct economist'[10] they were slaves to.

SADC was one arena where the future direction of regional integration was sharply debated. SADC launched an FTA in 2008, based on negotiations under the SADC Trade Protocol adopted in 1996.[11] The SADC Trade Protocol negotiations had been based on principles of asymmetry and differentiation. These meant that, as the largest economy, South Africa (actually all of SACU) had made more extensive tariff cuts more quickly than other partners. By 2005, South Africa and SACU had already fulfilled all of their obligations.

When I first began participating in SADC ministerial meetings there was a fierce debate under way on the modalities to establish both a customs union and a monetary union. This was largely driven by the organisation's secretariat, which pointed to the fact that the 2003 summit had adopted a Regional Indicative Strategic Development Programme (RISDP) covering the period 2005–2020.[12]

Among other things, the RISDP envisaged the establishment of a SADC customs union by 2010 and a monetary union by 2016. Participants in a Ministerial Task Force on Regional Integration were tasked with overseeing the implementation of these milestones. As the RISDP had been adopted at a summit, ministers were told they had no powers to amend timeframes, even though several expressed serious reservations about both their desirability and their realism.

Two consultant reports were commissioned to provide 'technical guidance' to these discussions. The first[13] was by a consortium of mainly South African researchers. It argued, quite correctly, that a move to a customs union would provide no additional gains for intra-regional trade over those already existing under the FTA. Strongly influenced by open regionalism, it nevertheless argued in favour of a move to a customs union on the grounds that this would allow a reduction in tariffs towards the rest of the world and thus further integrate the region into the world economy. Some spurious calculation suggested that the region would derive hundreds of millions of dollars as a result. On the basis of this, the report then made proposals on the structure of the CET. This would be a 'simple' four-band schedule, with tariffs in each band significantly lower than those in force at the time.

The other study was by a Tanzanian consortium. This also proposed a simple four-band tariff structure. However, in contrast to the first study, it proposed that a SADC CET significantly increase average tariffs compared to existing applied rates – to an extent that would almost certainly have led to its being challenged in the WTO. Another feature of the second proposal was that it also proposed a redistributive sharing of the revenue raised from tariffs weighted in favour of smaller economies.

The South African delegation consistently opposed these proposals, on two main grounds. First, from the standpoint of regional development, we argued that they were driven by a wrong paradigm and that adopting a CET at this time would not advance intra-regional trade or industrialisation. Second, from a South African national-interest point of view, either of these proposals would have required the decommissioning of a policy tool important for industrial development – tariffs. We also argued that we should eschew simplistic ideas that you became 'more integrated' if you adopted a 'more advanced' institutional framework when the objective conditions did not exist to make this an operational reality. Sometimes we encountered voices telling us that this or that region was 'more advanced' because it proclaimed itself to be a customs union or economic community, whatever the actual state of real-economy integration there. From this debate we developed an important proposition, namely, that the next phase of African integration should prioritise broadening integration at FTA level beyond existing regional economic communities rather than seeking to deepen integration within RECs.

As things turned out, there were good reasons for adopting such a view, rooted in the efforts some of the more successful emerging economies were making to further their own industrialisation efforts in the changing circumstances of the world after the Great Recession. Many of these countries had, before the onset of the 2008 financial crisis, based their industrial strategies on the export of value-added products to the advanced industrialised countries. For many years after the Great Recession, however, growth in the developed world was insipid, with demand similarly flat. Moreover, in the post-recession circumstances, many governments in the developed world were ditching some of the ideas that had guided their predecessors during the heyday of neoliberalism, in particular those that held that they were moving into in a post-industrial world driven by financialised services and that they could, therefore, dispense with manufacturing and renounce industrial policy. In the post-recession period, developed-country governments of all political expressions instead returned to avidly pursuing their own reindustrialisation, facilitated by a return to overt industrial policy. The developed world, in short, was looking less and less likely to be open to receiving ever more exports of manufactured products from more and more parts of the developing world. Faced with this reality, a turn to the domestic market became the strategic choice of several of the most dynamic emerging economies, including China and India, both with large populations.

In the case of Africa, however, colonialism had divided the continent into 54 different countries, none of which had either the population size or the level of domestic demand to sustain on its own serious economic diversification and industrialisation. Even within established RECs the agglomeration effects were modest. SADC, for example, had a combined population of 277 million and a combined GDP of US$575.5 billion in 2010.[14] But together the numbers in several RECs combined pointed to a potential regional market that could sustain deeper diversification and support the emergence of regional value chains. The 26 countries of SADC, the East African Community (EAC) and the Common Market of Eastern and Southern Africa (Comesa), for example, had a combined population of 626 million and a combined GDP of US$1.2 trillion.[15] At the level of the continent as a whole, the numbers looked even more promising – 1.2 billion people and a combined GDP of US$3.4 trillion.[16]

Southern Africa's move towards the prioritisation of broadening integration across RECs was, in the end, not really an outcome of policy debates in ministerial task teams. It began as an almost incidental consequence of overlapping customs union processes in both SADC and Comesa. Many members of SADC were also members of Comesa, and one, Tanzania, was also a member of the EAC. In the early 2000s, Comesa announced its intention to establish a customs union by 2008, even though its membership included several members of the EAC, while one, Eswatini (then Swaziland), was a member of SACU. The question of overlapping membership of separate RECs, each supposedly on track to establish customs unions (by definition, no one country can be part of more than one), led to the calling of a tripartite SADC-Comesa-EAC summit in Kampala, Uganda, in 2009. That summit, convened during the short presidency of Kgalema Motlanthe, resolved to 'rationalise' the integration efforts of the three RECs. Specifically, it agreed to work towards the negotiation of a tripartite free trade area (TFTA) embracing countries in the three RECs, and also towards the eventual merger of the three RECs into a single organisation embracing all members – dubbed a 'super REC'.[17]

The second tripartite summit was held in South Africa in 2011. We put considerable effort into preparing for this. The FTA negotiations, we insisted, must be member state-driven, not delegated to 'experts'. The approach, we argued, needed to be informed by the development integration paradigm, and thus embrace an industrial development as well as an infrastructure pillar. Trade in services, strongly pushed for by some participants, became a Phase 2 priority, while establishing free movement of businesspersons was placed on a separate but parallel negotiating track in Phase 1. Our view was that the timeframe should only be indicative, and the consensus at ministerial level was that this should set a target of three to five years to conclude the negotiations. In the summit this was cut down to three years.[18]

When the third tripartite summit convened in Sharm El Sheikh, Egypt, in June 2015, the negotiations on the free trade area had not only not been concluded but were far behind schedule. But significant progress had been made in developing a framework agreement for Phase 1, and this was opened for signature at the summit. Several annexes to the agreement had, however, not then been legally 'scrubbed' (checked). The framework set an overall ambition of reducing duties to zero on 85 per cent of tariff lines. Importantly, it specified that the TFTA would not reopen the FTAs already in existence within the three RECs, but rather would focus on negotiations between those members of the broader tripartite region that did not have preferential arrangements between them. Little progress was reported on the industrial development pillar or on the protocol on movement of businesspeople, but there was some advance in the 'North–South

Corridor' road and rail programme (the infrastructure pillar).

The AU, meanwhile, had drawn the obvious conclusion from the tripartite process that the rest of the continent needed to be drawn into a similar exercise. Within days of the 2015 tripartite summit, an AU summit held in South Africa agreed to launch negotiations for the establishment of an African Continental Free Trade Area.

The diminishing momentum of the TFTA, coupled with the energy and drive mobilised towards the AfCFTA, has in many respects led to the former's being eclipsed. There were, in fact, a number of reasons for the TFTA's slowing progress. Part of it was that the external funding on which negotiating sessions depended began to dry up once the AfCFTA was announced. But there were also deeper issues that the AfCFTA will no doubt confront once it moves into operationalisation. The exchange of commercially meaningful detailed commitments raised real issues of direct concern to domestic interest groups. Calibrating these in ways that would be seen to lead to credible 'win-win' outcomes necessarily involved consultations with domestic stakeholders, as well as technical assessments of offers and requests. These take time, particularly when relatively larger and more significant trading partners are involved. Countries with smaller economies and little current involvement in trade with parties beyond their immediate neighbours also needed to be persuaded to deploy personnel to participate in meetings. Both these issues were evident in the fact that it was only in May 2019 that officials concluded tariff schedule negotiations under the TFTA between SACU and the EAC – a development that nevertheless potentially represents a significant breakthrough for African regional integration at operational level.

African regional integration, prioritising as it is the establishment of a large continental FTA, is in my view broadly moving in the right direction. The energy and drive with which processes have been taken forward has also injected the necessary political will to move the AfCFTA beyond the point at which many earlier initiatives

The first AfCFTA ministerial summit, held in Niamey, Niger, in 2017.
President Mahamadou Issoufou of Niger is in the front row (centre).
I am standing fourth from left.

became stuck – the adoption of declaratory statements of intent. The AfCFTA is now being operationalised. All this is positive and welcome. At the same time, however, many challenges remain to be confronted before the AfCFTA fulfils its promise, not just of increasing intra-regional trade but also of becoming a vehicle to facilitate the emergence of regional value chains that enable the continent to move to higher value-added production. I will discuss my view on some of these matters in the concluding chapter.

It is important, however, to record here that we sought to apply some of the principles we espoused in negotiations at a more practical and operational level. In 2016 we established a new unit called Trade Invest Africa (TIA), led by Lerato Mataboge. This sought, in particular, to promote investment-led trade on the continent. The idea here was to identify infrastructure projects where investments by South African companies, particularly in partnerships with local companies, could both create demand for South African inputs and promote local-company participation. The first venture undertaken by TIA was an energy-focused mission to Zambia. Another aspect of the work of TIA – now incorporated into the Trade and Investment South Africa (TISA) division headed by Mataboge as a deputy director-general – was the promotion of a 'Guideline for Good Business Practice in Africa' by South African companies.[19] Broadly based on the United Nations Global Compact, this rests on adherence to 12 pillars that would serve as a guide for South African companies operating on the rest of the continent to emerge as good corporate partners. Although voluntary, the Guideline was signed on to by many of South Africa's major companies and was also well received by other African countries.

The world's oldest customs union

The other regional body we are part of is the Southern African Customs Union. SACU is, in fact, the world's oldest customs union, predating the EU by more than 50 years. The year 2010 marked the centenary of its existence. In the run-up to this milestone, the secretariat planned a commemoration in which the theme was to be celebrating how the union had managed to remain in existence for so long, despite facing many challenges. Only Dr Hage Geingob, who later became President of Namibia but was at the time Minister of Trade and Industry, and I pointed out that for most of its existence SACU had been a colonial and apartheid arrangement.

SACU in fact initially embraced South Africa and the so-called High Commission territories – Botswana, Lesotho and Eswatini (then Swaziland), known collectively as BLS. Under colonialism, the BLS territories had been administered out of South Africa by the British High Commission. Economically, they were once almost totally

Meeting civil rights icon the Reverend Jesse Jackson in New York in 2018, with DTI colleagues Lerato Mataboge (left), the head of Trade Invest Africa, and Wamkele Mene (right), then Chief Director: Africa Economic Relations.

integrated into South Africa, with no customs borders, the tariffs in force in South Africa applying in BLS, South African currency serving as legal tender, and there being unrestricted movement of people across borders (though subject to the influx control regime developed in South Africa during the periods of segregation and apartheid). As indicated in Chapter 2, after the conquest of German South West Africa during the First World War, Namibia became incorporated virtually as a fifth province of South Africa.

Until the 1960s, apartheid South Africa had ambitions to formally incorporate the High Commission territories. Had it achieved this, it would been able to portray the racial division of land in a greater South Africa as an equitable 50:50 split instead of the manifestly unfair 87 per cent for whites and only 13 per cent for Africans in homelands. By the mid-1960s, apartheid repression had made it impossible for Britain to agree to any such transfer, and so the BLS countries were 'prepared' for independence later in that decade. At

BLS independence, the economic union of SACU was in fact loosened. All three independent countries eventually adopted their own currencies, though Lesotho and Swaziland remained members of a looser Common Monetary Area.

A new formal SACU agreement was also negotiated after BLS independence in 1969. A key feature of this was the maintenance of the CET and of South Africa's unfettered right to set tariffs applying to all of SACU. In return, customs and excise duties collected throughout SACU were paid into a common revenue pool and distributed according to a weighted formula that was intended, in part, to 'compensate' BLS for the price-raising effects of being drawn behind South Africa's then relatively high protective tariff walls, as well as for the loss of fiscal discretion in having no say in tariff-setting. This arrangement can be described as a relationship of convenience held together by a redistributive revenue-sharing formula. Over time, the BLS countries, and particularly Botswana, argued that they were being inadequately compensated, and apartheid South Africa – then desperate to be seen as involved with some independent African countries – made upward adjustments to a formula that provided Lesotho and Swaziland at least with the major part of their budget revenue. Namibia was, until its independence in 1990, treated as economically part of South Africa, but thereafter became part of SACU on the same terms as the others. SACU had for all these years absolutely no developmental aspirations or pretensions and not one cent of the revenue collected and shared went to support any cross-border project of any description.[20]

After South Africa's democratisation in 1994, discussions began on how to reform and 'democratise' SACU. These culminated in the adoption of a new SACU treaty in 2002.[21] Until 1994 there had been few formal meetings (none at political level) and no permanent secretariat running the organisation. The new treaty provided for regular meetings at ministerial level (involving both trade and finance ministers) in a Council chaired by each country in rotation. Council meetings were preceded by meetings of officials in what was called the Commission. A permanent executive secretariat was also established, based in Windhoek, Namibia. The basic architecture of the revenue-sharing formula was carried over, though with a new element added – a developmental component based on levels of development. Although the structure of the formula was not identical to that of its predecessors, it grandfathered in a similar weighting in favour of BLNS (the BLS countries plus Namibia) as the previous formula. A final feature of the new treaty was that it envisaged the development of common policies, including for industrial development and trade, and, based on these, foresaw the establishment of new institutions. Among these were national tariff boards in each country, with a joint SACU tariff board answerable to the Council responsible for taking final tariff decisions based on consensus. This part of the treaty was, however, suspended pending the establishment of these boards, and in the meantime ITAC was delegated to continue to set tariffs on behalf of SACU.

By the time of its centenary, SACU was already looking increasingly anachronistic. A relationship of convenience held together by a redistributive revenue-sharing formula remained its hallmark as meetings in the new structures became characterised more by bickering than by efforts to generate genuine cross-border cooperation. Our SACU partners were still suspicious of South Africa. Often we were confronted with ahistorical accounts of how South Africa was using SACU to undermine their own development efforts, citing real episodes during the apartheid years as though they were current policy. Strategic conversations revealed an attitude of indifference, even hostility, to the existence of South Africa's industrial base and the approach to many issues tended to be seen by some of our partners through the lens of its impact on the common revenue pool. For example, a presentation on South Africa's automotive programme, the APDP, was met with calls for South Africa to 'compensate' the common revenue pool for the revenue lost due to the tariff rebates provided under the scheme. Although we had agreed to negotiate external trade agreements as a bloc, we found that as soon as the EU applied pressure during Economic Partnership Agreement negotiations (see below), everyone went their own way, leading some in our ranks to initial the interim agreement, while we and Namibia did not. Meanwhile, transfers to the rest of SACU from customs and excise revenue collected in South Africa were steadily rising, reaching R43.2 billion in 2012/3 and R51.7 billion in 2014/5 through an arrangement that saw South Africa retaining slightly less than half of the common revenue pool, more than 95 per cent of which was collected in South Africa.[22]

Ahead of the centenary celebrations, we made a presentation suggesting that SACU was at a crossroads: it could either advance along a path of developmental integration or become increasingly irrelevant if it stayed where it was. That debate led to agreement to develop a SACU work plan. This would include an industrial development pillar. Tariffs would be seen as a tool of industrial policy. We would work together more closely on external trade negotiations, and we would establish a regular summit of heads of state to provide strategic guidance. Unfortunately, the new programme soon became enmeshed in the same old challenges. Instead of trying to chart how we could cooperate on defined industrial projects to realise the potential of regional value chains, the issue of SACU industrial policy became a demand that each country must submit its national programmes for approval by SACU. Also elusive was any agreement that part of the funding for potential cross-border industrial or infrastructure projects would come from the common revenue pool: instead South Africa was expected to provide 'additional resources' that left no (other) member 'worse off'. With no progress on any of these issues, National Treasury eventually formally called for a renegotiation of the revenue-sharing formula. At the same time, and in the midst of increasing signs that our partners had little interest in defending South Africa's industrial base, we were presented with reports that all countries were ready to establish their national tariff boards and that the mandate to ITAC to set tariffs on behalf of SACU would be withdrawn by the end of 2013.

Our response was to elevate both matters to the summit and to limit our engagements with SACU for the next two years. We saw tariff-setting, as indicated above, as an important tool of industrial policy. The vast majority of tariffs set in SACU concern industries and sectors that exist in South Africa but not in the rest of SACU. Our experience with the debate on SACU industrial policy gave us little confidence that our SACU partners, except perhaps Namibia, would be inclined to follow an approach similar to that we had adopted. At best we *might* be able to reach agreement on industries in which we all had a stake (and these were few, mainly agricultural). But while we were more than ready to improve consultation in such cases, the architecture envisaged in the treaty would have thrown all tariff decisions upon the mercy of a consensus decision in which four countries that together had less than ten per cent of either the population or GDP of South Africa would have had a veto over all tariff decisions. Besides, the process would be slow and cumbersome, as a study commissioned by the SACU Secretariat confirmed. With a strong possibility that many of our partners would take a revenue- and consumption-driven approach to tariff decisions, we saw this as potentially decommissioning tariffs as a tool of industrial policy. Besides, as we pointed out in various bilateral meetings, the existing revenue-sharing formula (at least minus the developmental component) was based on grandfathering in compensation for being drawn behind South Africa's (now much lower) tariff walls and loss of fiscal discretion. The moment common tariff-setting kicked in, we suggested, the justification for these components of a revenue-sharing arrangement skewed in their favour would disappear absolutely and totally.

I left office in 2019 with South Africa's having formally tabled proposals to review both the tariff-setting and revenue-sharing arrangements of the 2002 treaty, but with an absolute deadlock on both issues. Even a 'consensus-building' proposal to establish a

Participants in a SACU ministerial meeting held in Gaborone, Botswana, in June 2018. Then Minister of Finance Nhlanhla Nene is standing directly behind me.

R1 billion fund to support some visible SACU infrastructure pro-grammes could not command agreement, because although South Africa indicated a willingness to contribute the biggest part, others would also have had to contribute. Meanwhile, specific demands from other members for exemptions from tariffs on wheat and sugar, to support industries looking to access the South African market, were posing new challenges. On a more positive level, trade ministers did manage to come together to negotiate a post-Brexit deal with the UK, essentially rolling over on a bilateral basis the arrangements in place under the Economic Partnership Agreement with the European Union (see below). My understanding is that SACU is now operat-ing on a 'pragmatic' understanding that the big controversial issues are shelved. How long this can last remains to be seen.

Other trade issues

In the case of other trade issues, one of our biggest challenges and headaches was the World Trade Organization negotiations. In one or other capacity, I participated in every WTO ministerial meeting from Seattle in 1999 to Buenos Aires in 2017. In addition, I attended numerous preparatory, 'informal' and regional meetings on WTO matters. I therefore had the opportunity to witness up close and personal the transition from hegemonic multilateralism to outright mercantilism, and the transformation of the WTO from a behemoth driving neoliberal reform to a moribund institution facing an existential crisis. I have written about this at length elsewhere[23] and will not repeat the detail here. The only point to make for now is that South Africa never looked likely to benefit directly and commercially from anything proposed in the WTO. Even the deal emerging, but not finally agreed, from the Doha Round negotiations would have seen commercially meaningful additional market access in just one agricultural tariff line (in Japan), while requiring significant payment in the form of reduced tariffs in Non-Agricultural Market Access (NAMA). As a result, we were obliged to adopt a largely defensive stance in the WTO – defensive of the policy space we needed to create jobs.

After African regional integration, the next priority we identified in the fourth administration was the promotion of South-South cooperation. On the trade front, we engaged with discussions already under way between SACU and Mercosul/Mercosur (embracing Brazil, Argentina, Uruguay and Paraguay, with Venezuela joining later) and between SACU and India to establish preferential trade agreements. Our approach was based on the proposition that as we were all industrialising countries and regions, there would be many areas where we were directly competitive, but we could also identify areas where we were actually or potentially complementary. The task of South-South cooperation, we suggested, was to prioritise the complementarities, to

Attending a World Trade Organization ministerial meeting in Davos in 2018. I am standing to the right of Roberto Azevêdo, who in August 2020 stepped down as Director-General of the WTO. In the middle row behind me and to the right is Xavier Carim, the former South African ambassador to the WTO.

build practical investment and project cooperation around these, and to construct any resulting trade agreements accordingly. We advanced similar propositions with other developing and emerging economies, including China, which in 2008 emerged as our largest single trading partner in both imports and exports.

In 2009 Brazil, Russia, India and China formed a grouping called BRIC. This followed, but was not informed by, the writings of Jim O'Neill of Goldman Sachs, who coined the acronym 'BRICs' to describe fast-growing emerging markets that were becoming a major dynamic force in the world economy.[24]

South Africa was already a member of IBSA (India, Brazil, South Africa). In 2010 the BRIC summit was held in Brazil back to back with that of IBSA, and there was a joint IBSA/BRIC business forum attended by trade ministers from all sides. It was an excellent opportunity to advance a request that South Africa be admitted as a member of BRIC. In a significant diplomatic achievement, the other BRIC members eventually agreed, and we participated in our first meeting as a member of BRICS, as it became known, in New Delhi in 2011.

BRICS membership drew us into the most significant grouping of emerging economies, but we realised from the start that South Africa had been admitted because the other BRICS members needed a partner from the African continent. This was seen as imposing responsibilities on us to ensure that our BRICS membership benefited the continent as a whole. South Africa joined at a fortunate moment. BRICS had not yet developed its programme for intra-BRICS cooperation, and we were thus able to contribute to shaping it. Among other things, we put forward our perspective of building cooperation and trade relations on the basis of identified complementarities. These and other discussions, meanwhile, led to a view that BRICS needed to establish a funding mechanism to support projects, to work to promote trade without recourse to third-country currencies and to establish a cooperative mechanism to mitigate the effects of volatility on currency markets. South Africa eagerly embraced all of these work streams. At the first BRICS summit held in Africa, in Durban in 2013, it was agreed that finance ministers would work to negotiate the establishment of a BRICS New Development Bank, as well as a contingency reserve arrangement to deal with currency and balance of payments volatility. The establishment of the bank was announced at the 2014 summit, held in Fortaleza, Brazil. Each BRICS member would contribute US$100 million to the capital base. The bank's headquarters would be in Shanghai, China. An Indian national would be the first president and the first regional office would be established in Johannesburg. The bank was formally launched, with the vice presidents and board members all appointed, at the 2015 summit, held in Ufa, Russia.

At the Durban summit in 2013, there were two further innovations. A permanent BRICS Business Council was established to provide an ongoing engagement on promoting business cooperation. Patrice Motsepe became the first chair of the council, and

In conversation with Patrice Motsepe (right), first chair of the BRICS Business Council, and Deputy Minister of Trade and Industry Bulelani Magwanishe (left, head turned) on the margins of the BRICS Business Forum, Johannesburg 2018.

did a sterling job of establishing a discipline of regular interactions and concrete work on project cooperation. There was also an outreach summit, organised at the initiative of President Zuma, between BRICS leaders and leaders of African RECs to discuss how the BRICS programme could reinforce the African agenda. This initiative was followed at the summits in Brazil and Russia, where the hosts organised similar outreach summits with their respective regions. Another initiative we pioneered was the commissioning of a study on potential complementary intra-BRICS trade based on revealed comparative advantage. This study was adopted at Fortaleza in 2014, but unfortunately has yet to underpin any serious trade arrangement between BRICS partners.

BRICS has continued to meet regularly, and to promote cooperation, despite increasingly evident divergences among its members. In my view, it is still important as the most significant grouping of 'emerging economies' in existence, even though it has definitely not

A bilateral meeting with the Indian delegation, led by Suresh Prabhu (left), Minister of Commerce and Industry, on the fringes of the WTO Ministerial Conference, Buenos Aires, December 2017.

yet become the kind of systemic alternative some of us might have hoped for.

Our BRICS work was accompanied by the promotion of stronger bilateral ties with each individual BRICS partner. During President Zuma's state visit to China in 2010, we negotiated a Comprehensive Strategic Partnership Agreement, the highest level of bilateral cooperation. The declaration establishing this spoke not only of increasing trade but also of working together to address the 'structural deficit' in our bilateral trade. By this we meant that if one took the top ten products in our respective export baskets, ours was dominated by ten unprocessed mineral commodities; China's basket, by contrast, started with cellphones, followed by nine other value-added products. Concretely, China agreed to work with us to promote more value-added sales in China, as well as investments in value-added production. Over the next few years, we took value-added trade fairs to China, though with limited results. We requested China to send inward buying missions, and some came, but these focused too much on 'traditional imports', such as wool and wine, in our view. Around the middle of the last decade, China moved from being a net absorber of FDI to becoming a net investor in countries abroad. We noticed and welcomed this trend, and, through agencies such as InvestSA, led by Yunus Hoosen, worked to realise investments by Chinese companies such as Hisense (televisions and refrigerators), FAW (trucks and cars) and BAW (vehicles), as well as a manganese sinter plant, and more. Beyond BRICS, we put considerable effort into promoting stronger trade and investment ties with countries in the Arabian Gulf and Indonesia, among others.

While a considerable amount of our time and effort was expended (with varied but limited effect) in developing new forms of relations with 'non-traditional' trade partners, we also had to deal with issues in relations with our long-standing established trading partners in the developed world.

Shortly after South Africa's democratic transition, negotiations began on what became the Trade, Development and Cooperation Agreement (TDCA) with the EU. The background to this was that, under apartheid, South Africa had no access to any preferential scheme with the EU and conducted its trade with its largest trading partner on Most Favoured Nation terms (MFN), which actually were the least favourable terms available. After 1994, the democratic government requested access to an arrangement 'as close as possible' to the non-reciprocal preferential access offered to the ACP countries under the then existing Lomé Convention. The response from the EU was to the effect that South Africa was not a 'typical' ACP country and that its inclusion in Lomé potentially threatened the waiver the arrangement operated under in the WTO, to the disadvantage of other ACP countries. Instead, the EU proposed the negotiation of an FTA on the grounds that this would offer South Africa a legally secure basis to ensure the improved access to the EU market it wanted. The preliminary discussions on this approach were conducted as though the EU had no offensive interests (the pursuit of further market opening) in the South African market and was only interested in 'helping' the country's development. In discussions on the framework, it was agreed that the FTA would be both asymmetrical (meaning the smaller economy, South Africa, would have longer to fulfil its obligations) and differentiated (the obligations themselves would be less onerous than those of the larger and stronger EU). The subsequent detailed negotiations lasted until 1999.

South Africa won the title of the agreement, and managed to ward off any strong political conditionalities (with clauses merely referring to each other's constitutions). But it was definitely not the case that the EU refrained from pursuing partisan commercial interests. It left out, or agreed only to tariff rate quotas on, a number of agricultural and agro-processing products where South Africa was competitive. I recall that during this time the Netherlands assumed the then rotating presidency of the EU. The theme it chose for its six-month presidency was promoting consistency between the EU's developmental agenda and its other programmes. This did not stop cut flowers being inserted into the list of products to be excluded from duty-free access under the FTA. In fact, the EU's overall coverage of duty-free entry of agricultural products was only a little over 60 per cent. By contrast, South Africa agreed to remove duties on over 85 per cent of EU agricultural imports. In NAMA the percentages were reversed, with South Africa gaining 97 per cent duty-free access, while the EU was granted a little less than 70 per cent. These obligations were to be phased in over five years by the EU, with South Africa having up to 12 years for a few tariff lines. Other provisions included South Africa's renunciation of export taxes on mineral products, with the exception of the diamond levy then already in force.[25] The EU's ambition here was later spelt out more clearly in its 2008 Raw Materials Initiative.[26] The fundamental objective was to ensure that EU companies continued to have access to raw materials from the developing world, unhindered by the deployment of any policy tools, such as export taxes, to promote beneficiation. The South African negotiators at the time followed a practice we later decided to reverse, of offering to freeze policy space not currently being used without seriously considering whether this might be required in the future. The TDCA negotiations were concluded in 1999 and the agreement entered into force in 2000.

Meanwhile, conversations were under way between the EU and the ACP countries on the future of Lomé. As an MP, I was deployed for many years to the ACP-EU Joint Parliamentary Assembly (JPA) and through this had an opportunity to witness some of what became a very one-sided dialogue. Most of the discussions, in fact, focused on issues of human rights in ACP countries. While many real issues were raised, the way they were approached (through resolutions tabled by major European parliamentary groups) led to overbearing self-righteousness being met with over-defensiveness, not just by delegations who were the direct subject of resolutions but also by many other ACP delegations fearing their turn might be next. At some stage I found myself elected as co-vice president for human rights on the JPA's Bureau. This required me to submit a draft report. I pondered over this for some time, and then decided to try to rebalance the debate by writing about human rights issues in the EU. I used the same sources as those used in resolutions on issues in ACP countries (such as Amnesty International and Human Rights Watch) and focused on the impact of racism and the then ongoing war on terror. Writing as diplomatically as I could, I concluded:

> While the EU has a number of admirable programmes to combat racism and xenophobia (mainly of an educational nature or involving the making of recommendations to member states), these clearly have not proved sufficient to stem a worrying trend towards heightened xenophobia and racism in Europe. What human rights organisations are pointing to is the possibility that

127

a passive approach by the EU towards charges of a lowering of human rights standards in the name of the 'war on terror' could exacerbate such trends. In addition to the direct impact on the dialogue on migration envisaged by [the Cotonou Agreement], such trends could also impact negatively on the overall evolution of an EU-ACP partnership by fuelling a negative sentiment towards the 'third world', of which the ACP is part.[27]

When this report was tabled at the Bureau, no one challenged the points made, but the majority on the EU side decided to restrict its circulation to members of the Bureau rather than to the JPA membership at large, as had been the practice up to then. A recommendation for a more substantial dialogue focusing on causal factors and longer-term issues did, however, feed into a decision to establish committees to deal with issues more substantially and table at plenary a limited number of resolutions that had been processed in committees.

It was into this milieu that the parliamentary debate on the future of EU-ACP relations was inserted. Only a few of us felt confident enough to engage in what became a very one-sided dialogue. This began by reflecting on the fact that, despite the Lomé preferences, ACP exports to the EU had not grown, and most ACP countries only took advantage of a few of the available preferences. Although a number of quality research reports had been produced showing that this was primarily because of the underdeveloped production structures of most ACP countries, as well as because many Lomé preferences were more generous on primary products than they were on value-added goods,[28] this research was ignored by the European Commission (the EU's executive branch), which developed its own alternative narrative. This proclaimed that the reason ACP countries could not make better use of Lomé preferences was because they were non-reciprocal, and what was required therefore was a shift to a reciprocal trade regime. *Post hoc ergo propter hoc* (after this, therefore because of this) is taught in Logic

101 as a form of logical fallacy. Yet that was exactly what informed the narrative that underpinned the passage from Lomé to what were called Economic Partnership Agreements (EPAs). Reciprocity was required because non-reciprocal preferences had not resulted in an increase in the proportion of ACP exports to the EU. To my horror, when I was appointed to the executive, I found ministerial-level EU-ACP engagements were not much better than those at parliamentary level. In the end, the ACP could not resist and began negotiations for EPAs. During this debate something of an irony began to emerge with regard to the TDCA. Originally presented as something crafted to accommodate South Africa's 'exceptionality', the TDCA became recast as a model for all 'normal' ACP countries to follow.

By 2012, the last of South Africa's tariff phase-downs under the TDCA kicked in. In the context of depressed growth in Europe after the 2008 financial crisis, these consolidated the transformation of a small surplus in South Africa's favour into a ballooning deficit. In 2012 South Africa exported goods to the EU worth R143 billion, while imports were valued at R238 billion, meaning there was an imbalance of R95 billion in the EU's favour. By 2015 this imbalance had risen to R104 billion as imports reached R320 billion while exports rose to only R216 billion.[29] Frozen potato chips, poultry products and a host of other agro-processed products, including several based on subsidised inputs, were among the 'new' import items flooding the South African market.

Meanwhile, by 2007 EPA negotiations were well under way. The architecture developed mostly by the EU envisaged two stages of negotiations: in the first, parties would negotiate 'interim' EPAs with FTAs covering trade in goods and some policy commitments; in the second, there would be negotiations on trade in services and binding commitments on competition, investment and intellectual property. The EU indicated it would offer 'duty free, quota free' access to its market for all products from all participating ACP countries (except South Africa) and would implement this immediately on the initialling of interim EPAs. Existing non-reciprocal preferences would, however, be withdrawn at a defined end date (which ended up being extended several times). This meant that from the end date, countries failing to agree an interim EPA would be subject to the WTO MFN duty.

The implications of this for our SACU partners were stark and dramatic. Namibia and Botswana had both exported beef to the EU under a Lomé quota that provided duty-free access for defined tonnages. Eswatini had a quota for sugar exports to the EU, which then paid higher than world market prices. Initialling the EPA meant the removal of the quotas, meaning that these countries would then be able to export duty-free to the EU all that they could. Not initialling meant the prospect of withdrawal of the preferences and reverting to WTO MFN duties. This would have meant paying 90 per cent tariffs in the case of the beef exports and Eswatini's having to accept the lower world market prices for its sugar exports, if indeed it could find a market.

We decided to participate in the official SADC EPA group. This was, in fact, only one of several EPA groups in which SADC member countries participated. A number of SADC members preferred the Eastern and Southern Africa (ESA) group coordinated by the Comesa secretariat, and Tanzania was in the EAC group. The SADC EPA group consisted of the five SACU countries plus Mozambique and Angola. The fact that SADC members participated in several EPA groups meant that SADC actually had no idea whether or not obligations accepted by its members were harmonised. Given that with the TDCA in place, South Africa had no legal obligation or pressing trade imperative to participate, our motivation for choosing to do so was twofold. First, we hoped it would result in the harmonisation of the terms of our trade relations with an important trade partner with those of our partners in the region – to the benefit of regional integration. Second, we sought to secure some improvements for ourselves compared to the TDCA.

I was deployed as Deputy Minister to the SADC EPA ministerial engagement with the EU, held in November 2007 in Brussels. The date was significant. The end of that year was the deadline then set by the EU for the initialling of interim EPAs, and the withdrawal of non-reciprocal Lomé preferences. Although the negotiations had been going on for some time, we went into the November 2007 ministerial with many issues still unresolved. In its preparatory meeting, the SADC EPA group had developed a list of over 20 textual changes it was unanimously agreed were essential before we could initial. These included apparently technical issues such as the definition of 'parties', which unless changed could have allowed the EU to act against all members of the group in the event of a dispute with any one of them. Another critical issue was that the BLNS countries were expected to provide market access better than that provided for under the TDCA for 54 EU products, while South Africa, which would not be given 'duty free, quota free' access, would not. No account had been taken of the impact of this differential treatment on the SACU CET and the broader coherence of SACU, nor how practically it would be administered. The SADC EPA group also agreed that there should be no obligation to enter into the trade in services and the other Phase 2 negotiations. It proposed, instead, that there should be a reference only to general cooperation on these matters, while allowing those that felt so inclined to proceed with negotiations for binding commitments.

The EU team at the November 2007 meeting was led by the then Trade Commissioner, Peter Mandelson. A larger-than-life personality, with a reputation as an 'operator', Mandelson refused to budge on most of our issues that the meeting began considering one by one. After several hours, a bored and irritated-looking Mandelson said that he was keen to move on to discuss the Phase 2 matters and in any case could only stay a further hour. Someone asked him when we could then reconvene and he replied that he was a busy man and could only fit us in 'next year' – after the expiry of the deadline. For the next hour or so the meeting continued, following the agenda, until Mandelson announced that his time was up and left the meeting. The majority of our colleagues looked flabbergasted. No one shared my view that we should offer Mandelson an award for amateur dramatics. Instead a delegation was dispatched to beg him to come back. After a while he did, but said he could only stay two more hours, after which he would have to leave for good. It was during those two hours that our group fell apart and visibly divided itself in front of the EU delegation. Several of our group felt they had no option but to initial the unmodified draft interim EPA. Three did so over the following two days, and one other did so later on. Three of us (Namibia, Angola and South Africa) said we could not. We never blamed our neighbours for their decision, reserving our criticism for the heavy-handed approach of the EU. In an ACP meeting held later, one delegate described a similar experience in another group as 'negotiating with a gun to one's head'. 'Not so,' said another. 'It was a bazooka.'

The effect, nevertheless, was that this episode added to the divisions within SACU and SADC. Mandelson resorted to demonising us publicly, at one time publicly saying that South Africa's role in the EPA process had been 'deeply negative'.[30] Xavier Carim, Faizel Ismail and I all came in for personal chiding at one point or another. One effect of this was that we drew closer to Namibia and Angola. In particular, we strongly resisted suggestions that Namibia's preferences be withdrawn, and worked to ensure that SACU as a whole endorsed a similar position. Mandelson was eventually replaced as EU commissioner while several of us were attending an ACP summit in Accra, Ghana. When the news reached us, many delegates broke out in an undiplomatic but heartfelt cheer. Mandelson's replacement was Baroness Catherine Ashton, a much more personable individual, who offered to take another look at the concerns of Angola, Namibia and South Africa. Like all commissioners, she was restricted by the very tight EU bureaucracy. I once met with her in her office in Brussels and recall her saying in reply to one of our proposals, 'I think

I can do that.' Behind her, however, were officials from the bureaucracy who shook their heads, leading her finally to ask, 'Oh, can't I?' Eventually, through discussions with Cathy Ashton and her successor, Karel De Gucht, we agreed to draw a line under the divisive interim EPA episode and move together into negotiations for a final EPA. Some of our long-standing concerns over the text were eventually accommodated, and we were able to agree that participation in negotiation on the original Phase 2 matters would be purely voluntary.

Over the next few years, and in a much more constructive spirit, we engaged in discussions on improving our own market access (given that the EU made it clear we would not get the 'duty free, quota free' access offered to all other participants). We requested improved terms for wine, sugar and canned fruit, among other commodities. The EU asked for very limited additional access for a few minor agricultural products, but insisted that we pay by recognising a long list of product names as geographical indications (GIs). These were names that could only be used by producers of those products located in a specific geographic region. In the TDCA, South Africa had already agreed to give up using names like 'port' and 'sherry' that were deemed to be geographical indications reserved for producers of fortified wines from Oporto in Portugal and Jerez de la Frontera in Spain, respectively. The EPA list was longer and included names of cheese and ham products, as well as other alcoholic drinks. In the end we conceded on a list that included very few names currently in use in South Africa. The few exceptions, such as feta cheese, exempted existing producers. In return we also secured recognition as GIs in the EU of the names of some South African wines, as well as rooibos and honeybush herbal teas and Karoo lamb. The other issue where we sought improvement was to claw back some of the policy space conceded in the TDCA that limited the imposition of export taxes. The small improvement we won here was hard fought. I recall engaging on this matter with then Commissioner De Gucht on

A consultative meeting of the SADC EPA group and EU Trade Commissioner Cecilia Malmström (second from left), held in Cape Town in 2018.

the margins of the EU-Africa summit held in Brussels in 2014. De Gucht said I must understand that he could not allow EU firms to be denied access to the raw materials they needed. I replied by quoting from the summit declaration then awaiting adoption, which spoke of both sides' acknowledging Africa's ambitions to industrialise and add value to its resource base. De Gucht responded, 'Oh, we don't pay any attention to that.' Although I used that Freudian slip to try to push for tactical advantage, De Gucht had inadvertently revealed something quite profound about the realpolitik of trade negotiations: the victories won by developing countries in summit declarations or preambles to trade agreements and the like actually have very little bearing on the positions pursued by interlocutors in negotiations on matters of detail.

The EPA between the EU and the SADC EPA group was eventually signed at a ceremony in Kasane, Botswana, on 10 June 2016. The EU Commissioner for Trade at the time was Cecilia Malmström. For us, the EPA represented a small but significant improvement over the TDCA and allowed harmonisation with our neighbours. Over time, the large deficit with the EU has reduced to a more manageable €105 million in 2018, with exports of €24 072 million and imports of €24 177 million, according to EU figures.[31] When I left office, however, there were still a number of tensions and disputes with the EU, most prominent among them the EU's demand for us to remove a special safeguard measure limiting the import of poultry 'spare parts' (brown meat, bone-in portions).

AGOA renewal and post-AGOA

The US African Growth and Opportunity Act (AGOA) is the final issue dealt with in this chapter. AGOA was signed into law in May 2000 by President Bill Clinton after years of campaigning by the Congressional Black Caucus and supporters in the US Congress. AGOA provided significant non-reciprocal trade benefits to African countries identified as meeting prescribed standards of democratic practice and economic governance. Specifically, AGOA added 1 600 tariff lines to the duty-free access applied under the US Generalized System of Preferences (GSP) and also provided that these were not renewable annually, unlike under the GSP. South Africa became an AGOA-eligible country after concluding the TDCA negotiations with the EU (a point whose relevance will emerge later). Over the years, South Africa, as the most diversified of AGOA-eligible countries, made use of the largest number of tariff lines. Among other products, motor vehicles assembled in South Africa entered the US duty-free. AGOA was enacted for a fixed term of 15 years expiring in 2015. From about 2013 onwards we became involved in a number of engagements about the future of AGOA.

In these engagements, we discovered that a number of influential voices in the US had begun to raise the same kinds of issues, in a similar way, as the EU had in the debate that led to the transition from Lomé preferences to EPAs. These pointed to the fact that the vast majority of AGOA beneficiaries were using only a few of the preferential tariff lines available. African exports to the US as a whole, in fact, amounted to one per cent of total US imports, with more than 60 per cent of that made up by mineral products – the largest by far being oil.[32] The idea that there needed to be a move to reciprocity began to be floated. Another view, supposedly similar but actually contradictory, argued that 'more advanced' countries with a broader trade profile ought to be 'graduated out' of AGOA preferences, which should be reserved for 'poor countries' and in some versions exclusively for Least Developed Countries (LDCs). South Africa, as the most diversified economy among AGOA-eligible countries, and using the broadest range of AGOA preferences, including on auto products, was a prime candidate for 'graduation'. However, as the then US Secretary of State, John Kerry, pointed out in his speech to the 2014 AGOA Forum in Washington, the auto preferences benefited both sides. A Ford engine manufactured in the company's Struandale plant in South Africa and incorporated into a panel van manufactured in the US contributed to the creation of 800 American jobs.

We used every possible opportunity to engage in this debate. In addition to formal engagements with our counterparts in the United States Trade Representative's office, we also became involved in lobbying members of Congress. Our main message was that the fundamental reason for the limited use of tariff lines by most AGOA beneficiaries was not the non-reciprocal nature of the preferences but capacity constraints. SACU had, in fact before my time, engaged in exploratory talks with the US on the possibility of an FTA. As indicated above, we had enough problems with the TDCA and EPA negotiations, but at least the EU's perspective on FTAs allowed some element of asymmetry, differentiation and exclusion of some lines. The US model, by contrast, was much less asymmetrical and differentiated and sought much higher levels of product coverage. It also sought binding commitments to align investment, intellectual

Meeting US President Barack Obama during his state visit to South Africa in 2013. In the centre is Minister of Economic Development Ebrahim Patel.

property and other laws to US models. With there being no harmonisation on any of these matters within SACU, both sides finally unanimously agreed not to pursue the talks any further. In the debate on AGOA renewal we put forward the proposition that the US should not see itself as just in competition with the EU in Africa. There were now many other competitors, none of whom were trying to foist EPA-like arrangements on the continent. We pointed out that AGOA had built goodwill for the US – unlike the EPAs, which had done the opposite for the EU. We suggested that the priority for the US in seeking commercial opportunities lay in investing in projects to promote industrialisation and infrastructure development.

With regard to South Africa specifically, we pointed to the fact that our bilateral trade with the US had continued to grow throughout the post-2008 period, unlike that with the EU, which dipped sharply after 2008. We added that our trade with the US was relatively balanced, and that AGOA preferences had led to our export basket's containing not just primary products but some value-added goods. Besides, we pointed out, there were then more than 600 US companies invested in South Africa, several benefiting from AGOA preferences. We used all of these arguments to put forward the proposition that 'AGOA ain't broke, so we don't need to fix it', adding that without South Africa, AGOA would be a pale shadow of what it ought to be.

Of course, we were not indifferent to AGOA's limitations. There were product lines that we were perfectly capable of utilising but were not included in AGOA preferences because of the competition African producers potentially presented to interests in the US. For example, AGOA covered canned pears, but we could not get it extended to cover canned peaches, a product where South Africa is highly competitive. I was told that the reason for this was that we would never be able to persuade members of Congress from Georgia (whose official nickname is the 'Peach State') to agree. South Africa was also excluded from the 'third country fabric' provisions applicable to other AGOA members. These allowed eligible countries to import from third countries the textiles used in the manufacture of clothing products exported to the US under AGOA. While we sought improvements, and at one stage were told by Michael Froman, the then US Trade Representative (a cabinet-level appointment although the incumbent has the title of Ambassador), that he would push for these too, our priority was to retain access to AGOA preferences for a reasonable period (which African ministers proposed should be 15 years).

The canned peaches issue highlighted something very important about the US legislature, which, rather than the administration, was ultimately required to pronounce on the future of AGOA. Its strongly entrenched district system, and frequent elections, made legislators very susceptible to special-interest lobbying. Senators Chris Coons (Democrat, Delaware) and Johnny Isakson (Republican, Georgia), the two most prominent members of the Senate dealing with the AGOA dossier, also happened to come from poultry-producing states. They informed us around 2014 that they would not support South Africa's inclusion in a renewed AGOA unless we removed the anti-dumping duty (ADD) on US poultry products that had been in force since 2001. The reason for imposing the duty arose from the differing consumption patterns in the developed and developing worlds. More affluent consumers in the developed world tend to favour white meat, meaning that poultry producers there have a surplus of brown meat. As this is virtually unsaleable for human consumption in home markets, it is often aggressively pushed into developing-country markets at very low prices. The alternative is to turn it into pet food at even lower prices. The South African anti-dumping duty was applied to all US bone-in portions after the US failed to cooperate in a potential company-based investigation following WTO rules. We were convinced that the duty was imposed legally, but the US insisted it was not. In addition, the US wanted us to remove their beef from sanitary and phytosanitary (SPS) restrictions, imposed at a time when they had an outbreak of bovine spongiform encephalopathy (BSE or 'mad cow' disease), as well as to remove pork from other SPS restrictions imposed to counter other diseases. Several SPS measures in the US that restricted access for South African meat products to the US market were also put on the table, although these did not command the same attention from our US interlocutors.

The 'three meats' soon became the subject of much engagement and fervent diplomatic lobbying. This included a phone call from then US Vice President Joe Biden (previously Senator for Delaware, an important poultry producer) to then Deputy President Cyril Ramaphosa. As usual, this lobby could count on a ready hearing from much of the South African commercial press, as well as the opposition in Parliament. An organisation calling itself the Association of Meat Importers and Exporters (AMIE), which in fact did very little exporting, hired the former leader of the opposition, Tony Leon, as its public liaison officer. The USA Poultry and Egg Export Council,

At the Capitol building in Washington, DC, standing between Senators Chris Coons (left) and Johnny Isakson (right).

In 2014, during the lobbying over the future of AGOA, I met with Representative Karen Bass of California, in her office in the Capitol building.

the main demandeur on the US side, was an associate member of AMIE. Yet we had to endure article after article presenting the issues as a debate between different 'sides' of the South African poultry industry. There were also other ambitions on the US side. Ambassador Froman informed us that the US wanted South Africa to reduce the MFN duty on over 280 products, identified by the US as 'of interest', to the level applicable to the EU under the TDCA. We responded by arguing that any such move would apply not just to us but to all of SACU as well. We added that South Africa had been included in the original AGOA after the start of the TDCA negotiations in full knowledge that we were likely to end up with an FTA with the EU. Besides, we pointed out, an MFN reduction would more than likely benefit parties other than the US. A Private Security Industry Regulation Bill, our draft intellectual property discussion document and a Protection of Investment Bill were also all identified as 'concerns'. None of this was presented as anything other than a quid pro quo we were expected to pay to remain in AGOA.

Looking at the list of demands as a whole, and taking into account the relatively small margin AGOA offered over the GSP, as well as the fact that AGOA access was not going to be improved, to have paid all of this would have rendered the cost-benefit of staying in AGOA a lot less attractive. We decided to try to limit the list of issues on which we would engage to the 'three meats'. We proposed 'agreeing to disagree' on the legality of the poultry ADD and offered instead to facilitate an engagement between our respective poultry associations to negotiate a quota providing access for a defined tonnage within the ADD. This, we were clear among ourselves, was not a matter of justice but of power, but we calculated that if we could obtain agreement on a quota manageable to the local poultry industry, we could retain AGOA as a net-positive arrangement for the South African economy as a whole. Several engagements had taken place but no agreement had been reached by the time the AGOA reauthorisation debate started unfolding in the US Congress. I appointed former ambassador to the WTO Faizel Ismail as a special envoy to facilitate and drive the negotiations, as Senators Coons and Isakson began threatening to remove South Africa from AGOA. Finally, they settled on insisting that South Africa be subject to an 'out of cycle review' within 30 days of the signing into law of the AGOA Bill (which otherwise basically rolled over the previous Act for a further ten years). Finally, in a focused negotiating session held in Paris in June 2015, agreement was reached to admit an initial 65 000 tonnes of US poultry products subject to resolution of SPS matters, in particular in relation to avian flu.

That agreement undoubtedly saved AGOA for South Africa. But a debate then ensued on future relations after 2025. Michael Froman commissioned a discussion paper that was circulated at the AGOA Forum in October 2016.[33] It spoke of a global trend towards reciprocity and suggested that this would need to be the basis of US-Africa trade relations after the expiry of the current AGOA mandate in 2025. While the paper identified several possible options for a reciprocal agreement with individual African countries, RECs or the continent as a whole (including an EPA-type arrangement), the clear preference was for a comprehensive 'modern' FTA based on the Trans-Pacific Partnership (TPP). This provided for a comprehensive FTA covering trade in goods and services, with little asymmetry or differentiation, and binding commitments on investment, intellectual property, competition and electronic commerce. Ironically, given the history of its relations with the US, Vietnam's inclusion in the TPP was held up as a model for future US-Africa trade and investment cooperation.

Africa and AGOA were clearly not priorities for the Trump administration. I attended the first AGOA Forum under the new administration, held in Washington in July 2018. During this visit, I also had bilateral meetings with both Robert Lighthizer, the US Trade Representative, and Commerce Secretary Wilbur Ross, as well as with Senators Coons and Isakson. The background to these bilateral meetings was the imposition, on 'national security' grounds, of unilateral punitive tariffs on steel and aluminium products (so-called Section 232 tariffs) originating from some countries, including South Africa, while exempting others in like circumstances. There was also a threat at the time to extend Section 232 tariffs to automotive products. We argued that South Africa supplied less than half a per cent of US steel imports and around one per cent of its aluminium imports, and could not be causing disruptions in the US market. Cutting these off would, however, cost jobs in South Africa. We warned that the agreement on the poultry quota indicated that this arrangement would stay in force as long as South Africa remained in AGOA. We pointed out that stakeholders were threatening to ask a court to decide whether the Section 232s on steel and aluminium amounted to our removal from AGOA benefits. We suggested that any extension of the tarrifs to automobiles, where more exports with more jobs were involved, would almost certainly result in a court requiring that we remove the poultry concession.

At the AGOA Forum itself, Lighthizer appeared to be under-prepared on issues that were clearly not priorities. He indicated, however, that the US wanted a few countries to volunteer to begin FTA talks. He said there was no a priori model but expected this to emerge from the negotiations. The then Deputy Chair of the AU Commission indicated in the forum that countries had agreed at the AU summit to refrain from third-country trade negotiations until the AfCFTA was in place. Several individual delegations made similar remarks at the formal sessions. In the bilateral meetings, however, we were told that whatever they were saying in public, several countries were indicating privately their desire to sign on. I indicated both publicly and privately that we would not be volunteering. At the second AGOA Forum of the Trump administration, held after my time, the US indicated that it saw the US-Mexico-Canada Agreement (USMCA), the amendment to the North American Free Trade Agreement (Nafta), as a potential model for a US-Africa post-AGOA arrangement.

143

10

Legislative highlights:
A decade of parliamentary engagements

Parliament provided an important forum for reporting on work done, for policy debate and, of course, for the passage of legislation.

The first iteration of the IPAP was launched with a parliamentary ministerial statement in 2010. The response from the ANC and its alliance partners was overwhelmingly positive and it was generally well received by manufacturers. Joan Fubbs was the chair of the Trade and Industry Portfolio Committee from 2009 to 2019. A hard worker with a strong personality, Fubbs provided solid leadership to the committee and created a platform for real debate.

At first, the opposition parties had no real alternative to propose to the direction we were taking. In the portfolio committee, the Democratic Alliance (DA) contingent was initially fairly positive about the IPAP. Its Trade and Industry spokesperson in the first part of the fourth term, Kobus Marais, was apparently removed because he was seen as too uncritical of the work of the DTI. He was replaced by Tim Harris, a young ally of the then DA parliamentary leader, Lindiwe Mazibuko. Harris, while critical of some details, actually said he supported industrial policy and much of the IPAP, even though, he said, drawing on a comment attributed to Tony Leon, in liberal circles this was a bit like selling a pork sausage at a bar mitzvah. At this time, a more intense neoliberal critique in fact came from Mario Oriani-Ambrosini of the IFP, who tended to prefer leaving such matters to the vagaries of 'the market' alone. In due course, Harris was redeployed to the Finance Portfolio Committee. He was replaced by Wilmot James, who was part of a project trying to reposition the DA ideologically to appeal to a larger black constituency. While seeking to retain the essential neoliberal core values, this involved, among other things, providing some conditional support for broad-based black economic empowerment (B-BBEE), which had hitherto been frontally opposed by the DA.

For some time, even before I became a minister, I had developed a strong feeling that much of what passed as BEE was deeply problematic. I had no doubt that the aims and intentions of BEE were both laudable and necessary. Greater inclusion, part of which involved drawing many more people from the historically oppressed black population into leadership positions in the economy, was a matter of both correcting past injustice and creating a more sustainable basis for economic progress by drawing on the skills and talents of all of our people and not just those of a once-privileged minority. At the same time, it was increasingly evident that too much of what was being called BEE involved drawing black people into some kind of agency, intermediary or indeed merely public relations role. The result was that the commanding heights of management, leadership and ownership continued to be dominated by so-called pale males, while many black businesses were left scrambling for government tenders. A more productive form of B-BBEE had to be found. In this quest, I was sensitive to the need to avoid trying to drive a reform agenda without adequate debate and consultation. Early in the fourth term, I reminded President Zuma that the B-BBEE Act 53 of 2003 provided for the establishment of a BEE Advisory Council chaired by the President. No such body had, however, been appointed up to then. President Zuma responded quite quickly and appointed the Advisory Council in 2010. Most of those appointed were the Presidency's choices and a number of ministers also participated. The DTI served as the council's secretariat.

By 2013, following debate and discussion in the Advisory Council, we developed amendments to both the 2003 B-BBEE Act and the Codes of Good Practice. Essentially the debates in the Advisory

Council had identified two main problems in what was in fact a lacklustre performance of B-BBEE since the passage of the Act. The first was that 'fronting' was pervasive and much more sophisticated than the stereotypical appointment of a junior employee to a nominal position of authority but with no real power. BEE share deals increasingly included small print that in myriad ways deprived empowerees of real powers and influence over the core ownership and management of supposedly 'empowered' companies. While these practices were potentially susceptible to prosecution under the common law offence of fraud (in most cases, being undertaken to claim some incentive or regulatory benefit to which the entity was not entitled), in practice prosecution was difficult. The other main weakness was that while the codes allowed points to be earned for supplier and enterprise development or for skills development, in practice not many entities actually scored points in these parts of the scorecard. Yet, properly structured programmes in these areas held out the promise of transferring real competencies that would enable empowerees to become significant players in the productive sectors. Supplier and enterprise development held out the potential of drawing black-owned companies undertaking productive activity into supply and value chains, while skills development could mean building capacity for leadership positions in the core areas of operation of companies.

The 2013 Broad-Based Black Economic Empowerment Amendment Bill[1] created the statutory offence, subject to criminal penalty, of 'fronting practices'. These included, but were not limited, to any initiative:

(a) in terms of which black persons who are appointed to an enterprise are discouraged or inhibited from substantially participating in the core activities of the enterprise;

(b) in terms of which the economic benefits received as a result of the broad-based black economic empowerment status of an enterprise do not flow to black people in the ratio specified in the relevant legal documentation;

(c) involving the conclusion of a legal relationship with a black person for the purpose of that enterprise achieving a certain level of broad-based black economic compliance without granting that black person the economic benefits that would reasonably be expected to be associated with the status or position held by that black person ...[2]

The Bill also established a B-BBEE Commission to receive and investigate complaints about fronting, as well as to monitor and evaluate the implementation of B-BBEE.[3] It further provided for the development of regulations on the conduct of BEE verification agencies, some of which were alleged to be charging excessive fees to inflate enterprises' BEE performance. The parliamentary portfolio committee took the initiative to revise a clause in the 2003 Act pertaining to the way state agencies were expected to implement the Act and its codes. The 2003 Act said that all state entities should 'take into account, and as far as reasonably possible,' apply the codes. This was recognised as what is known in trade-negotiation jargon as 'best endeavour' language, meaning there was no legally binding obligation and entities had wide discretion in deciding whether or not to apply the codes. The committee amended this provision to read simply that the entities 'must apply' the codes.[4]

When the Bill came before the National Assembly, Lindiwe Mazibuko – rather than the DA portfolio spokesperson – announced that her party would reverse its previous stance on empowerment legislation and conditionally support the Bill. By the time the Bill was tabled in the National Council of Provinces, we had already published our proposals to revise the codes. These created a new category of 'supplier development' (amalgamating two previous categories) and required that there would need to be performance at a prescribed sub-minimum level here, as well as in skills development and ownership. The penalty for not meeting the sub-minima would be a downgrading of one level on the overall scorecard. This was intended to encourage performance more broadly across the score-card, as well as to incentivise the adoption of business models promoting stronger symbiotic relations between large and small companies, such as those practised in a number of Asian countries. As there were only eight levels on the scorecard – and level eight was 'non-compliant' – this was a significant disincentive to deals that did not reach the sub-minima in prescribed areas. Another element in the revised codes was that they provided for automatic recognition of defined small black-owned enterprises. These could no longer be required by companies with whom they were doing business to pay for expensive verification assessments to confirm that they were black-owned. Our argument was that an affidavit would be sufficient for procurers doing business with such entities. If they suspected fronting, they could go to the BEE Commission. This move alone cut costly red tape for many actual and potential BEE suppliers to larger companies.

When the B-BBEE Bill came before the National Council of Provinces, the DA announced that they would now oppose the very Bill they had supported with great fanfare in the National Assembly. This, they said, was because they could not agree to the content of the revised codes. This justification was patently spurious. During the debate in the National Council of Provinces, I said that I knew this was not the real reason. I suggested that having put their toe into the water of empowerment, they were now retreating to their comfort zone of tolerating race-based privilege. Some years later, I discovered that this episode was, in fact, a dress rehearsal for a bigger drama that engulfed the DA in 2019 (see Chapter 14).

In her autobiography, former DA leader Helen Zille indicated that when she learnt of the original decision on this issue in the Na-tional Assembly, she tore into the parliamentary caucus, telling them that they had no right to depart from the party's established policy and support race-based legislation.[5] Within a short time, her former protégé, Mazibuko, vacated her position as parliamentary leader, ostensibly to take up a study opportunity in the United States – leading to the coining of the euphemism 'off to Harvard' to describe later removals of individuals from DA positions. Wilmot James was left having to engage in verbal gymnastics to explain the DA's position on empowerment. At one stage, he said the party was in favour of 'developmental economic empowerment' but would oppose any kind of ethnic-based programme. This led to jibes such as 'Is it to BEE or not to BEE? Or to DEE or not to DEE? That is the question.'

Another Bill that generated some controversy in the fourth term was the Intellectual Property Laws Amendment Bill.[6] This provided for a system and process of recognition and protection of 'indigenous knowledge' in intellectual property (IP) laws – covering copyright, trademarks, performers' protection and designs. Indigenous knowledge (IK) refers to traditional works, collective knowledge and genetic resources developed as part of the heritage of communities that was referred to by international bodies such as the World Intellectual Property Organization (WIPO) as 'traditional knowledge'.[7] There have been many instances around the world of indigenous knowledge being appropriated by commercial interests for private profit without any benefit accruing to the communities from which that knowledge originated.[8] Yet WIPO informed us that there was little prospect of reaching agreement on a proposed international convention on this matter in the near future. This, I understood, was because it was being linked to the issue of the international recognition of geographical indications, about which there was no consensus.[9] That being the case, we decided to incorporate protections for IK into our IP laws. Even though we later agreed that the National Indigenous Systems Office established by the Protection, Promotion, Development and Management of Indigenous Knowledge Bill,[10] introduced by the Minister of Science and Technology in 2016, offered a more elegant and workable way of managing claims for recognition of IK than the National Trust established by the Intellectual Property Laws Amendment Act, I make no apology for promoting the broader principle of incorporating recognition of indigenous knowledge into intellectual property law.

The strong pushback against both this principle and the content of the Intellectual Property Laws Amendment Bill was driven largely by private legal practitioners active in the field. This tells us much, in my view, of the state of IP expertise in South Africa. Private practitioners made good money from established systems and practices. I recall once talking to officials responsible for registering patents in the Companies and Intellectual Property Commission (CIPC). They told me that the CIPC at the time charged about R500 to register a patent. But the submissions were drawn up by private lawyers who charged many tens and often hundreds of thousands of rands to prepare them. Most patents registered (more than 95 per cent, in fact) were on behalf of international clients applying for an extension of rights into South Africa that they had first registered elsewhere. The local legal fraternity were very conventional and conservative in their views on IP matters, and not just on the Bill. Virtually any complaint about any aspect of IP reform coming from a multinational company or Western government found a ready echo in such quarters. The main reasons this lobby advanced for opposing the incorporation of IK recognition into intellectual property law were that IK related to collective rather than individual rights, and that existing copyright and other IP laws provided for time-bound recognition whereas IK recognition was in perpetuity. They proposed instead that there be *sui generis* legislation to protect IK. We retorted that even if we went this route, there would have to be provisions for dealing with potential conflicts with IP law, and we could not leave the boundaries to be decided by (no doubt lucrative for some) litigation.

Opposition parties, unsurprisingly, showed themselves ready to embrace the views of 'experts' opposing our Bill. One of these, Professor Owen Dean of Stellenbosch University, was indeed not shy in claiming credit for his own intellectual property. He pointed out even in public that he was, in fact, the author of a Private Member's Bill to establish an alternative *sui generis* system tabled in the name of Wilmot James and therefore sometimes referred to, erroneously, as 'Wilmot's Bill'.[11]

A draft discussion paper on broader IP policy published in 2013 generated a similar response. Given the importance of the issues involved, we decided to develop actual policy papers step by step, beginning with issues that were most pressing and drawing on international as well as national expertise.[12] The Phase 1 policy, adopted in May 2018, focused particularly on issues of IP and public health.[13] Among other things, it proposed moving towards a system of substantive search and examination of patent applications. The issue here was that what we had to date was a 'depository system' that simply registered mostly foreign patents, as described above. There was no capacity to assess the validity of submissions in terms of whether or not they met thresholds of adding real new knowledge. However, as international experience demonstrated, the practice of 'evergreening' patents was gaining ground in several sectors, including in the pharmaceutical industry. Evergreening meant making some small, cosmetic change to a patented product just before the expiry of its 20-year patent life, and then registering for a new patent what was essentially the same product. In this way, the patent life of a product (giving exclusive rights to the patent holder and preventing the manufacture of generic versions) could be extended for a further 20 years. The Phase 1 policy envisaged calibrating the roll-out of substantive search and examination with the development of technical capacity in the CIPC and establishing a pre- and post-patent objection system, beginning with health products. Steps to identify and train personnel in the CIPC to undertake this task were well advanced by the time I left office. Other proposals included using flexibilities already available under the WTO's 2001 Annex VI (Declaration on the TRIPS Agreement and Public

Health), and some other international conventions. A somewhat different set of IP issues arose in the processing of the Copyright and Performers' Protection Amendment Bills at the end of the fifth administration. I will return to this later in the chapter.

Opposition forces, of course, always sought to capitalise on any issues of mismanagement, corruption or bureaucratic inertia that emerged. One of the first such issues to be raised after I was appointed concerned the distribution of lottery funds. There were indeed bureaucratic blockages that meant distribution was often very slow. We took up this issue through a process that started with reform of internal processes, followed by changes in regulations and eventually amendments to the Lotteries Act 57 of 1997.[14] Among other things, the Lotteries Amendment Act 32 of 2013 ensured that distributing agencies would be full-time and act independently, and that no member could have any personal interest in any entity applying for funding. These reforms, I believe, had a positive impact, and the lotteries issue gradually moved offstage as the process of administering and distributing funds greatly improved.

Over time, occasional issues of mismanagement and corruption did emerge, more often in the agencies reporting to the DTI than in the DTI itself. Our attitude was that when credible allegations were made, there would be zero tolerance and we would respond with forensic investigations and, as warranted, cancellations of contracts, suspensions, disciplinary processes and the laying of criminal charges. The first issue of alleged impropriety I had to deal with was in respect of an ICT tender awarded by the then Companies and Intellectual Property Registration Office (Cipro), the predecessor of the CIPC. After investigation, which established little evidence of real value given in return for sizeable upfront payment, I decided to cancel the contract, leading to a long saga of court cases before we were finally vindicated. An appearance on this matter in Parliament's Standing Committee on Public Accounts (Scopa) indicated huge lacunae in the system of qualifying companies for ICT tenders in government as a whole.

Given that most of the problems of this sort that we confronted were in agencies rather than within the DTI itself, we eventually embarked on a process of reviewing whether the system of relatively autonomous structures with boards was appropriate for all the different entities that reported to us. I felt that most of these had been structured during the early post-1994 period on the basis of assessments of 'best practice' in other jurisdictions. This was at the height of the neoliberal restructuring of states, which sought to promote relatively autonomous agencies in many areas of economic governance. We concluded pragmatically that regulatory bodies did not need to have separate boards and that some could be brought into the department. This process began with the National Regulator for Compulsory Specifications (NRCS), the body responsible for setting compulsory minimum technical standards and for combating the import or sale of harmful products that do not meet these. The NRCS was reestablished as a trading entity within the department after instances of corruption were uncovered implicating its erstwhile chief executive officer (CEO) and board.

Of course, whatever we did to combat corruption would be met with an allegation from the opposition that it was not enough. This we accepted was the norm of party politics, but at the start of the fifth term this discourse began to take on new dimensions. In the fifth term, Wilmot James was replaced as DA Trade and Industry spokesperson by his deputy, Geordin Hill-Lewis. Hill-Lewis's deputy was a new MP, Dean Macpherson. Both were staunch ideological neoliberals and also set out to be more combative than their predecessors. They progressively ditched the cautious narrative on the IPAP and became much more negative. The IPAP was presented either as a statist departure from the NDP or as ineffective, or both. In this narrative both the NDP and the IPAP were caricatured: the NDP as being market fundamentalist, the IPAP for allegedly being a statist attempt to 'pick winners'.

The DA was, however, in a bit of a bind on this matter. In the

Western Cape, where they controlled the provincial government, many of the projects and investments they wanted to claim in events or photo ops in fact drew on the IPAP and other national government programmes. These included the partial turnaround of the clothing and textile industry, advances in the film industry, the manufacturing of wind towers and other green energy equipment, the Saldanha oil and gas servicing Special Economic Zone, several agro-processing and aquaculture projects, television manufacturing and business process service industries. Even Alan Winde, then Western Cape MEC for Finance, Economic Development and Tourism (and premier at the time of writing), acknowledged the role of the DTI in some of these.[15] We frequently challenged the DA cohort in the portfolio committee to identify precisely what it was in the IPAP they disagreed with, and surmising it to be localisation and developmental trade decisions, challenged them to have the courage to go out and tell firms benefiting from these measures in the province that they opposed them. Of course they never did, preferring the more opportunistic course of claiming the successes in the province while disowning the policy tools that gave rise to these.

The newly formed Economic Freedom Fighters (EFF) initially deployed their deputy leader, Floyd Shivambu, to the portfolio committee. Shivambu was an articulate and serious-minded individual who had read and was conversant with some of the writings of heterodox economists on industrial policy (see Chapter 8). Sometimes he raised real issues, such as that of base erosion and profit shifting, that became the subject of a hearing held jointly by the Finance and Trade and Industry portfolio committees. But his solutions were almost always populist and demagogic – for example, in insisting that nothing significant could be done to curb illicit outflows from the mining sector unless the state took over the mining industry.

Increasingly, as the fifth term unfolded, the single-minded focus of all components of the opposition centred on one issue – corruption. The context of this was, of course, the looming crisis of state capture, discussed further in Chapter 12. The DTI was not a particularly easy target for such a narrative. We had a record of acting against allegations, and after 2015 in every year bar one achieved a clean audit both for the department and for most of the agencies reporting to it. Nevertheless, the DA began to conduct their own independent 'oversight' visits to agencies, including arriving unannounced at agency offices and demanding to be provided with any and all documentation. Their access to parts of the media allowed the DA to claim to be the champions of 'clean government', uncovering our alleged unwillingness to act decisively. The difference between them and us, as I often told them in Parliament, was that we had to follow due process and respect the rights of accused but not convicted people, which they did not. Claims of inefficiency in the delivery of services were also sometimes raised. But the approach of the opposition in encountering these was not to channel them to the DTI for resolution, but rather to hold them back for some grandstanding opportunity on a public occasion.

The Protection of Investment Bill and other legislation

At the beginning of the fifth term, we tabled another major piece of legislation, the Protection of Investment Bill.[16] The background to this was a review of the bilateral investment treaties (BITs) that had been negotiated with some EU member countries, a few African countries, Argentina, Cuba, South Korea and China. Most of these BITs (and all of those with EU member countries) dated back to the period between 1994 and the entry into force of the Constitution. They were negotiated in the expectation of attracting FDI. The review, which began under my predecessor and was completed in 2010, concluded that there was no correlation between the existence or nonexistence of a BIT and FDI. We had no BITs with the US,

Japan or India, yet we received quite significant FDI from these countries. Conversely, we received little or no FDI from several countries with whom we had signed a BIT.

The BITs in force were all based on what has become known as 'old generation' or OECD-model agreements – so named as they were based on a model developed by the Paris-based Organisation for Economic Co-operation and Development (OECD). These agreements offered expansive definitions of investments to be protected, of 'direct and indirect' expropriation, of 'fair and equitable treatment', of the 'national treatment' to be accorded to foreign investors and of the 'fair market value' compensation they would be entitled to in the event of transgression. These broad definitions underpinned extensive guarantees to investors to preserve conditions both for their present and future expectations of profitability. They also gave private investors the right, in the event of dispute, to take governments to international tribunals, most of which are established under the International Centre for Settlement of Investment Disputes (ICSID) system. Analyses of the ICSID system revealed that it was becoming increasingly litigious and that the monetary value of awards was rising sharply. The number of investor-state disputes dealt with rose from 38 in 1996 to 706 in 2018. The average cost of litigation was US$8 million and the average award in the event of an adverse finding was US$522 million. In the event of default, unrelated foreign assets of the state concerned could be seized.[17] Among issues being brought to the ICSID system were matters challenging the rights of governments to regulate in the broader public interest. These included cases initiated by multinational tobacco companies challenging health-policy-driven regulations in Uruguay. The claim here was that these regulations undermined the expectations of profit guaranteed by BITs. Although this case was eventually decided in favour of Uruguay, it took six long years of expensive litigation, and highlighted the expansive nature of rights provided for by the investment treaties. In 2010 I attended an UNCTAD World Investment Forum in Xiamen,

China, and heard a panel discussion where an ICSID arbitrator said governments should not blame the panels for their rulings but rather look at the treaties they had signed.

In South Africa we had had similar if less dramatic experiences. One company initiated a process when it did not automatically receive a new-generation mining right; another cited 'physical security' provisions to seek compensation from government when it became a victim of crime; and a third involved an individual who had become a private investor in the SARB and threatened to pursue a case when he wanted to cash in his shares and claim a massive payout because the Bank had built up its reserves. Our conclusion was in line with, but also somewhat ahead of, a general trend of dissatisfaction with the established system.

There was one immediate challenge. In 2012 BITs with several EU countries reached their expiry date. We faced a stark and urgent choice. We could give notice of our intention to lapse these BITs, which in fact all had 'survival' clauses preserving the rights of existing investors for at least another decade. Failing this, the treaties provided for their automatic renewal on their existing terms for another ten or, in a few cases, 15 years. We decided to opt for the course of lapsing. This led us into a sharp public polemic with then EU Trade Commissioner Karel De Gucht. On several occasions, De Gucht publicly admonished us for this move, suggesting it would lead to an outflow of EU investment. We were forced to respond, explaining the rationale and clarifying that it was not an indication of any intention to expropriate EU investments.

The last time I met with De Gucht was during the World Economic Forum meeting in Davos in 2014, the year he left office. I had read that he had expressed concerns about some of the issues being raised in various arbitration panels, in particular in a context where some of the investment proposals tabled in negotiations then under way for a Transatlantic Trade and Investment Partnership (TTIP) could open EU regulations to many more similar challenges from US transnational corporations. I asked him to elaborate. He referred to the tobacco case, then still ongoing, and said the EU would not allow such processes to undermine its right to regulate. I then asked him what he thought we had been grappling with all these years. He said nothing!

The policy framework that underpinned our decision to exit the BITs did not say we would never enter into bilateral investment agreements ever again. It established an interministerial committee to consider this possibility, if there were compelling political or economic reasons and clear benefit to South Africa. But it also said that any such bilateral agreements would be very different to those under the 1990s OECD model.

However, as the aim was not to have a proliferation even of new-generation bilateral agreements, it was proposed that we introduce a generic law applicable to all investors, foreign and domestic. The Protection of Investment Bill (and later Act) provided BITs-type protections to all investments. These were, however, drafted in such a way that there was a better balance with the state's right to regulate, which was specifically provided for, subject to the Constitution and applicable legislation.[18] All investors were guaranteed 'fair administrative treatment' and 'legal protection of investment' in accordance with the property clause (Section 25) in the Constitution.[19] Foreign investors were guaranteed that their 'investments must not be treated less favourably than South African investors in like circumstances', and that they could 'repatriate funds subject to taxation and other applicable legislation'.[20] Government was also required to accord foreign investors and their property physical security at 'a level … generally provided to domestic investors in accordance with minimum standards of customary international law and subject to available resources and capacity'.[21] In the event of disputes, foreign investors were guaranteed access at their request to a domestic mediation process operated by the DTI. They were then required to exhaust all domestic legal processes before the government could consent, subject to guarantees of fair administrative processes, to international arbitration.[22]

*At the China International Import Expo in Shanghai in November 2018,
I met with leaders of major multilateral bodies. From left are José Ángel Gurría,
Secretary-General of the OECD, Li Yong, Director-General of the United Nations
Industrial Development Organization, and Mukhisa Kituyi,
the Director-General of UNCTAD.*

James Zhan, UNCTAD's Director of Investment and Enterprise, appeared before the portfolio committee and hailed the Protection of Investment Bill as 'timely and in line with global trends'. He said that it 'would achieve the appropriate balance of rights and obligations between investors and the state'. He also welcomed the 'dispute avoidance' mechanism provided for in the mechanism on domestic mediation.[23] Predictably, however, the DA opposition and a few vested interests argued that the Bill provided for reduced rights for investors compared to OECD-model BITs. We replied that this was hardly the point. Investors from countries with which we had no BITs would receive codified rights they had never had before. In the case of the others, the idea was precisely to achieve a better balance with the right to regulate. Besides, by the time of the Bill's passage much of the concern about potential expropriation had dissipated. In practical terms, we found this debate had very little impact on investment decisions. Mercedes-Benz, for example, announced its biggest-ever investment in South Africa just after the lapsing of the BIT with Germany.

A footnote to this saga was an evident willingness by the DA to whip up concerns of foreign investors for partisan party-political advantage, even when real concerns were not very evident. This was part of the shift towards a more combative stance evident in the fifth term. When he was DA spokesperson on Trade and Industry, Wilmot James offered a bipartisan approach on campaigning to retain access to AGOA, which we welcomed. His successors were, however, happy to bash us with every critique and concern raised in this debate, as well as that on AGOA. At one point, in fact, this threatened to add fuel to an already raging fire that could have seen South Africa out of AGOA. On one occasion I was accused of risking our continued AGOA access because I had allegedly become a prisoner of the local poultry industry and had only been saved from a disaster by the intervention of Faizel Ismail. This was absurd; Ismail and I were part of the same team. I retorted on one occasion that I hoped that the claim that I had become a puppet of the poultry industry was not driven by the fact that the DA's former leader, Tony Leon, had become a consultant to the meat import and export association AMIE.

Other legislation passed over the decade included an Amendment Bill that enabled the Companies Act 71 of 2008, passed under my predecessor's leadership, to come into force. The Companies Act was a major piece of legislative reform, providing for, among other things, 'business rescue' for companies in distress, instead of the previous 'judicial management', which almost always was a step towards liquidation.

I left office disappointed that we had not been able to complete reforms of gambling and liquor legislation. We had hoped to be able to reposition the National Gambling Board as a national gambling regulator in a context where there was evidence of growing non-observance of legislation. But at least the portfolio committee rejected a DA Private Member's Bill, tabled in the name of Geordin Hill-Lewis, that would have legalised online gambling. We took the view that this was not desirable. A proliferation of websites and internet cafés offering sports betting and online casino games would potentially undermine the fixed-line casinos that at least built hotels and conference centres as a requirement of their licences, and thus created jobs. The proliferation of more gambling activity, potentially targeting lower-income people, was also a major social concern. We certainly did not want to follow the likes of the UK and Australia, where a proliferation of gambling activity has been associated with increasing incidence of problem gambling.[24] In support of his Bill, Hill-Lewis argued that it was better to regulate an activity we could not prevent. We disagreed, arguing that while we might have difficulty controlling wagers on internet websites, we could use banking regulations and the anti-money-laundering system to block payment of winnings and this would be a major deterrent.

Alcohol abuse is no small matter in South Africa. A World Health Organization (WHO) study found that 31 per cent of the population aged 15 and older consumed alcohol, and that the drinking population consumed an average of 28.9 litres of pure alcohol per year – the fifth highest in the world. Some 59 per cent of drinkers were classified as heavy or binge drinkers. Research published in the journal *BMC Medicine* found that 62 300 adults died from alcohol-attributable causes in 2016, which represented about one in ten of all deaths in the country.[25] The tangible financial costs of harmful alcohol use (including the costs of road accidents and costs to the health system, both falling on the state) were estimated at R37.9 billion or 1.6 per cent of GDP in 2009, while adding intangible costs (such as loss of productivity) brought the total cost of the harm to the economy to an amount equal to between 10 and 12 per cent of GDP.[26]

A draft Liquor Bill, published for public comment in 2016,[27] proposed introducing a civil liability for damages attributable to someone found not to have taken reasonable steps to ensure they were not supplying liquor to, among others, unlicensed retailers, underage drinkers, already intoxicated consumers or evidently pregnant women. The Bill would also have allowed for a tightening of regulations on alcohol advertising, as well as on the location and conduct of retail liquor outlets in residential areas. More controversially, it proposed a public debate on raising the minimum legal drinking age (MLDA) from 18 to 21 years. There were good medical reasons for making such a proposal. The human brain is not fully developed until the mid-20s, and the part of the brain that is not fully developed is the prefrontal cortex, which affects decision-making, impulse control, rule-learning and social behaviour, among other things. It is also one of the areas of the brain most impacted on by alcohol consumption, explaining why excessive drinking by young people is particularly associated with harmful behaviour.[28] In the United States, where individual states had during the 1970s and early 1980s progressively raised the MLDA from 18 to 21 (to meet conditionalities on federal funding for road-building projects), research found that in states where the MLDA had been so raised, the percentage of fatally injured drivers in the 16–20 age group declined from 61 per cent in 1982 to 31 cent in 1995 as the total number of alcohol-related fatal road injuries also declined.[29] Conversely, New Zealand's decision to lower the MLDA from 20 to 18 was associated with a significant increase in drinking by 16- to 19-year-olds, as well as with increased abuse.[30]

The public consultations on the Liquor Bill revealed, predictably, that there was strong support from health professionals, social workers and community and faith-based organisations but strong opposition from the liquor industry at all levels – from large manufacturers to small tavern owners. The Free Market Foundation was also present at several consultations that I attended, arguing that the Bill amounted to an unwarranted intrusion into consumers' right to choose. They, and others, also argued that the Bill was unconstitutional as the Constitution prescribed the age of majority as 18. Yet gun ownership regulations set a minimum age of 21 years (and imposed other restrictions) on the grounds that gun ownership in South Africa, unlike in the USA, is not a right. In the end, the Liquor Bill was not deemed urgent at the end of the fifth term. It remains to be seen how this important issue will be dealt with in the sixth Parliament.

The Copyright and Performers' Protection Amendment Bills

The last issue to be dealt with in this chapter is two intellectual property Bills that passed through both Houses of Parliament in the fifth term, but which President Ramaphosa referred back to Parliament in June 2020, namely, the Copyright and Performers' Protection Amendment Bills.[31] The background to these is that in 2001 the two Acts were amended to strengthen provisions for the collection and payment of 'needle time' royalties to performers and musicians. These are royalties payable for the public performance of commercially released recordings. I remember well the day this legislation passed through the National Assembly. As the then chair of the portfolio committee, I was listening to the debate in the House when someone whispered to me that an attack had taken place on the World Trade Center in New York – it was 11 September 2001 (9/11). Despite this legislation, which was signed into law in 2002, we continued to receive complaints from artists and performers that they were not being paid. In response to this, we requested retired judge Ian Farlam, who later chaired the commission of inquiry into the Marikana massacre, to lead a small commission of inquiry into this matter and to make recommendations.

The commission issued its report in 2011.[32] It found that despite the enactment of the 2002 legislation, 'not a cent had been paid in royalties to musicians and record companies'.[33] There were many reasons for this, including disputes over rates and methods of payment, as well as insufficient monitoring of local content by broadcasters. But there were issues in the law as well. Definitions in the existing law identified those entitled to needle-time royalties as composers and authors, and did not specifically mention performers. There was also a need to define minimum standards for contracts based on 'a general recognition in the industry that many of the contracts between record companies and artists and between music publishers and artists ... were unfair to the artists concerned'.[34] Particularly in the early stages of their careers, artists desperate to get a recording contract were signing away rights to royalties. I heard artists reading out some of these contracts during one of the engagements on the 2018 Bills. There was also a 'crisis of credibility' in the collecting societies (the bodies formed to collect royalty payments on behalf of those entitled to receive them).[35] This encompassed governance and mandate issues, particularly as existing institutions collected royalties due to all stakeholders, while only paying them over to their clients.

The two Amendment Bills aimed in the first instance at addressing the recommendations of the Farlam Commission. Under the legislation, collecting societies would have to be accredited by the CIPC. To gain accreditation they would have to show that they were subject to the control of the authors, performers or copyright holders on behalf of whom they collected royalties, and to meet other governance requirements.[36] Authors and performers would have to be allocated a 'fair share' of royalties in contracts, and the minister would be empowered to make further regulations in this regard.[37] A Copyright Tribunal, consisting of three judges appointed by the Judge President of the Supreme Court of Appeal and five retired judges, would be established to adjudicate on applications made under the Bill or disputes arising from copyright matters, including over royalty shares in contracts.[38] The Bill also sought to give effect to the provisions of the WIPO Marrakesh Treaty to Facilitate Access to Published Works for

Persons Who are Blind.[39] Hearings on the Bills, which we acknowledged needed significant improvement in technical drafting during the committee stage, predictably heard proposals for many other amendments to copyright law. We urged the committee to try to limit itself to the issues raised in the original Bill, with an undertaking that we would consider other matters in the broader IP reform.

In the hearings, though, a persuasive argument was advanced to allow some flexibility in the application of copyright. The United States and some other jurisdictions had 'fair use' provisions in their law that allowed limited use of copyright material for defined purposes without permission of copyright holders or payment of royalties. Others, in the UK tradition, allowed only 'fair dealing' – restricted to private use only. 'Fair use' meant that satirists such as Trevor Noah, broadcasting in the US, could use excerpts from Fox News, for example, without their permission. Another US-based satirist, John Oliver, often remarked that items about Britain in his show could not be rebroadcast in the UK due to copyright law there. The committee developed its own South Africa-rooted approach to this issue in Section 13.[40] This allowed limited fair use or reproduction of parts only of copyright material for defined purposes. These were:

(i)   Research, private study or personal use ...

(ii) criticism or review ...

(iii) reporting current events,

(iv) scholarship, teaching and education,

(v)   comment, illustration, comedy, satire, caricature, cartoon, tribute, homage or pastiche,

(vi) preservation of and access to the collection of libraries, archives and museums, and

(vii) ensuring proper performance of public administration.[41]

Again, the limits of this could be tested by the Copyright Tribunal. Most of the controversy surrounding these Bills focused on the 'fair use' provisions. Journalists, libraries and educationalists, including the South African Democratic Teachers' Union (Sadtu), were strongly in favour. Publishers, booksellers and filmmakers were fervently opposed. Performers and artists were divided. In addition to claiming that this would damage the publishing industry, some argued that it would open creative work to pirating by the likes of YouTube (something we said was not just not our intention but something we would actively combat if it occurred).

The controversy over fair use also spilled over into the attitude towards the 'Farlam issues' in the Bills. Those most fervently opposed to fair use also opposed those provisions. However, in one meeting I attended I noticed a strange coalition in that regard. Opposition was voiced both on populist grounds, that the provisions did not go far enough and that there should be the equivalent of 'expropriation without compensation' to ensure that no one other than authors and performers had rights to royalties, and on neoliberal grounds, that the provisions amounted to an intrusion into the unfettered right to contract. Speakers articulating either position drew cheers and applause from all organisations opposed to the Bills, whatever position they had articulated in their own input. Even though, as indicated above, fair use provisions would take South African law closer to the US model, the Bill came also to be raised as a 'matter of concern' by US interest groups and the US administration. I was led to understand that this was because there were doubts about South Africa's capacity to administer such a system and fears that it might result in further piracy of US copyrighted work.

The Bills passed through both Houses of Parliament before the end of the fifth term, but in June 2020 President Ramaphosa referred them back to Parliament. The President's referral letter acknowledged the 'noble objectives' of the legislation, but expressed reservations on certain procedural and constitutional matters. These included the tagging (classification) of the Bills, the retrospective provisions on royalty payments and the fact that he considered referral to the

National House of Traditional Leaders to be essential. The President also indicated that he felt that the fair use provisions had not been subjected to proper consultation.[42] It remains to be seen how the sixth Parliament will deal with this legislation. If, however, there is any long delay in reforming the system of sharing royalties and improving collection, artists will continue to be subject to unfair contracts that underpay them.

11

Results and prospects at the end of the fourth term

By the end of the fourth term, in 2014, small but significant advances had been recorded in placing the economy on a new growth path. The infrastructure build programme had clearly benefited from the establishment of the Presidential Infrastructure Coordinating Commission, and the term ended with R1 trillion actually spent on a range of programmes organised into 17 Strategic Integrated Projects. This was more than double the amount spent in any other five-year term. This programme was credited with having enabled South Africa to avoid joining several other mineral-producing countries (such as Brazil) in entering recession after 2012, following the end of the global commodity supercycle. In manufacturing, we were able to record some real successes as a direct result of the IPAP programmes. These included:

1 Investments reaching a record total of R25.7 billion in the automotive sector, supporting around 300 000 jobs, with the APDP broadened to embrace bus bodies, medium and heavy vehicles and minibus taxis;

2 The retention of 67 000 jobs and creation of 7 000 new jobs in the clothing and textile, footwear and leather industries, which had lost 45 000 jobs between 2000 and 2010. With the introduction of the Clothing and Textile Competitiveness Programme, government support focused on approved competitiveness-raising initiatives. Clusters focusing on quick response to retailer demands and technical textiles (tents, parachutes, sportswear, etc) were also supported.

Renowned film director Sir Ridley Scott (right) showing me round the setting for a TV series produced with support from a DTI incentive, Cape Town 2018.

3 Important advances in metals fabrication industries, driven by a combination of infrastructure spending and localisation programmes;
4 Significant investments in the agro-processing, household consumer goods, television manufacturing and pharmaceutical sectors, among others;
5 A fourfold increase in the value of film productions supported by the film rebate programme.[1]

We ended the term concluding that the experience of the IPAP between 2010 and 2014 had shown that 'industrial policy can and does succeed if it is well designed, adequately resourced and informed by robust and constructive stakeholder dialogue'.[2] But we had not yet remotely reached the stage of having sufficient impact decisively to create conditions for a new, productive, sector-driven inclusive growth path. There had been too little consistent application across government of IPAP Key Action Plans; localisation had been slow and industrialisation was negatively impacted by 'high administered prices' charged by state-owned companies (SOCs). In this regard, we were able to record some progress in adjusting port charges to reduce the negative impact of fees skewed to the disadvantage of value-added exports. But electricity was another matter. As we put it, euphemistically, 'our historical competitive advantage in cheap electricity has become a thing of the past.'[3] Privately, I also felt that while we were given the green light to do our work, we did not have sufficient coherent high-level support within government about the centrality of industrialisation and about the IPAP as a driver of it. Instead, it was too much regarded as a programme of one department. The objective need, therefore, was for a serious raising of our game and for entering the next term with further and bolder moves in driving both a productive sector-led new growth path and industrial policy in particular. New conditions were emerging, however, that looked likely to change the context, and not in a positive direction.

Developments in the labour movement: Marikana and beyond

The fourth term ended with significant organisational fragmentation and weakening of the trade union movement. Cosatu began the term with what it called an 'open door' attitude to government and government programmes. There were frequent invitations to ministers to brief Cosatu Central Executive Committee meetings, and regular interactions took place between some individual unions and ministers. During this time, we in the DTI took steps to strengthen ties both with Sactwu and the National Union of Metalworkers of South Africa (Numsa). Both unions made significant inputs into the design and implementation of the new programmes in the clothing and textile and motor industries, respectively. On reflection, one could conclude that there was insufficient attention

With my wife, Grace Constable, in support of a campaign against racism developed by Sactwu and Independent Newspapers.

on the part of unions to establishing and maintaining an appropriate stance of 'critical support' for the Zuma administration. The relationship at the beginning was too uncritical, with too little independent input on policy matters.

The first signs of a change came over what many considered to be an insignificant matter. Cosatu General Secretary Zwelinzima Vavi criticised the SACP's decision to allow its General Secretary, Blade Nzimande, to take up a position in cabinet as Minister of Higher Education and Training. At the same time, it was becoming apparent that several Cosatu affiliates were being wracked by factional conflicts ultimately traceable to contestation over access to resources in investment arms. Within about 18 months, Cosatu, led by Vavi, began to adopt an increasingly oppositional stance, shifting from a position that, in my view, was too uncritical, to its antithesis, one that was often overly critical.

Meanwhile, contradictions began to sharpen in the mining sector. The high point of the mineral commodity supercycle came in 2012. Mineral prices had progressively risen to reach record levels. According to Chinese statistics, South Africa supplied 37 per cent of China's imports from Africa, mostly in the form of primary mineral commodities. Mining capital reaped huge profits. Some of this was no doubt amassed offshore through a variety of transfer schemes. While a few companies, such as the Sishen Iron Ore Company, did engage in some profit-sharing initiatives, many others did not. One of the latter was Lonmin, the third-largest producer in the platinum sector.

At the same time, financialisation was taking on a new dimension. *Mashonisas*, operating both as small businesses and as part of the formal banking sector, were becoming increasingly involved in the highly lucrative provision of high-interest consumer loans to low-income working people. Credit providers were taking little risk as it was then easy to extract a garnishee order, meaning the repayment was deducted from workers' wages at source. According to an estimate made at the time, an increasing number of South Africans earning between R3 500 and R10 000 a month were finding as much as 40 per cent of their salaries deducted to service such loans. Indebtedness among mineworkers was known to be particularly severe, and an investigation by the National Credit Regulator established that most of the small loan providers in the Marikana area were not compliant with the law.[4] Under such circumstances, wage increases linked to inflation or a little above would have made little difference to workers' pay packets emptied upfront by garnishee orders. Not surprisingly, established institutionalised wage bargaining in an industry reaping huge resource rents was seen by increasing numbers of workers as not generating sufficient results.

All of these factors came to a head in 2012 at Lonmin's platinum mine at Marikana, near Rustenburg in the North West province. The Cosatu-affiliated National Union of Mineworkers (NUM) found itself increasingly challenged by a populist breakaway calling itself the Association of Mineworkers and Construction Union (AMCU). AMCU promised a militant campaign for very significant wage increases. By August of that year, rivalry between AMCU and the NUM had turned violent, with several NUM officials, as well as police members, being killed. As the tension deepened, a large contingent of riot police were deployed to the area. On 16 August 2012 police opened fire on a demonstration of AMCU supporters, killing 17, while 17 others were killed in other incidents on that day. A subsequent judicial commission of inquiry, chaired by Judge Ian Farlam, determined that the incident could, in fact, be described as a 'massacre'. The Farlam Commission found that there were significant weaknesses in public order policing. It made findings against the police leadership, Lonmin, the NUM and AMCU and made recommendations mainly on police procedures and conduct.

Marikana was a major catalytic event, as well as an enormous tragedy that should never have happened. One effect of Marikana was that it consolidated the domination of AMCU in the mining sector. AMCU went on in 2014 to lead a five-month strike in the sector, which yielded a result far lower than its initial demand while creating severe hardship for many of its members, who received no income for a long period of time. Marikana also reinforced divisions within Cosatu. Subsequent months saw a slow but steady progression towards a split in the federation, with spats between its President, Sdumo Dlamini, and General Secretary, Zwelinzima Vavi, becoming increasingly bitter. Eventually, Vavi was accused of impropriety in his relationship with a female staff member, while Numsa was accused of seeking to poach members from other affiliates (particularly the NUM). The eventual split in 2014 saw the exit from Cosatu of both Vavi and Numsa, with several other unions leaving shortly thereafter. Ultimately, the differences could be traced to matters of 'big politics': difference over whether to remain in the tripartite alliance under Jacob Zuma's leadership or to seek to establish an 'independent' trade union movement and, for some, a new workers' party.

Within the ANC, the relationship between the ANC Youth League, led by Julius Malema, and the Zuma leadership also began to deteriorate. The Youth League began to campaign for the nationalisation without compensation of the mining industry. Ironically, this drew support from some BEE empowerees in the sector. Weak and problematic transformation in the sector had resulted in share deals that gave empowerees little or no real influence. Worse, several of these deals were funded by loans that in the circumstances of falling profits left some empowerees 'under the water', meaning that the debt they owed was greater than the value of the shares acquired. In this context, the idea of a state takeover would have provided welcome relief for some in this predicament. The Youth League's campaign was, however, presented as a struggle to deliver economic freedom to the masses in general, and to young people in particular, through 'radical economic transformation' (later abbreviated to RET).

At around this time, in 2011, national government intervened to take over the running of the finances of Limpopo province, amid widespread allegations of mismanagement and corruption. The province was a Malema stronghold. In all of this, the Youth League's conduct reached beyond the bounds of regular debate. A style of arrogance and disrespect emerged, together with a developing personality cult around Malema. Malema became well known for outrageous statements and insults, providing grist to the mill of a press generally hostile to the ANC. At one stage during the ANC's 2010 National General Council (NGC) Malema and his allies stormed the podium, disrupting proceedings as well as hijacking the Economic Transformation Commission with orchestrated, insistent inputs demanding adoption of their nationalisation proposal. Finally, in 2011 the ANC leadership decided that enough was enough. Malema and some of his close associates were charged with bringing the organisation into disrepute, and in early 2012 they were expelled. The Disciplinary Committee's decision was upheld by an appeal body chaired by Cyril Ramaphosa, fuelling a steady stream of invective alleging that Ramaphosa, who was at the time on the board of Lonmin, was responsible for the Marikana massacre.[5]

These developments weakened not only the loose coalition assembled at Polokwane but also the ANC and the tripartite alliance. Hot on the heels of all of this came the revelation that nearly R250 million had been spent on security upgrades at the President's family residence at Nkandla in KwaZulu-Natal (see Chapter 12).

The debate on nationalisation of the mining industry led the ANC to commission a study on options for radical economic transformation in the sector. The report of this study was entitled 'State Intervention in the Minerals Sector' (SIMS).[6] It concluded that nationalisation was neither feasible nor desirable. Taking account of the Constitution and bilateral investment treaties, it argued that any such move would require the payment of compensation that would 'break the bank'. Instead, SIMS advocated moving along a path followed in about 30 other mineral economies, that of seeking to capture resource rents, and using the proceeds to support development. Specifically, the study proposed the introduction of a significant 'resource rent tax', which it estimated could yield R40 billion a year. It also argued for an accelerated effort to promote beneficiation of mineral products, and the establishment of a state-owned mining company.

Towards the end of 2012, the work on the National Development Plan,[7] led by Trevor Manuel, was completed. The NDP set out a comprehensive policy framework touching on most areas of government, including chapters on education, health, infrastructure, foreign policy and proposals to create a 'capable state' and fight corruption. Its economic chapter set a target of creating 6 million jobs and reducing unemployment by half by 2030. It had very little explicitly to say about manufacturing and no specific reference to the need to develop industrial policy. In fact, there was more attention given to service sectors. Targets for the reduction of inequality were also seen by the SACP and Cosatu as modest. The NDP generated considerable debate within the alliance. The SACP argued for not 'monumentalis-ing' it,[8] arguing that it should be seen as a living document that could be improved over time as some of its better recommendations were implemented. Some in Cosatu wanted to go further and explicitly reject the NDP. The federation's formal position was that the alliance needed to rewrite parts of it, specifically the economics chapter. The NDP was certainly a document that had different emphases to either the IPAP or the New Growth Path and one, moreover, that was open to different readings. We argued that its broad vision was one with which we agreed and that several of its objectives, for example in-creasing exports of diversified manufactures and stimulating a higher rate of industrial investment, would require a higher-impact IPAP. Without specifically mentioning the NDP, we also argued, based on a vast body of evidence, that service-sector growth was both more strongly rooted and of a higher quality if underpinned by a diversify-ing productive sector than if simply 'footloose', ie unconnected to the development of any productive sector.

The resolution on economic policy adopted at the ANC's 53rd National Conference, held in Mangaung in December 2012, devel-oped a neat compromise to accommodate all three programmes plus the infrastructure plan. It resolved that 'the National Development Plan is a living and dynamic document … and should be used as a common basis for the mobilisation [of all South Africans around a common vision of economic transformation]. Within the NDP vision, critical instruments and policy initiatives will continue to drive government's medium-term policy agenda. These include: the national infrastructure plan … the New Growth Path … the indus-trial policy action plan …'[9] The resolution also supported some of the proposals from SIMS and, as indicated in Chapter 8, captured the essence of the significance of industrial policy in the formulation 'transform the structure of the economy through industrialisation'.[10]

In addition, the Mangaung conference consolidated a view that had been emerging in debates within the alliance for several months.

This was based on an assessment that the biggest achievements to date in moving towards a national democratic society had been in the politico-social sphere rather than in the economic life of the people. Citizens had acquired extensive rights and freedoms, and the delivery of a number of social benefits had advanced rapidly, yet unemployment, poverty and inequality remained, while ownership and control of the economy still lay predominantly with monopoly capital. Earlier formulations had attempted to characterise the stages of the NDR as a first stage of political freedom, followed by a second stage of economic freedom. By Mangaung, the consensus had become that the NDR needed to enter a new phase whose main content would be 'radical economic transformation'.

The ideas developed in Mangaung were carried over into the ANC's manifesto for the 2014 general election. It called for radical transformation both in the approach to developing the productive forces and in changing the existing patterns of control of the economy. Specifically, it called for accelerated infrastructure development, better implementation of a higher-impact IPAP, localisation to increase to a target of 75 per cent of total procurement, greater focus on small business development and more effective transformation.[11]

12

The fifth administration: From radical economic transformation to state capture

As is well known, the defining feature of the fifth administration was a gathering crisis of corruption and what came to be called 'state capture', compounded by a series of poor decisions on specific issues. It began, however, with President Jacob Zuma pledging at his inauguration in May 2014 that the incoming administration would pursue 'radical economic transformation'. Zuma defined this as 'fundamental change in the structure, systems, institutions and patterns of ownership, management and control of the economy in favour of all South Africans especially the poor, the majority of whom are African and female'.[1]

As indicated in Chapter 11, this concept emerged from discussions within the ANC and alliance that were consolidated at the 53rd National Conference in Mangaung. Ahead of the 2014 elections, the ANC campaigned on a positive message, arguing that it had 'a good story to tell'. This was based on achievements over both the entire two decades of ANC government and the first five-year term of the Zuma administration. Among the latter was the R1 trillion spend on infrastructure.

The fifth Parliament, elected in 2014, saw the ANC marginally down on the number of seats it won in 2009. The DA achieved a small increase, but the new entrant, the EFF, emerged as the third-largest party, with six per cent of the vote. The EFF was formed after the expulsion of erstwhile leaders of the ANC Youth League and was led by its 'Commander-in-Chief', Julius Malema. It soon became apparent that the EFF was not going to play the conventional parliamentary game. Its MPs arrived at Parliament bedecked in red overalls and hard hats – representing something of a fancy-dress outing for individuals better known for their penchant for luxury watches and designer clothing. EFF MPs made it clear from the start that they would not respect parliamentary rules or conventions. Refusals to withdraw assertions ruled as 'unparliamentary' and spurious points of order became their stock in trade, with the chanting of slogans, leading to physical evictions, becoming later features of their conduct. South African politics had entered the era of populism, with a high level of personality cult thrown in. The parallels with the conduct of members of the Nazi Party elected to the German Reichstag in 1928 did not go unnoticed.[2]

All of this unfolded against the background of the continuing impact of the global economic crisis. The crisis that erupted in 2008–2009 can be likened to an earthquake emitting aftershocks felt long after the initial convulsion. Moreover, with the tectonic plates of the globalised world economy all being interconnected, the initial quake spawned shockwaves with multiple epicentres, the effects of which were felt unevenly in different parts of the world.

As indicated in Chapter 8, the initial epicentre of the global financial crisis was the financial sector of the United States. This was because of the extensive financialisation of the system and the fact that financialisation had moved furthest in the United States. Thereafter, while the developed world was mired in low growth and stagnation, dynamic economies in the developing world continued to grow, based on advancing industrialisation. Indeed, the turn to financialisation in the developed world, sometimes theorised as a move towards a post-industrial economy, allowed some emerging economies to advance their manufacturing sectors at the expense of those in the developed world. China was foremost among these. Since the 1990s China had pursued an industrial development strategy based on increasing exports of manufactured products to the developed world – starting with clothing and textile products. China benefited from the liberalisation brought about by globalisation – not least from the phasing out of the Multi-Fibre Arrangement between 1994 and 2005. It also capitalised on the partial withdrawal from active industrial policy by some developed countries. After 2008–2009, while several developed economies lurched into recession, China continued to experience double-digit GDP growth, which enabled it to emerge as the world's second-largest economy by 2010. By the start of the second decade of the 21st century, however, several developed economies began to revive their industrial strategies, perhaps drawing the lesson that those among them, such as Germany, that had never abandoned such policies were faring better. Cautious recovery became evident in the United States, in particular, based on reindustrialisation underpinned by cheap energy from shale gas.

The installation of the new administration in China in March 2013, led by President Xi Jinping, saw the development of a new strategy to adjust to these changing realities. Recognising that the space for continued growth from exports of manufactured exports to the developed world was becoming constrained, the incoming leadership defined a new strategic growth trajectory. This looked to domestic consumption as a new driver of growth, and aimed to move the Chinese economy further up the value chain into the high-tech, design, branding and high-quality service ends of global value chains. Reacting also to the real possibilities of 'overheating', meaning over-production of capital in some sectors, the new strategy envisaged a managed transition from double-digit growth to a 'new normal' of still high, but single-digit, GDP growth rates.

By 2013, it was already evident that these developments had abruptly halted the mineral commodity supercycle. For several years up until 2012, steady growth in demand for mineral products, driven in large part by increased demand from China, had increased prices for a host of mineral commodities. By 2012, these had reached record levels. But, in the years that followed, prices for one mineral commodity after another fell sharply as the commodity super-cycle definitively ended. The context this formed for the Marikana massacre was discussed in Chapter 11, but it also had broader longer-term implications. Mineral resource-based economies across the world, from Australia and Canada to Brazil and a host of developing countries, saw export earnings and growth rates falling.

South Africa, as an economy whose major source of foreign exchange earnings remained the export of industrial minerals, was no exception. The World Bank estimated that lower mineral prices cost the South African economy the equivalent of four per cent GDP growth between 2012 and early 2017.[3] On top of this was the impact of what was called a global 'glut' of steel – overproduction of steel relative to demand – leading to increased exports of cheap steel to markets across the world, and threatening steel production in several countries, including in South Africa.

Compounding all of this, the ANC-led government entered its fifth term with an own goal: an electricity crisis. This was long in the making. It dated back to decisions taken in the 1990s that there was no need to invest in new power stations as there was 'overcapacity', and perhaps also to a sense in some quarters that Eskom, the national electricity supplier, would be privatised and private investors would come in. The process of awarding tenders, and the vested interests that emerged from this, together with a failure to carry out proper preventive maintenance, on top of outright bad management at Eskom, led, by the end of 2014, to both planned and unplanned power outages (known euphemistically as 'load shedding').

The R1 trillion infrastructure build programme undertaken during the fourth term came to be recognised as one of the main reasons why South Africa managed to escape the fate of several peer countries (such as Brazil) that fell into recession after the end of the commodity supercycle. Certainly, the infrastructure build programme – for all the weaknesses of some of its projects – had operated countercyclically and the discipline created by the establishment of the PICC was beginning

Meeting President Xi Jinping in Beijing during President Cyril Ramaphosa's state visit to China in September 2018. To my right are fellow ministers Naledi Pandor and Senzeni Zokwana; to my left Derek Hanekom and Lindiwe Sisulu (head turned).

During President Ramaphosa's state visit to China, the South African delegation visited the headquarters of e-commerce and technology giant Alibaba, where we were addressed by the company's founder, Jack Ma (far right).

to have positive results. However, the major drivers of this programme were investments by SOCs. The 2014 Eskom crisis was but a harbinger of what became the defining feature of President Zuma's second term – a gathering crisis of corruption and state capture – that would impact profoundly on the performance of many public institutions, particularly SOCs.

Corruption had, of course, become a significant issue long before Zuma's presidency. The interface between government and the private sector in the area of government procurement (significantly expanded in many countries with the adoption of neoliberal policy prescripts favouring 'outsourcing' of an increasing range of services previously performed by public institutions) had in South Africa been characterised since apartheid days by high levels of rent-seeking. Levels of concentration and centralisation were widely recognised as being extreme in South Africa, compared even to the high global norms. This meant that there were generally only a small number of established suppliers in each sector, initially linked to conglomerates. These suppliers demonstrated a significant propensity to engage in collusive practices. This was underscored by the investigation by the competition authorities that uncovered extensive collusion and tender-rigging in contracts for the building of stadia for the hosting of the 2010 FIFA World Cup.[4]

After 1994, a new element was added – not, as some would have it, BEE per se, but BEE of a certain kind, and more particularly BEE fronting. While there were many black people who entered business as farmers, miners, industrialists or service providers, exceptionally high levels of concentration and centralisation erected formidable barriers to entry and required much persistent effort by new entrants. At the same time, many established white-owned companies saw the imperative to change their appearance and began to embark on BEE deals. While not true of all, many of these involved some element of BEE fronting (see Chapter 10). This generally took one of two forms. The first saw recruitment of black people (preferably with some 'struggle credentials') into nominally high-profile public relations positions in established white-owned companies seeking tenders. The second involved the formation of black-owned or black-led companies with the specific goal of acquiring tenders. The element of fronting crept in when these companies developed no real capacity to produce the goods or services tendered for, but merely served as intermediaries between government procurers and established white-owned or foreign suppliers who actually delivered the good or service procured. At their worst, some of these companies sought to position themselves as intermediaries for absolutely any tender – giving rise to the term 'tenderpreneur'. Government procurement, instead of being an opportunity for the negotiation of discounts for large purchases, became instead a reality of overpriced acquisition of goods and services, as excessive mark-ups were added to often monopolistic prices. Over time, instances emerged of purchases by government departments at prices many times higher even than high street shop prices, involving, among other items, computer equipment, furniture for offices or official residences, and even bottled water and drinking glasses hired for state dinners. All of this was compounded by numerous instances of officials and political leaders seeking and obtaining significant bribes and kickbacks to grant or receive tenders.

In other words, the exceptionally concentrated and centralised character of South African capitalism, with a strong resident white bourgeoisie, gave 'primitive accumulation' by an aspirant black bourgeoisie a particular character. It led some, but not all, to limit their horizons to the rent they could extract by becoming intermediaries in, and/or facilitators of, access to state tenders. After two decades in office, such practices were having a major deleterious effect on the ANC as an organisation. This had in fact been foreseen in many documents as one of the potential perils of incumbency.[5] To my knowledge, at least from the time of the report of then Secretary-General, Kgalema Motlanthe, to the ANC's Stellenbosch Conference, held in 2002, successive secretaries-general had warned that branch activities were becoming increasingly corrupted by ambitious individuals forming factions and cliques with the precise intention of using political position to secure personal access to state resources and tenders.[6] It was not that opposition-led government institutions were immune. Several instances of corruption came to light in various non-ANC municipalities.[7] But the fact was that, with its greater control of government in all three spheres, the ANC was the main target.

Compounding this was the reality of systems operating (or not operating) in ways that made attempting to fight corruption far from easy. Individuals implicated could count on slow procedures by an overstretched criminal justice system. This made the chances, if discovered, of ending up behind bars much less likely than simply losing a position, with a prospect of being able to find another somewhere else in government. As indicated in Chapter 10, shortly after my appointment in 2009, I cancelled an ICT tender in the then Companies and Intellectual Property Registration Office that was manifestly out of order. This resulted in a lengthy court process, during which a host of hostile articles appeared in sections of the press. The easier route, much more travelled, was simply to reach a settlement, involving a payout of yet more government money.

It was on this terrain that it emerged in 2012 that R246 million had been spent on upgrades at President Zuma's family residence at Nkandla in KwaZulu-Natal. Some R70 million of this was within the perimeter of the property, and the remainder was earmarked for the construction of facilities for police and other support personnel outside. At first, many of us in government and the ANC were inclined to give President Zuma the benefit of the doubt. He strongly asserted that he had not asked for the upgrades and that these had been insisted on by officials from various government departments. We all knew of instances where officials, particularly in the Department of Public Works, drove overpriced repairs and renovations to the official residences assigned to us as tenants without our knowledge or concurrence. Officials in the security cluster also assured us that all upgrades had been undertaken as matters of security. For example, I recall a briefing in which we were told that the 'fire pool' had no shallow end and could not possibly be used as a swimming pool (something that later proved to be untrue).

Even at the time, some of us doubted whether it was wise for the President to refuse to offer to make any repayment, but Zuma argued strongly that any move of this sort this would be tantamount to admitting guilt. As the media storm erupted, a government investigation was initiated. This concluded that there was indeed extensive corruption and overpayment in the project, but that neither the President nor any sitting member of the executive was culpable in this regard. The matter was then referred by the opposition to the Public Protector, Thuli Madonsela, who conducted her own investigation culminating in the issuing of a report, titled 'Secure in Comfort', a few months before the 2014 election.[8] The report found that there had indeed been extensive corruption and overpayment, and while it made no findings that directly implicated the President, it did conclude that he and his family had benefited from upgrades that were not in fact security-related. It accordingly recommended that the Minister of Police identify what non-security upgrades had been made, and that the President make a reasonable contribution towards the cost of these. As is well known, President Zuma referred the question of the status of the Public Protector's findings and recommendations to the Constitutional Court, whose ruling was still pending as the fourth Parliament and fourth administration ended their terms.

The Nkandla issue had a significant impact on campaigning for the 2014 election, and not just among urbanised middle-class voters. I recall many ordinary poor people raising it in door-to-door engagements, and we were all provided with speaking notes on the matter. Not surprisingly, it was seized on in opposition party campaigns. Nkandla, indeed, provided the DA with something of a lifeline after what might otherwise have been an electorally damaging internal conflict over the issue of the 2013 B-BBEE Act (see Chapter 10). The Nkandla matter also allowed the fledgling EFF to deflect attention from some very real, and still unanswered, questions about its leadership's alleged role in dodgy deals in Limpopo province.

After the elections, and with the Constitutional Court ruling still pending, the then Minister of Police, Nathi Nhleko, treated us to a 'bioscope' to demonstrate that all the upgrading at Nkandla was indeed security-related. I recall a scene where the local Nkandla fire service (a bakkie with a small hose) was shown to be unable to generate sufficient water pressure to quench a potential fire. A pump accessing the water from what appeared to be a regular swimming pool was presented as the answer.

The Constitutional Court ruled on 31 March 2016 that recommendations from the Public Protector were not merely advisory, and had to be implemented unless overturned by a judicial review. The court also found that the President had failed to uphold, respect and defend the Constitution in disregarding the remedial action called for by the Public Protector. The National Assembly was similarly admonished for passing a resolution assuming that what should have been binding remedial action (unless overturned by a court) had no legal force or effect.

Shortly after this ruling, and with no further consultation either with cabinet or the NEC, the President indicated that he would abide by it. Treasury was instructed to determine what a fair contribution from President Zuma personally would be, and he undertook to pay it. The bioscope rapidly became, in the phrase immortalised by disgraced former US President Richard Nixon, 'no longer operative'. But the damage had been done. Calls to 'pay back the money' became the slogan around which the EFF mobilised the first of its disruptive campaigns in Parliament. This was damage that could have been avoided had a decision to pay been taken as soon as the matter arose.

Nkandla, though, proved to be small beer compared to what unfolded later. Even as the payments were being made (financed by a loan from the VBS Mutual Bank, formerly the Venda Building Society, later identified as a vehicle for the looting of public funds), a string of increasingly serious allegations emerged of corruption and state capture linked to relationships between members of the Zuma family and other senior officials with an Indian immigrant family, the Guptas.

Meetings with businesspeople go with the turf of the position of Minister, and indeed of Deputy Minister, of Trade and Industry. Establishing relationships with business (and other) stakeholders is integral to the process of developing and implementing industrial policy. Seeking out investors is also a critical part of the department's work and engagement with the minister is often part of the process of securing investments. I also encouraged a stance of openness and real engagement with the many unsolicited requests and proposals that came our way. Occasionally these resulted in real gems, but more often they involved special pleading or lobbying from all kinds of businesspeople seeking access to incentives and offerings of the DTI. Navigating this terrain was a test of both diary management and diplomatic skills. I tried to pass on as many proposals and requests as possible into systems developed in the ministry that would direct these to appropriate channels. But inevitably I ended up seeing some, both on trips abroad and in the country. My own position when encountering lobbyists was to ensure that they well understood that I would not and could not intervene to direct officials to support any specific application. There were systems that established criteria for accessing particular programmes, and committees that received and adjudicated on particular applications. This view was rooted in a clear understanding of the division of responsibilities between the executive authority (the minister) and the accounting officer (the director-general). The role of the executive authority was to provide strategic leadership, including in the design of programmes, but the allocation of benefits to particular applicants had to be subject to processes under the control of the accounting officer. If anyone involved in such processes was found to be acting improperly, we adopted a stance of zero tolerance. If it ever came to applying flexibility, which happened very rarely, that would require concurrence between the executive authority and the accounting officer and follow discussion with the officials concerned. That approach was rooted in a view, which I held throughout my term, that the role of a minister was to build institutions and institutional capacity, including drawing into institutionalised processes new programmes such as the IPAP.

My own first contact with members of the Gupta family came shortly after my appointment as minister in 2009, when President Zuma asked if I would meet with his son Duduzane, supposedly to discuss some business ideas he wanted to pursue. I had known Duduzane since Mozambique days. He was a contemporary of my own older children and I had bumped into him from time to time since then. I had no problem in agreeing to meet him for what I thought would be a general discussion about opportunities for small businesses, perhaps culminating in a suggestion that he meet with the Small Enterprise Development Agency (SEDA). As it was a weekend, and I was told Duduzane would be leaving Cape Town soon, I suggested he call at my residence in Cape Town. When he arrived, he was accompanied by Ajay Gupta, whom I had never come across before – and about whom I certainly did not know then what I know now. Duduzane in fact said little in a conversation that was dominated by Ajay Gupta. He complained that the IDC was not responding to a request for support in the acquisition of a mine. He told me that the option to buy was due to expire and that if this happened hundreds of workers would be laid off. I gave him some version of the answer I gave to no end of people who approached me seeking personal (or ministerial) support for this or that project. I as minister could not and would not get involved in deciding whether any specific project would be supported for funding. Whether or not I had the skills, I did not have the time to carry out essential technical assessment of specific funding proposals, and such decisions were taken by teams of professionals operating according to a broad mandate set by the executive. The IDC had a board and well-established procedures. I said, however, that I would ask the IDC to make its own decision within a reasonable time, which I did.

The start of the fourth term was a time when we were actively seeking to strengthen and deepen economic relations with emerging economies, finally culminating in South Africa's becoming a member of BRICS. India, as a key emerging economy, and an increasingly active investor in manufacturing industries across the world, became a significant focus of attention. My then Indian counterpart, Anand Sharma, had been a leader of the Indian anti-apartheid movement. He was sent by the Indian Congress Party to observe our first democratic elections in 1994 and he was married to a South African from a prominent family well known for its contribution to our liberation struggle. Anand and I put a lot of effort into strengthening bilateral economic relations. This included working to strengthen and support the South Africa-India Business Council, then headed respectively by Patrice Motsepe and Sir Ratan Tata. Anand and I also hosted several broader bilateral business fora both in India and South Africa. The Guptas were present at several of these and I saw them on a number of occasions. On one such occasion, Ajay Gupta asked me if I liked Indian food. When I responded in the affirmative, he said I should come round to his house for dinner. I said something like 'that would be nice', thinking that would be the end of the matter. Sometime later, I received a call inviting me and my wife to come to dinner on some particular day. I replied that I was busy on that day. He responded by asking when, then, could we make it.

Eventually, I accepted a few dinner invitations. Mostly we talked generally about the economy and building stronger relations with India. Ajay Gupta, who was the host, projected an image of himself and his brothers as Indian investors with a capacity to serve as a catalyst for deepening ties with India. I tended to think, even at the time, that they were exaggerating their influence with serious Indian investors, but I could not ignore the fact that they were a factor in such relations. They were clearly close to the Indian High Commission and had some role in organising high-profile events. For example, in 2010 I attended a cricket match and cultural event held as part of the commemoration of the 150th anniversary of the arrival in South Africa of Indian indentured labourers. I went because I understood that my counterpart might attend. (He did not.) This was a full international match held at a ground in Durban bearing the name of the Gupta computer brand. The cultural event saw performances by some of the very best Indian artists. At some point I was told about their computer manufacturing business, which they indicated was involved in exporting products assembled in South Africa to India. I was invited, when next in Mumbai, to visit the depot from which computers assembled in South Africa were distributed to customers in India. During one or other visit to India, I went to this facility on a tour conducted by the local managers. At the end of the visit, the hosts gave me a laptop computer, the only gift I received from the Gupta family. I accepted it but shortly afterwards donated it to SEDA.

I was reminded once that a delegation from the Gupta family visited the DTI, and, having been told how the department's programmes worked, were overheard saying as they left, 'There's nothing here.' I attended the well-known Sun City wedding in 2013, in part because again I was led to understand that a number of business and political figures from India would be present. In the event I was introduced to a few legislators from one of the states and some businesspeople, who clearly had neither the inclination nor the capacity to become serious investors in South Africa. I was already at the wedding when I first heard about the controversial authorisation for the chartered jet carrying guests to land at the Waterkloof Air Force Base. I felt very embarrassed but, as I was already present, tried to be a polite guest and stayed until the end. I have had no personal contact with the Guptas since then.

At some stage the family image underwent a makeover as they 'transitioned' from presenting themselves as Indian investors to projecting themselves as 'patriotic' South Africans committed to promoting radical economic transformation. As this unfolded, they became bolder and bolder in their demands, and more people were drawn into their patronage network. Their particular focus was on tenders issued by public entities, especially SOCs. The basic modus operandi, it is now clear, was to use political influence, kickbacks and backhanders to ensure they received lucrative tenders, and then to divert upfront payments abroad using a variety of money laundering techniques. As indicated earlier, the use of fronting and kickbacks to secure tenders was nothing new, but up to that point had usually involved some level of delivery of the goods or services procured, albeit at high cost. The Gupta model took this to next stage – to outright looting and repatriation abroad of funds with little or no delivery. I only became directly aware of this as journalists and whistleblowers began to publish revelations in 2016–2017, but I had become cognisant of the indirect effects of state capture a bit earlier when it began to impact on our efforts to roll out industrial policy.

Local content designations were a hard-won policy tool that we began to apply in 2011. Localisation, in which public authorities determine that they will give some or other preference to locally manufactured products in procurement processes, is a key industrial policy tool that had been applied by all successful industrialising countries. Indeed, it is a measure applied even in many developed countries, giving rise to much hypocrisy in the form of not practising what is preached and decidedly not preaching (particularly to developing countries) what they themselves were practising. The United States, for example, in its 'Buy America' legislation requires all railway equipment procured by Amtrak to be both mined and manufactured in the US.[9]

In terms of the regulations implemented after 2011, the DTI was charged with identifying local content requirements that would apply to purchases of defined products by all public entities. These were then turned into practice notes by National Treasury, after which the applicable designation became binding. Local content designations specified that some part, or all, of a product procured had to be produced in South Africa. Between 2011 and 2019, 23 products or sectors were subject to local content designations under these regulations, and between March 2015 and September 2018 some R71 billion was spent on designated products – an amount that could otherwise well have been spent on imports.[10] Localisation designations covered, among other things, textiles and clothing, furniture, electrical and telecoms cables, canned and processed food, buses and transformers, and various other inputs into infrastructure programmes.

One of the biggest and most significant procurements linked to the infrastructure development programme was the locomotive and railway wagon tender. This called for the procurement of 1 064 locomotives, subject to local content requirements. The introduction of these designations had a number of positive results including the gearing-up of production facilities in South Africa by both South African and foreign-owned companies, and investments by actual or potential manufacturers of railway locomotives. During a visit to the United States, I met with executives of GE, who told me that their company had never before manufactured a locomotive outside the United States. They had, however, established a manufacturing plant in South Africa to enable them to qualify to become part of the locomotive tender. GE's local managers were quite positive about their experience in South Africa, and later this led to the company's doing something similar in India. There were also important positive benefits from the designations for smaller manufacturing businesses, including those that were black-owned. In 2016 we launched that year's IPAP at the Guestro Naledi factory in Benoni. This was owned by a black industrialist, Sibusiso Maphatiane, who had acquired a run-down foundry, and had used a DTI incentive, as well as an IDC

The Industrial Policy Action Plan (IPAP) for 2016 was launched at the Guestro Naledi factory in Benoni.

loan, to modernise the equipment in the facility. The factory was manufacturing wheel castings for locomotives and wagons that were part of the locomotive and wagon tender.

Over time, we observed significant non-observance of localisation designations. In part this could be attributed to bureaucratic inertia driving a general lack of commitment to seek out local suppliers. But there were also an increasing number of allegations of irregularly awarded tenders, corruption and looting. Without exception, all such cases had in common the fact that they involved the acquisition of imports rather than locally produced products. One of the casualties of such a process was Guestro Naledi, which failed to get orders in the later phases of the railway procurement programme. Products that it had earlier supplied were now procured fully imported. Guestro Naledi went into business rescue and the company was only saved by reorientating itself to export markets.

I raised this concern repeatedly. Then Minister of Public Enterprises Lynne Brown arranged for me and some of our team to meet with Siyabonga Gama, the then CEO of Transnet. Gama told us that the problem was that the applicable localisation designation pre-scribed general percentages but was not sufficiently precise to ensure that each tenderer localised the same components, in this case wheel casings. While taking the general point about the need for greater precision in the design of designations, I was not convinced that this was the whole story. I therefore actively encouraged the portfolio committee to organise public hearings when they raised the matter with me. The committee heard many allegations of irregularity in tenders being a major factor. I also encouraged our team to engage the Auditor-General with a view to making noncompliance with localisation designations an audit finding (and this is now happening). I also repeatedly expressed a view that all improperly issued tenders should be cancelled and reissued in order to, among other things, comply with localisation requirements.

Another deleterious impact on our work arose from what became known as the 'shenanigans' in SARS. During the fourth administration we had become aware of significant illegal imports of clothing and textile products. One of the key techniques was the practice of under-invoicing, in which the declared value of the product was understated to customs officers. As indicated in Chapter 7, it was calculated at the time that there was in fact up to a 60 per cent divergence between the value of such products recorded as exports to South Africa by authorities in China and the value recorded as imports from China by our own customs officers. This meant that importers paid far less in duties than they should have, to the detriment of competing local manufacturers. Discussions in Nedlac led to the development of a 'reference price' system. Under this system, customs officers were provided with a minimum indicative value for each product – and this was the basis on which duties were levied even if the invoice recorded something less. For some time, this system worked quite well and we saw a welcome reduction in the entry of under-invoiced products.[11] However, as instability in SARS began to unfold, we began to hear either that those administering the scheme were no longer there or that there was a general non-implementation of the system. By 2018 it was apparent that under-invoicing was back with a bang.

Beyond these specific instances, the declining reliability of services, coupled with increased service charges by SOCs (both at least partly the result of state capture), began to impact seriously on industrial development. Electricity supply and cost, undoubtedly linked to the crisis in Eskom, rapidly became a major issue, impacting negatively not just on energy-intensive users, such as smelters, but also on a broad range of industrial customers. Indeed, over the course of a little more than a decade South Africa moved from being an investment destination where a reliable supply of affordable energy could be punted as a competitive advantage to one with a reputation as an unreliable provider of expensive electricity.

Port charges were another issue we tried to grapple with, particularly the skewed tariff schedule that penalised exporters of value-added products with higher tariffs than those paid by either importers or exporters of unbeneficiated mineral commodities. These issues we captured in successive iterations of the IPAP under the euphemistic heading of 'high administered prices'.

Faced with all of this, the job of leading a government department charged with trying to place the economy on a new growth path became less and less personally satisfying. As various problematic cabinet reshuffles unfolded, I started to read or hear that I was one of those about to be fired. I was already in my late sixties, and more than once from a personal perspective contemplated resigning. The reason I did not was, in the first instance, based on a concern about what would happen to the DTI if I did. Given the kind of appointments then being made, and hearing rumours about potential replacements, I worried about what would happen to the institutions we had tried to build if I left under those circumstances. Besides, at a political level I took my cue from the evolving positions of the SACP, and these included not abandoning any site of power. That decision I felt had consequences for my own profile in the evolving struggles within the movement against state capture. I supported the SACP positions as they evolved towards calling on Jacob Zuma to step down. In one ANC NEC meeting, I stated explicitly that I was a member of the Central Committee of the SACP whose position on the issue was well known and that I was not someone who would be part of one decision in one organisation and then support something else in another organisation. But my role was that of a supporter and follower, rather than a leader, of these processes.

Faced with such circumstances, and with little prospect of early resolution, we in the DTI focused on doing what we could, consistently aware that our efforts to promote industrial policy were now both well below potential and less than what was needed to place the economy on a more inclusive, higher value-added growth path. We kept up the discipline of issuing IPAPs as three-year rolling action plans. We also engaged in an intense, two-year-long process of developing a master plan to take the automotive industry to 2035. This was to serve as the basis for the post-2020 phase of the APDP (see Chapter 7). The Automotive Master Plan was developed through an inclusive process that drew representatives of the automotive assemblers, component manufacturers, the main union (Numsa) and government into an iterative series of engagements based on research findings introduced by a facilitator, Justin Barnes. The research established the point that while the motor industry had made progress, measured by output and investments, since the introduction of the APDP in 2010, the automotive manufacturing ecosystem in South Africa was in fact fragile. In particular, the level of locally manufactured components was small in comparison with competitor locations – being only 39 per cent of the total value of vehicles assembled. The Master Plan accordingly set a target of raising the average level of local content to 60 per cent by 2030, as well as increasing the number of vehicles produced to one per cent of world output by 2035 – meaning an increase from 600 000 to 1.4 million units – and doubling employment to 240 000. After much discussion and negotiation, the APDP was amended in particular by changing one of its sub-programmes (the Volume Assembly Allowance) into a Volume Assembly Localisation Allowance that would reduce payments to manufacturers unless they increased local content.[12] Another master plan process initiated before I left office involved the clothing and textile sector, and I am pleased to note that the suggestion we made to extend this methodology to other sectors is now being carried forward.

A further important initiative was the launch of the Black Industrialists (BI) programme. As indicated in Chapter 10, the amendments to B-BBEE legislation made after 2013 generally sought to bring about a shift towards a more substantive and productive form of B-BBEE – through tightening provisions against fronting and establishing a B-BBEE commission to combat such practices, as well as requiring sub-minima in enterprise development and skills development in assessments of B-BBEE scorecards submitted to qualify for various benefits. But we were also well aware that the manufacturing sector was among the least transformed of all sectors in the economy. The BI programme was a specific response to that reality.

Developing the BI programme was long process that saw much lobbying, including from rent-seekers. I eventually decided to take what I knew was a very inadequate draft to cabinet, hoping for critical input from colleagues. One came from the then Deputy President, Cyril Ramaphosa. I pushed him to elaborate on his comments and he eventually agreed to a lunch meeting with me and some of our officials. Out of this we developed some of the criteria for entry into the programme. Beneficiaries had to be majority black-owned businesses operating in IPAP sectors. Owners had to have a personal stake and be taking risk (have 'skin in the game') in industrial companies. By February 2019, the DTI had supported 138 black industrialists with an incentive grant.[13] I visited a number of these, and it was a real pleasure to meet individuals who had

*At the opening of the Yekani electronics manufacturing plant in East London,
with then Eastern Cape Premier Phumulo Masualle (left) and
Yekani CEO Siphiwe Cele (second from left).*

taken advantage of the opportunities created by democracy to
acquire skills and experience that enabled them to establish businesses in agro-processing, clothing and textiles, and various component
manufacturing businesses, among others. One case I cited frequently
was that of Yekani Manufacturing and Technology, whose CEO is
Siphiwe Cele. I participated in the opening of their new plant in
the East London Industrial Development Zone in June 2018. This
was a R1 billion investment in an electronics manufacturing plant
that was creating an additional 1 000 decent jobs.[14] This would be
a remarkable investment whoever was undertaking it. The fact that
it was driven by a black South African spoke volumes about the
potential still lying untapped.

Beyond pushing forward with our key programmes, we also
resolved, in a context of witnessing several public entities failing,
that we would ensure that we left to our successors a functioning
department and associated institutions. One element of this was
what we called 'Operation Clean Audit'. The record before this was

not so bad. Like many departments, the DTI had been receiving audits that were financially unqualified but with findings on technical matters rather than on matters involving misappropriation of funds. Several of the entities reporting to the department were similarly positioned, while a few of the smaller ones had obtained 'clean audits' (meaning financially unqualified with no findings). The then Companies and Intellectual Property Registration Office and the National Regulator for Compulsory Specifications were outliers in receiving qualified audits in some years.

Operation Clean Audit involved setting the goal of moving to clean audits across the portfolio. This required the department and all entities to specifically identify how they would address issues raised by the Auditor-General both in previous reports and in preparing for each year's audit. We ended our term with the DTI achieving a clean audit in four of the five years of the term, and the majority of entities doing likewise. One of the latter was the Companies and Intellectual Property Commission which achieved a clean audit in 2017/8 – a remarkable achievement given that its predecessor, Cipro, had had qualifications.

As is well known, state capture was not confined to direct theft and the corrupting of incumbent officials and public representatives. It extended to encompass allegations of individuals being offered bribes by members of the Gupta family to take up positions they did not then hold, including cabinet positions. Two individuals who said they declined such offers were Vytjie Mentor and Mcebisi Jonas.

I had worked with Mcebisi Jonas, first in his capacity as MEC for Economic Development in the Eastern Cape and later as Deputy Minister of Finance. He was, in my opinion, one of the very best MECs with whom I interacted in intergovernmental meetings. He was both committed to the development of his province and a gifted analyst and writer on broader policy issues. I also interacted with him on several occasions when he was Deputy Minister of Finance, and found him to be someone with a much broader and more progressive perspective than many Treasury officials. I was with him at a SACU meeting in Botswana when the Sunday newspapers reported that he had been offered the Finance Minister's job by members of the Gupta family, along with a not inconsiderable bribe of R600 million. At the SACU meeting, I said something like, 'I've been reading about you in the Sunday papers.' He smiled and then showed me the SMSes setting up the meetings. Based on that and what I knew of him, I had no doubt that he was not making things up. Later I publicly said that I regarded him as a person of integrity.[15]

These allegations were serious. They amounted to taking corruption to levels previously unknown – certainly in South Africa and probably even on a world scale. While there are many examples around the world of private corporate interests gaining benefits they should not be entitled to, or exerting influence over government leaders, there has never, to my knowledge, been any case anywhere where the interviewing of potential candidates for cabinet positions was outsourced to representatives of private corporate interests offering candidates bribes for favours.

By 2015–2016, it had become glaringly obvious that the influence of the Gupta family was extensive and pernicious. According to research conducted later for the South African Council of Churches, a family that arrived in South Africa in the early 1990s reputedly with R1 million had looted a fortune of no less than R40 billion[16] – most of it taken offshore. The knock-on impacts on the economy, arising from the damage caused to the functioning of public entities, was of course many multiples of that figure – a calculation that, at the time of writing, still has to be done.

Towards the end of her term, Public Protector Thuli Madonsela conducted an investigation into the allegations of state capture. Her report, entitled 'State of Capture',[17] was published in October 2016 and recorded a number of damaging allegations, including widespread corruption and awarding of dodgy tenders to Gupta-linked companies. It also pointed to allegations against particular members of cabinet, and referred to claims that bribes and cabinet positions had been offered to both Mcebisi Jonas and Vytjie Mentor by members of the Gupta family. The Public Protector's report called for the establishment of a judicial commission of inquiry to further investigate the many allegations recorded in her report. As President Zuma was himself implicated, the Public Protector called for the Chief Justice to nominate the judge to head the commission.

The report and the allegations included in it were extremely damaging to the ANC and the alliance. This damage was further compounded by the publication, over several weeks in 2017, of leaked emails between Gupta-led companies and various leaders in government and state-owned companies. Over time, two narratives emerged within the ANC and the alliance. The first called for 'self-correction', including the urgent establishment of the judicial commission of inquiry called for by the Public Protector.

The second narrative, in practice, sought to slow down the process of establishing the judicial commission. Arguments advanced in this quest included that there were important constitutional issues at stake in the appointment of the chair (normally the prerogative of the President), and that ministers named, who had taken the Public Protector's report on judicial review, needed first to have their day in court. Another argument that emerged was that the issue of state capture that needed to be investigated should not be confined to the actions of the Guptas, but should also include other instances in the apartheid period, involving, among others, members of the Rupert family. One of the techniques of populist discourse is what has been dubbed 'what aboutism'. This involves responding to a critique on any particular issue by asking 'what about?' something else – as if the latter could justify the former. There was much 'what aboutism' in the responses to charges of state capture. The main one was to respond to charges of state capture involving the Guptas with the retort, 'What about the Ruperts?' as though the evident state patronage supplied to Anton and Johann Rupert during the apartheid days could in any way justify the actions undertaken to support Gupta looting.

Another narrative that emerged in this context was that the issue of state capture was being used as part of a broader agenda of 'regime change'. The real target, it was said, was not an individual (Zuma) but the ANC as an organisation. The aim, it was asserted, was to dislodge the ANC from government and thereby thwart the advance of the National Democratic Revolution. The existence of a regime-change agenda, at least in some forms, cannot be doubted. Apart from the obvious fact that this was by definition the main goal of opposition parties, it was also evident that many domestic- and foreign-funded NGOs, parts of the press, capital and some foreign interests had this as an implicit, if not explicit, objective. A number of papers emanating from both the ANC and meetings of former liberation movements spoke of the threat of 'colour revolutions' – a reference to events that had driven incumbent regimes from power in various countries in the Middle East and North Africa, as well as in Ukraine and Georgia. All of this was accompanied by a shift in neoliberal discourse suggesting that 'good governance' should see not only presidents respecting two-term limits but also individual parties not remaining in government 'too long'. This kind of discourse was directed at Chama cha Mapinduzi (Party of the Revolution) in the 2014 Tanzanian elections and even by former supporters at the Botswana Democratic Party in the same year. This was of course a variant within the overall neoliberal paradigm, holding that states everywhere should be composed of strong 'independent' institutions coexisting with frequently changed governments, delivering weak regimes unable to advance any agenda of fundamental change.

The real point, though, some of us felt, was how to act in the face of such an agenda. We pointed out in various debates within the ANC that whatever the underlying intentions or objectives, the narrative driving most successful regime change was corruption. Take, for example, the overthrow of President Viktor Yanukovych of Ukraine in 2014. The big geostrategic objectives in that case were not hard to see: to shift Ukraine from the Russian sphere of influence to that of the EU and NATO. But the discourse that drove Yanukovych from power in Ukraine was that the Yanukovych regime was corrupt, and this had at least some base in reality.

The gathering crisis was further exacerbated by a number of bad decisions, especially on appointments. The firing of Finance Minister Nhlanhla Nene in December 2015 was the first of the prominent episodes in this respect. I always found Nene to be both a competent colleague and someone who was open-minded and ready to address the challenge of bringing National Treasury into a new and more co-operative relationship with those of us in real-economy departments. Like many, I was shocked when he was fired. The notion that he was being redeployed to head the African regional office of the BRICS New Development Bank soon proved hollow. No such offer was ever made. His replacement for a weekend, Des van Rooyen, showed more of the real reason. Van Rooyen was treasurer of the uMkhonto we Sizwe Military Veterans' Association, and although he was whip in the Finance Portfolio Committee, he clearly did not have the track record or the gravitas to take on the job. I was attending a WTO meeting in Nairobi that began during his 'weekend in office' and was asked by colleagues from neighbouring countries who he was and what he was like. They were astounded when I replied quite truthfully that I did not know him personally.

On that occasion, Zuma was obliged to back down by reappointing to the position the Finance Minister of his first term, Pravin Gordhan. Gordhan held the position for less than 18 months before being fired, along with his deputy, Mcebisi Jonas, in March 2017. This unleashed even more fire. Markets crashed and rating agencies downgraded the country's sovereign debt rating, citing 'political uncertainty'.

But while these were the most prominent of the problematic appointments, there were also others in what became an increasingly unstable administration. A study commissioned by the South African Institute of Race Relations and published in August 2017

With President Zuma and then Minister of Finance Pravin Gordhan during a bilateral visit to Lesotho in June 2016

found that there had been 126 changes in the executive (involving 62 ministerial and 63 deputy ministerial positions) and 138 changes of directors-general in 38 national departments.[18]

By the time of the local government elections in August 2016, it was clear that the ANC was facing a moment of reckoning. Elected in 2014 with a 62 per cent majority, the ANC found itself receiving only an overall average of 54 per cent in the August 2016 elections. The party lost its majority in most of the large metropolitan municipalities (with Johannesburg, Tshwane and Nelson Mandela Bay falling to opposition coalitions). With Cape Town already in DA hands, the ANC was left in charge of only Ethekwini, Mangaung and Ekhuruleni (and in the last-mentioned it depended on coalition partners). In terms of budget controlled, before the 2016 election the ANC controlled 82 per cent of total municipal operating budgets and 83 per cent of total municipal capital budgets. After the election, these numbers fell to 42 per cent and 45 per cent, respectively.[19]

There were many local issues that impacted on this result, including unhappiness at service delivery and processes of choosing councillor candidates. But there was also an evident overall sense that ANC leaders had become corrupt, remote and elitist. At its meeting held immediately after the local government elections, the NEC declared that it had heard the concerns of the people and would humble itself before them. It pledged to embark on a path of self-correction, both on the local issues and corruption. But, as with many such pronouncements, there was no discernible implementation.

By 2016 the malaise within the ANC had come to impact on alliance relations. Cosatu had already split, largely on the issue of divisions around relations with the ANC under Zuma (see Chapter 11). This was a massive blow that seriously weakened the influence of the working class within the alliance and, in my estimation, opened the way for the eventual emergence of a form of aspirant capitalist populism as a major discourse within the ANC (see below and Chapter 14). The SACP remained loyal to the alliance but with increasing dismay at developments within the ANC. In a number of bilateral meetings, Zuma was asked to cut his ties with the Gupta family. Finally, at one NEC lekgotla, the SACP's then Second Deputy General Secretary, Solly Mapaila, bravely said in front of a large audience of leaders and officials that the elephant in the room was the Guptas. Thereafter, the SACP threw its weight behind the campaign against state capture, including mobilising and participating in a range of anti-state capture broad-front activities.

Emerging in this context, and ahead of the ANC's mid-2017 policy conference, was a renewed focus on radical economic transformation. As indicated earlier, the idea itself was not new and had been mentioned by President Zuma in his 2014 inauguration speech. The idea and the definition offered by Zuma quoted earlier actually commanded broad support within the alliance. It, after all, embraced a number of elements of what needed to be done. The reference to bringing about fundamental change in the structure of the economy,

With Isithwalandwe Andrew Mlangeni and Dr Zweli Mkhize at an event in Soweto in July 2017. Mlangeni, the last surviving Rivonia trialist, died on 21 July 2020, aged 95.

for example, could be interpreted as calling for a move to higher value-added activities, as well as for creating new opportunities in a more diversified and less concentrated economy. The emphasis on promoting greater inclusiveness in ownership, leadership and effective participation in the economy was also critical. But in the circumstances existing in 2016–2017, it also spawned a form of populism easily identifiable as speaking to the aspirations of potential rent-seeking capitalists. The discourse associated with this kind of position held that at the heart of all the shortcomings in the performance of the economy was the fact that it was 'not in the hands of the black majority'. The solution to all issues was, accordingly, the transfer of existing assets to black individuals.

But this new-found radicalism also had its element, in Marx's famous adage, of history repeating itself, once as tragedy and then as farce. Several individuals who, as ANC and government leaders, had defended GEAR, and who had been part of decisions allowing South African-based companies to move offshore, were now supposedly leading a charge to 'transform' the finance sector and wage war on (white) monopoly capital. While real issues were sometimes raised, such as the lack of transformation of the financial sector, proposals as to what was to be done were generally more rhetorical than substantive. In the case of the financial sector, their target missed fundamental issues such as financialisation, the proliferation of speculative-bubble activities and the failure to provide finance to support productive activity. Often the trigger for broadsides against the financial sector was the closure of Gupta bank accounts and a search for more asset-seizing. Proposals on the evidently important issue of land reform gravitated towards changing the Constitution to allow expropriation without compensation. There was much less reflection on how to ensure that prospective beneficiaries became productive farmers rather than either failures or rent-seekers.

The same kind of vague populism characterised the debate on (white) monopoly capital as the principal adversary of the National Democratic Revolution. Much time and energy was spent on this issue during the July 2017 policy conference. While many insisted that the word 'white' be inserted, the report eventually adopted at the Nasrec conference sent the issue back for further consideration. It was not easy to discern from the ritualistic inputs of most of those insisting on the white-monopoly-capital characterisation what the strategic significance of this would be. While there could be no doubt that ownership of the domestic economy as a whole remained largely white and that this needed to change, the concept of monopoly capital in the age of globalisation clearly embraced foreign investors, including foreign investors, for example, from Asian countries. Moreover, those insisting on this characterisation had little to say about what needed to be done to combat the negative effects of excessive concentration and centralisation. The call for stronger measures to reduce concentration tended to come from those less insistent on the white-monopoly-capital construct, leading several of us to conclude that the central issue for many white-monopoly-capital militants was the whiteness rather than the monopoly character of white monopoly capital, and that the main solution sought was a greater share of the pie rather than fundamental structural change. This characterisation, it eventually transpired, originated at least in part from a public relations strategy devised by the UK-based Bell Pottinger company to deflect attention from the growing criticism of the activities of the Guptas.[20]

All of the above shaped the context for a leadership elective contest at the ANC's 54th National Conference, held at Nasrec in December 2017. This was driven by two competing policy platforms. The first, which supported Nkosazana Dlamini-Zuma's election as party president, promised a programme of 'radical economic transformation', including accelerated land reform, an undefined transformation of the financial sector, a loosening of public procurement rules to allow more tenders to be awarded to black business, etc.

The second platform, personified by then Deputy President Cyril Ramaphosa but also embraced in varying degrees by other candidates, such as Lindiwe Sisulu, Zweli Mkhize, Jeff Radebe and Mathews Phosa, emphasised 'cleaning up' the ANC and ending state capture. Allegations in this regard were frankly acknowledged as having substance, and it was argued that the future of the movement and of the NDR depended on ending such practices and returning to the core values and principles of the ANC. This platform did not reject the idea of radical economic transformation but tended to have a less populist, more strategic and nuanced approach to it; for example, it was Ramaphosa who spearheaded the call for stronger competition legislation that would move beyond sanctioning abuse of dominance and embrace actual deconcentration. In proposing this, Ramaphosa cited numerous analyses, including by the IMF, which cited excessive concentration as a major factor impeding both broader participation and more robust economic growth.

Never before had the ANC entered a national conference with as much at stake. The result was a near stalemate in the balance between the contending forces, but with one decisive outcome: the election of Cyril Ramaphosa as party president. Ramaphosa, however, was part of 50:50 split in the top six, between his supporters and those of Zuma, while the NEC was similarly divided. Of considerable significance was the failure of any of the SACP officials to make it on to the ANC's NEC – the first time this had happened since the days of Moses Kotane.

13
Politics and economics in the early Ramaphosa era

The near stalemate between the main platforms in the elections at the 54th National Conference could have resulted in impasse and indecision. But the Ramaphosa platform won the top prize, the presidency, albeit by a small majority. Ramaphosa himself is a consummate strategist, negotiator and consensus builder. He frankly declared that if people wanted a dictator, he was not that person.[1] His approach, rather, was what he described as the tried and tested South African way of dealing with seemingly insurmountable problems: engage with all interested parties and find a solution. This did not mean going into an engagement in a vacuous way with no idea of its desired outcome. Rather it meant testing pre-existing propositions through engagement, being open to other proposals and leading discussion towards a conclusion that would draw broad buy-in in ways that often had the effect of creating an unassailable reality, rendering a contrary decision untenable.

I saw something of this up close in the preparatory meeting for the delegation travelling to the 2018 meeting of the World Economic Forum in Davos. Ramaphosa, then ANC President but not yet President of the Republic, was tasked with leading the delegation. At the preparatory meeting, he was asked by the CEO of one of the development finance institutions how the delegation could credibly present its investment message at Davos while the issue of the appointment of a new Eskom board remained unresolved. The easiest response would have been to say the matter needed to be attended to and would be in due course. But Ramaphosa seized on this remark to agree that it needed to be resolved in the less than a week that remained before travelling to Davos, and he undertook to engage with Zuma to ensure that this happened. Arriving in Davos with this done, and an indication of his authority under his belt, he responded to questions about the Presidency of the Republic by speaking of the necessity of a 'difficult conversation' back home.[2]

Against the background of continuing revelations in the media on the extent of state capture and corruption, opposition to the idea that Zuma deliver the 2018 State of the Nation Address (SONA) began to grow within the ANC, the alliance and the public at large. This, plus the predictable threats by the EFF to disrupt the address if it was delivered by Zuma, led to an unprecedented decision to postpone the SONA. All of this created more than an opportunity; it made imperative an early NEC decision to call on Zuma to step down. Although there were definitely forces in the NEC opposed to such a move, by the time the NEC met on this issue it would have been impossible to have taken the opposite decision except at great cost. After some prevarication, Zuma eventually stepped down on 14 February 2018. One can only imagine how differently things might have worked out had Ramaphosa chosen to follow a course recommended to him by many commentators on other issues later on and simply tried to assert his authority as President of the ANC and insist that Zuma stand down in his favour.

When Ramaphosa finally delivered the SONA on 16 February, the day after being elected President, he spoke of a 'new dawn'. Quoting from the title of a hit tune by Hugh Masekela, he called on social partners to 'Thuma mina' (lend a hand) in getting the country moving again. Ramaphosa's election and his inaugural speech were extremely well received, leading the press to coin a phrase capturing the mood in these early days – 'Ramaphoria'. Specifically, the new President announced a number of summits to be held before the end of the year, including a Jobs Summit and an Investment Summit aimed at raising the level of domestic and foreign investment

The group photo of DTI staff, members of the portfolio committee and stakeholders taken after my last budget vote debate in 2018, on the steps of Parliament.

Speaking in the National Assembly during the SONA debate, February 2019.

by US$100 billion over five years. To this end, four 'investment envoys' were appointed to scour the world to promote investment in South Africa. Another early initiative was the Youth Employment Scheme (YES), a private-sector-driven programme aimed at creating one million internship and small enterprise opportunities for young people.

The various summits were all duly held in a much better spirit than comparable events under Zuma. The investment summit in October 2018 recorded R290 billion of verified commitments, meaning the initiative looked well on track to potentially achieve the US$100 billion target.[3] UNCTAD's *Global Investment Trends Monitor*, published in January 2019, reported that global FDI flows had declined by 13 per cent to US$1.3 trillion in that year, but the flow to South Africa had increased by 446 per cent to reach US$7.1 billion.[4] In other words, in the first year of the Ramaphosa presidency, South Africa had bucked the global trend. But, despite all of this, the underlying reality was one of a stagnant economy with a faltering infrastructure investment programme and serious operational and financial weaknesses in the performance of public institutions and SOCs. Early 2019 saw the return of power cuts (load shedding) as the public became increasingly aware of the acute crisis in Eskom.

Ahead of the May 2019 general election, the ANC campaigned on a platform emphasising its commitment to ending state capture and corruption, fixing damaged public institutions and creating a capable developmental state as the essential components of creating conditions for the achievement of higher levels of more inclusive growth. It went into the campaign with new, much more credible appointments having been made to the leadership of institutions such as SARS and the NPA. The Commission of Inquiry into State Capture and Corruption, chaired by Deputy Chief Justice Raymond Zondo, which had actually been appointed by Zuma, meanwhile began to hold televised public hearings. While testimony given before the commission implicated a number of senior ANC politicians and officials in serious allegations of corruption, many also felt that it demonstrated that South Africa's constitutional order had both been tested and was holding, and that under the new leadership wrongdoers would eventually be held accountable. Quoting from what he said was his favourite film, *The Guns of Navarone*, Ramaphosa told one election meeting that the 'fuse had been lit' as far as those involved in state capture and corruption were concerned.

The ANC was returned as the largest party in the sixth Parliament of the democratic era, with 231 seats out of 400 (58.2 per cent). This represented an increase over the percentage of the national vote attained in the 2016 local government elections but a decrease on the 249 seats (or 62.1 per cent) it had won in the national elections in 2014. The DA also lost ground, winning 84 seats (21.2 per cent) compared to the 89 (or 22.2 per cent) it had won in 2014. But the EFF increased its numbers from 25 seats (or 6.3 per cent) to 41 seats (or 10.3 per cent). The ANC election team acknowledged, privately, that Ramaphosa's personal appeal (beyond that of the ANC) had been worth at least ten per cent of the vote the party had won, meaning that without him at the head of the ticket, the ANC could well have come in below 50 per cent.

The sixth administration took office against a backdrop of economic stagnation. The 'stimulus package with South African characteristics' announced in 2018 was not really recognisable as a stimulus package in the meaning generally understood elsewhere. It included neither a fiscal stimulus nor quantitative easing of any kind. Indeed, in many respects the 'stimulus with South African characteristics' seemed little more than the new name for Zuma's Nine-Point Plan, which had been announced in 2015. Certainly, it had little discernible impact in igniting a higher level of inclusive growth.

It was in that context that Finance Minister Tito Mboweni began a process, on his own initiative, of developing new proposals to ignite economic growth. At the outset, he called on the advice of some members of the 'Harvard Group' put together by National Treasury during the Mbeki administration. These included Professors Ricardo Hausmann and Dani Rodrik, as well as representatives of the OECD, World Bank and other agencies. The critique of the members of the Harvard Group was that while government said jobs were its priority, in practice the focus was blurred by too many other, and sometimes conflicting, goals.

The proposals eventually tabled by Mboweni in the name of National Treasury were titled 'Economic Transformation, Inclusive Growth and Competitiveness: Towards an Economic Strategy for South Africa'. The paper called for a number of 'growth reforms'. These included 'modernizing network industries', 'prioritising labour-intensive growth in … agriculture and services' and 'implementing focused and flexible industrial and trade policy'.[5] Significantly absent were any proposals for significant changes in the conduct of fiscal or monetary policy.[6] Fiscal policy would instead focus on 'consolidation' – and in particular on bringing the debt-to-GDP ratio back below the threshold of 60 per cent. The Medium Term Budget Policy Statement delivered by Mboweni on 30 October 2019 indicated that this would be achieved by moving over the next three fiscal years to a primary budget surplus of one per cent through R326 billion worth of cuts (starting with the government wage bill, and real reductions in social and university subsidies).[7]

The Treasury paper, in fact, had a rather difficult passage through the formal decision-making structures of the ruling party. It had not been developed in ANC structures or government and this led to its legitimacy being questioned on process grounds. Beyond this was the reality of a divided NEC. What came to be called the 'RET populist' faction still had significant influence within the ANC. Faced with the prospect of a Ramaphosa presidency, they managed at Nasrec to secure the passage of several important resolutions on economic policy matters. These included pursuing an amendment to the Constitution to allow expropriation of land without compensation and fully nationalising the SARB by ending private shareholding in it.

Ramaphosa skilfully embraced the first resolution, on land reform, and defended it in numerous engagements, including with sceptical foreign audiences. He argued that land seizures were the 'original sin' of colonialism, that the issue would not go away and indeed had to be addressed through bold land reform. He said that South Africans would find the way forward in the same way they had resolved the question of majority rule – through dialogue. But he was noticeably wary of the nationalisation of the SARB, seeing this as a move that would achieve little at potentially high risk. For the RET populists, changing the character of both the SARB and the Treasury were critical, and they were extremely averse to any ideas emanating from Treasury. A paper commissioned by the DTI towards the end of my term argued that an expansionary macro-economic policy stance was imperative to underpin more effective industrial policy and propel the economy to higher levels of more inclusive growth.[8] This was discussed at an internal Economic Trans-formation Committee meeting but not tabled at the February 2020 NEC lekgotla, which eventually adopted a slightly modified version of the Treasury paper.

The SACP noted that the Treasury paper marked a shift to macroeconomic exceptionalism.[9] The GEAR debate had been characterised by macroeconomic fundamentalism. As indicated in Chapter 7, the essence of this was a perspective that held that macroeconomic policy was the royal road to growth and develop-ment. For those influenced by neoliberalism, on the one hand, this meant an orthodox macroeconomic policy based on the neoliber-al 'ready reckoner' seen as being applicable to all economies at all times: the budget deficit must be less than three per cent and de-clining; inflation must be limited to single digits and declining; and public debt must be below 60 per cent of GDP. For those influenced by neo-Keynesianism, on the other hand, growth would

In conversation with Nobel economics laureate Joseph Stiglitz, Cape Town 2017.

With Nhlanhla Nene, Christine Lagarde (then IMF Managing Director) and President Cyril Ramaphosa, New York 2018.

be driven by some vague and often undefined deficit spending. As argued in Chapter 7, insufficient attention was paid by either side to the structural transformation of the productive base of the economy – and to the critical question of moving to higher value-added activities through industrialisation. The move to macroeconomic exceptionalism did at least genuflect in this direction.

Thus, while some of its detailed proposals were problematic, the Treasury paper did at least recognise the fundamental imperative to structurally transform the productive base of the economy. The central problem was that the steps to be taken in this regard were expected to deliver in a context of what the SACP called growing 'austeritisation'. This had never been achieved anywhere. In an interview given during a visit to South Africa, Nobel economics laureate Joseph Stiglitz warned that 'austerity has never worked … there's no such thing as an "expansionary contraction" … austerity is contractionary, it leads to downturns – period'.[10] He went on to suggest a tactically flexible approach to avoiding austerity in the face of enormous pressure to conform:

> Unfortunately, capital markets don't have the sophistication that academic economists do. So Moody's might not share the same view of debt and deficits. As a result, this requires more institutional innovation, ingenuity, and careful design. For example, a greater role for development banks … Second, to think about areas where you can focus on domestic resource mobilisation … tax policy, to aggressively support local production … spend in ways that have high multipliers, but also where you don't run into constraints.[11]

A major driver towards austerity was the threat of a ratings downgrade. At the start of 2020, only one of the three international credit rating agencies, Moody's, kept South Africa's sovereign rating at an 'investment grade'. But on 1 November 2019, it changed its out-look from 'stable' to 'negative' meaning that Moody's was consider-ing joining Standard & Poor's and Fitch Ratings in downgrading the sovereign rating to 'sub-investment grade' or 'junk status' at its next assessment in March. The implications of a downgrading to junk status by all three agencies would be that many institutional inves-tors would be prohibited by their fund rules from investing in South African bonds, while those that could still do so would expect to receive a higher rate of return. In other words, a credit downgrading would directly increase the costs of borrowing by government, and indirectly impact negatively on the ratings of other entities operating in South Africa, including SOCs and banks.

February and March 2020 saw further steps in a steady march to-wards austerity. The budget delivered in February was wise enough to resist the temptation (much anticipated) to impose new taxes on the poor by once again raising the rate of VAT. Instead it announced that government would seek to cut expenditure by R261 billion over three years. This, in particular, would target the government wage bill. A notice issued the day before the budget indicated that government would seek to cut the public sector wage bill by R160 billion over existing estimates, including by engaging unions to avoid paying the increases for 2020/1 provided for in the three-year wage agreement still in force. The austerity budget had avoided the possibility of a Lebanon-style mass protest response to the imposition of unpopular new taxes, but this was at the expense of a probable confrontation with public-sector workers and their unions. As indicated in Chapter 11, the labour movement had been severely weakened by develop-ments during the Zuma administration, but with Cosatu's main base and largest affiliate being public-sector workers, it could not but re-spond critically to the budget. Meanwhile, the leadership of the Public Sector Bargaining Forum pointed out that an agreement remains binding unless both parties agree to change it, leading some to opine that 'the government's grand plan to cut the public wage bill would seem to be on a road to nowhere, at least for this year'.[12] It remains to be seen how this issue will unfold.

A few weeks after the budget, Statistics South Africa reported that the South African economy had entered a 'technical recession', with negative growth of minus 0.8 per cent and minus 1.4 per cent recorded in the third and fourth quarters of 2019, respectively.[13] This was followed by a further contraction of two per cent in the first quarter of 2020.[14] Unemployment in the third quarter of 2019 predictably rose to 29.1 per cent on the strict definition, rising to 38 per cent, or more than 10 million people, on the 'expanded' definition, which includes discouraged job seekers.[15] In the first quarter of 2020, it rose again to reach 30.1 per cent on the strict definition, taking the numbers of unemployed persons up by 344 000 to reach a total of 7.1 million people.[16] This came amid a cascade of announcements of further retrenchments and plant closures.

The new leadership at Eskom, meanwhile, warned that unless the utility carried out a preventive maintenance programme that would inevitably lead to load shedding episodes over the next 18 months at least, its output would be cut by 8 000 megawatts by mid-2021.[17] Struggling South African Airways was placed in business rescue in December 2019, with serious job cuts seen as essential to any salvaging of the airline, while regional airline South African Express hovered on the brink.

This 'crisis before the crisis' was unfolding before South Africa, along with the rest of the world, was struck by the COVID-19 pandemic caused by the novel coronavirus SARS (severe acute respiratory syndrome) CoV-2. This was, first and foremost, a health emergency posing a major threat to human life, and the government of President Ramaphosa began by responding with exemplary leadership and statesmanship. Its decision to impose the initial strict lockdown was taken without hesitation, manifestly guided by science, reached after consultation and communicated to the citizenry in addresses that were well-reasoned, empathetic and inspiring. The way difficult decisions were taken, including the imposition of a strict lockdown, was in sharp contrast to the often denialist, narcissistic and partisan manner that leaders in other countries approached the pandemic. The government's response generated a hugely positive reaction among the people, and no doubt contributed to a higher level of compliance with measures recommended by medical experts than might otherwise have been the case.

But, while first and foremost a health emergency, COVID-19 also had major implications for all national economies and indeed for the world economy as a whole. In March 2020, UNCTAD warned that a decade of debt and austerity had rendered many national economies unable to cope with the implications of this emergency and that the world economy would plunge below its recessionary threshold. On a 'preliminary downside scenario', UNCTAD suggested that this could shave US$2 trillion off global income, with developing countries (excluding China) suffering a hit of US$220 billion.[18] In the month between mid-February and March 2020, portfolio outflows from the main emerging markets surged to US$59 billion – twice the level witnessed by the same countries at the onset of the global financial crisis. To counter these effects, UNCTAD called for a US$2.5 trillion support package to support developing countries in coping with the impact of COVID-19.[19] For its part, the IMF predicted that the 'Great Lockdown' recession would be the steepest for almost a century, with the world economy contracting by three per cent in 2020.[20]

In South Africa, it is widely accepted that COVID-19 will turn 2020 from a year of insipid growth into an actual contraction – with both the World Bank and National Treasury estimating that the contraction could reach more than minus seven per cent.[21] On 27 March, the very day the initial lockdown came into effect, Moody's delivered its verdict, downgrading the sovereign rating to one level below investment grade, thereby bringing the ratings of all three major rating agencies into alignment and ensuring some additional portfolio outflow as the costs of borrowing increased.

14
Conclusion: Towards a new deal for the new dawn

As I conclude this work, a health emergency of enormous proportions is engulfing the world. While a few are still hoping for an early return to 'normal' as the coronavirus pandemic passes, many others are recognising that the post-COVID-19 world will be very different from the one before. A global recession is inevitable. The only questions are, how severe will it be, and how long will it last? Many are now predicting that the impact will be worse than that of the Great Recession that began in 2008, and may even match, or surpass, that of the Great Depression of the 1930s.[1] In a world of high and growing inequality, it is inevitable that the impact of a global economic downturn will be particularly severe on the unemployed (whose ranks will swell), and on lower-skilled and lower-paid workers, particularly those in service sectors and in developing countries. The other question is, how will governments around the world respond? Stimuli and unorthodox policy responses of one sort or another (including income grants) are already being mobilised even by fiscally conservative administrations.[2] What remains to be seen is the impact this will have on politics and policy choices and thus on the political economy of the world in the years ahead. The answer to that question will determine the extent to which, to paraphrase Fidel Castro's remark on the impact of the battle of Cuito Cuanavale, the history of the world economy in the 21st century comes to be written in two parts – before and after COVID-19.

Even before the coronavirus emergency, South Africa was in midst of one of its worst-ever crises of economic stagnation, in fact its longest slump at any time since the Second World War. Analysts agreed that GDP growth, even before the shutdown and social distancing, would be less than one per cent in 2020, and possibly even less than half a per cent.[3] With a population growth rate of 1.4 per cent,[4] these figures meant that on average living standards were already in decline. Now 2020 looks certain to be a year of significant contraction – with even National Treasury, which normally comes in on the 'more optimistic' side of the spectrum, predicting it will reach minus 7.2 per cent of GDP.[5]

Again, even before the coronavirus emergency, productive sectors (manufacturing, mining, agriculture) were all recording flat or declining output. Consumer demand, as measured by various consumer confidence indices, was likewise flat and declining. Continuing power cuts and the energy crisis were striking a further blow to an already stagnant economy, hastening more plant closures and job cuts. All of this was seriously exacerbating the pre-existing crisis of unemployment, poverty and inequality. The statistics remain to be released, but the lockdown and social distancing measures can only have added significantly to the already large number of the unemployed.

Decisions taken at any particular conjuncture are shaped by the balance of forces existing at the time. Decisions taken, however, also have consequences that impact on the future. The context in which decisions are being taken by the ruling party and the ANC government under the leadership of Cyril Ramaphosa is one shaped by state capture and corruption, as well as by massive pressure to adopt austerity policies. Zuma's legacy, and the collective responsibility of all of us occupying leadership positions at that time, is one of public institutions deeply damaged by state capture and corruption. This has weakened the capacity of the state to intervene in the economy in manifold ways, including by undertaking public investment. This in turn has enhanced the power of finance capital, in particular of lenders in banks and funds. This was evident in the way in which the decisions of the ratings agencies (whose role is to advise investors and lenders) hung like a sword of Damocles over fiscal policy decisions – driving a steady march towards austerity.

Measures to end state capture and corruption taken thus far have not seen any high-profile prosecutions. But steps have been taken that could eventually lead to such an outcome, and these have predictably produced a backlash. Some of those potentially at risk of prosecution still have influence within the ANC leadership, and it is reported that former beneficiaries of overpriced contracts are also beginning to mobilise against what they see as steps that could exclude them from tenders.[6] Masquerading as champions of an anti-white monopoly capital 'radical economic transformation', these forces have falsely posited a linkage between resistance to holding suspected beneficiaries of state capture accountable and radicalism. This has fuelled an antithetical narrative, suggesting that the other side of the coin of fighting corruption and restoring good governance is a neoliberal version of 'structural reform'.

The SACP has argued that, in many respects, politics within the ANC has become reduced to a contestation between two aspirant capitalist factions. The first is a group of more established earlier-generation empowerees now firmly ensconced enough to favour 'playing by the rules'. This grouping, which emerged during the heyday of neoliberalism, also tends to hanker after the 'golden years' of the Mbeki administration. They tend to speak of 'nine lost years' under Zuma. Their nostalgia for this era also often embraces the supposed 'sound fiscal management' of GEAR. The second faction are less secure, more recent arrivals or aspirants, more dependent on rent-based tenders awarded through political connectedness. They feel left behind, and have less respect for Treasury rules, pushing in particular for amendments to procurement rules to allow easier access to overpriced tenders. This also spills over into a broader antagonism to both National Treasury and the Reserve Bank. Changes in ownership purportedly to end the dominance of white monopoly capital tend to be seen not as one element to place the economy on a more inclusive growth path, but rather as the magic bullet to be pursued virtually to the exclusion of all else.

Contestation between these forces has emerged as the main shaper of intra-ANC politics, largely because the influence of the working class and the poor (repeatedly identified as the main drivers of the NDR) has sharply diminished. The split in Cosatu has visibly reduced the influence of this alliance partner, also allowing for a greater marginalisation of the SACP. As suggested in Chapter 12, the same phenomenon has also been behind the emergence of radical nationalistic populism both inside and outside the alliance (in the latter case in the form of the EFF).

A progressive way forward must decisively reject corruption, but it must also say no to neoliberalism. Progressive economists around the world are united in the view that austerity won't work in promoting even meaningful growth, regardless of who benefits from it. In Chapter 13, we quoted Joseph Stiglitz, who argues that austerity leads to contraction. Austerity also tends to widen inequality, as its first casualties tend to be redistributive programmes in government budgets. Austerity should not be confused with trimming perks for senior officials or ensuring greater value for money by cutting rent-seeking. These measures should all be part of normal, prudent management of public funds. Austerity involves as its defining characteristic the prioritisation over all else of the achievement of predefined macroeconomic balances even to the extent of cutting redistributive programmes and withdrawing from any real stimulus. Experience elsewhere has shown that austerity tends to unleash a vicious cycle. Cuts made to restore fiscal numbers promote stagnation. Stagnation reduces revenue collection, which leads in turn to more cuts. An alternative needs to be rooted in a recognition that the route to fiscal sustainability must be through moving decisively to propel the economy onto a higher level of more inclusive growth and drastically reducing unemployment.

The post-COVID-19 reality will be one that objectively requires real economic stimulus. More than that, the coronavirus crisis has revealed weaknesses and lack of preparedness in health care systems across the world. COVID-19 was the first WHO-declared pandemic caused by a coronavirus, but it was not the first cross-border flu-like epidemic. In 2002–2003 the SARS epidemic infected 8 000 people living in 29 countries or territories, killing 774.[7] The H1N1 (swine flu) virus outbreak in 2008–2009 killed more than 18 000 people in 214 countries and territories.[8] There have also been other, more contained outbreaks of flu-like viruses, as well as of even more deadly haemorrhagic fevers such as Ebola. That one or other such disease would reach pandemic proportions was predictable. Yet health care systems across the world were short of medical ventilators and even personal protective equipment for front-line health workers.

The world is also already experiencing an increasing number of extreme weather events – linked to climate change. These will be part of our reality even if (and this is a huge 'if') political will is eventually found to contain global warming to below catastrophic levels. Floods and other hydrological events quadrupled between 1980 and 2004 and doubled again between 2004 and 2018. Extreme temperature-related events, such as droughts and forest fires, more than doubled between 1980 and 2018.[9] The year 2019 was the second hottest year on record, with 2016 being the hottest and 2015, 2017 and 2018 making up the rest of the five hottest years on record.[10] The same year saw some of the most extreme weather in 20 years, with 7 million people displaced from their homes by flooding in the first six months of 2019.[11] Extreme weather was a factor in 26 of 33 food crises recorded in that year, and was the main driver in 12 of these.[12] Again, evidence of huge underpreparedness for these emergencies abounds. An obvious example is the catastrophic bush fires in Australia in 2019–2020, which revealed too few firebreaks and insufficient fire-fighting capacity. Worse were the more under-the-radar cases of food crises in some of the poorest countries of the world.

Both the health and the climate emergencies point to the urgent necessity for massive public investment programmes to build more resilient systems, as well as to add more resilience to existing infrastructure – even as work proceeds to address causal factors. Such programmes will need to have a strong redistributive bias towards the poor and poorer countries. During the South African lockdown, for example, the directive for people to stay at home and maintain social distancing came up against the harsh reality of people living many to a room in shacks in informal settlements. In *The Condition of the Working Class in England*, Friedrich Engels showed how the squalid conditions of the working class in 19th-century Britain led to the spread of diseases such as smallpox, typhus and cholera to the bourgeoisie.[13] New, innovative ways to unleash public investment programmes to build greater resilience across the world are clearly emerging as an imperative for the benefit of most of humanity. Properly structured and funded, they could also be drivers of a recovery from the COVID-19 crisis very different from that which was pursued after the Great Recession of 2008. In recent years, a growing number of progressive economists, politicians and activists have called for a 'Global Green New Deal' to drive a move beyond austerity. The period that followed the Great Recession, they argue, saw the imposition of austerity in many countries. This choked off the prospect of a recovery leading to 'inclusive growth across the world economy'. Instead, the introduction of various measures, undertaken in the name of stimulus, disproportionately benefited powerful vested interests. These included bank bailouts totalling US$16.8 trillion in commitments, with US$4.6 trillion actually paid out by 2015 in the United States alone.[14] There were also tax incentives and relief for higher-income earners, quantitative easing, which in practice underpinned credit extension heavily concentrated in speculative activities,[15] and the retention or introduction of 'light touch' regulation in respect of rent-seeking and monopoly conduct.

The result was a 'a spluttering North, a general slowdown in the South and rising levels of debt everywhere'.[16] Several countries or

228

territories were on the brink of entering recession in 2020 – even before the coronavirus struck. These included Argentina, Brazil, Hong Kong, Germany, Italy, Mexico, Turkey and the UK.[17] At the one end of the spectrum of an increasingly unequal global order, those benefiting from financialised speculation, rentier activity and the proliferation of 'winner takes most' markets prospered. According to UNCTAD, 'surplus profits' beyond those derivable from 'typical' business activities rose from 4 per cent of total global profits in 1995–2000 to 23 per cent in 2009–2015. For the Top 100 global companies, the share increased from 16 to 40 per cent.[18] At the other end of the spectrum, 'too many people in too many places [were] integrated into a world economy that delivers inequitable and unjust outcomes'.[19] Among other things, wage suppression led to a decline in the ratio of income from employment to GDP from the 61.5 per cent recorded in 1980 to 54.5 per cent in 2018 in the developed world, with a similar decline from 52.5 per cent in 1990 to just over 50 per cent in 2018 in the developing world.[20] Even the middle classes, in both the developing and developed world, found themselves facing increasing economic insecurity – fuelling in the developed world a right-wing, nationalistic populism that in fact offers few real answers to the problems facing people in this category.[21]

South Africa has been far from immune to these trends. The country's wages-to-GDP ratio fell from 57 per cent in 1993 to just under 53 per cent in 2010, despite labour productivity having risen by 73 per cent between 1994 and 2012.[22] Unemployment, on the narrow definition, meanwhile, oscillated between 22 per cent of the economically active population in the best of times to over 30 per cent in the worst of times – and that was before the lockdown, which we know means it is headed for much more than that. The fact that unemployment since 1994 has never gone below 22 per cent points to the fact that it is fundamentally structural rather than cyclical in nature. That it has remained stubbornly high, despite wage suppression, also surely negates the neoliberal myth that wage suppression offers some path to reducing unemployment. South Africa, however, faces specific challenges. Its fiscal numbers have fallen outside the norms of orthodoxy not because it has been investing 'too much' in inclusive growth-enhancing programmes, but because resources have been looted and public entities have fallen into financial and operational dysfunction. This has created a serious vulnerability to the demands of financiers and lenders.

The post-COVID-19 world looks set to present both an imperative and an opportunity to do things differently. Responses to the recession both within countries and globally are increasingly widely recognised as needing to take on more of the character of a 'new deal' if the threat of a lurch into depression is to be avoided.[23] The 'new deal' response to the Great Depression of the 1930s was rooted in 'a social contract [based on] relief from mass unemployment; sustained economic recovery; regulation of finance; and redistribution of income'.[24]

Before the onset of the coronavirus crisis, proponents argued that the elements of a Global Green New Deal in the third decade of the 21st century should include the following:

- Ending austerity through 'using fiscal policy to manage demand conditions, and making full employment a central policy goal. Monetary expansion should also be used differently, so as to finance public investments which add to inclusive and sustainable outcomes'.

- Enhancing public investment with a strong caring dimension. 'This would include major public works programmes for mitigating and adapting to climate change.'

- Raising government revenue, with 'a greater reliance on progressive taxes, including on property and other forms of rent income'.

- Establishing a new global financial register – to clamp down on tax havens and other forms of base-erosion and profit-shifting.

- A stronger voice for organised labour – to ensure wages rise in line with productivity as a significant stimulus to demand.

- Taming financial capital – to make 'financial institutions ... serve the broader social good'.
- Significantly increasing multilateral financial resources.
- Reining in corporate rentierism, including through stronger regulation of restrictive business practices, the establishment of a global competition observatory and generally designing competition policy to promote distributional objectives.[25]

Other interventions within the same paradigm called for a new multilateralism based on the following 'design principles':

1. Global rules should be calibrated towards the overarching goals of social and economic stability, shared prosperity and environmental sustainability, and protected against capture by the most powerful players.
2. States share common but differentiated responsibilities in a multilateral system built to advance global public goods and protect the global commons.
3. The right of states to policy space to pursue national development strategies should be enshrined in global rules.
4. Global regulations should be designed both to strengthen a dynamic international division of labour and to prevent destructive unilateral economic actions that prevent other nations from realising common goals.
5. Global public institutions must be accountable to their full membership, open to a diversity of viewpoints, cognisant of new voices and have balanced dispute-resolution systems.[26]

What I have suggested needs to be added, in the light of the COVID-19 crisis, is public investment programmes directed at building more resilience to meet potential future emergencies – including those arising from climate change and health emergencies. Since such programmes need to embrace the large part of humanity living in poverty in the developing world, something along the lines of the US$2.5 trillion programme to support developing countries called for by UNCTAD must be an urgent priority.

In South Africa, while the phase one support programme announced by government during the initial 'hard' lockdown was widely welcomed, per capita expenditure was in fact the third lowest of any country in the G20.[27] The R500 billion (equivalent to around ten per cent of GDP) announced for the second of three phases was initially widely hailed as beginning to be on the scale necessary to respond to immediate pressing socio-economic imperatives, as well as to revive some economic activity and save jobs.[28] But the Supplementary Budget presented in June was seen as falling short of delivering on this commitment. Critics argued that, coupled as it was with cuts to other programmes, it in fact delivered as 'new spending' only six per cent of what had been promised.[29] Certainly, the Supplementary Budget Review seemed to be at least as preoccupied with 'avoiding the looming crisis in public finances' as with responding to long-term damage to employment and the productive economy.[30] This points to the continuing contradiction and contestation within the administration – between those forces recognising the need for a decisive intervention on a sufficient scale to build a new economy, and those preoccupied with the need to retain as much as possible of austerity with the aim of returning fiscal numbers to the preordained ratios that much of the rest of the world has long since jettisoned in the face of the crisis.

One of the features of the coronavirus crisis is that it has unblocked inertia and led governments to do things previously said to have been impossible.[31] In South Africa, as already indicated, the President and government have built significant credibility for the way in which they initially responded to the health emergency and led the country in implementing necessary, but difficult, public health measures. This surely is something that can be built on in leading an economic recovery. This is hardly an original point. Many have already called on President Ramaphosa to use the authority and credibility built up in the COVID-19 crisis to push ahead with 'structural reform'.[32] For many, making this call no doubt means acting to deliver some version of the European Commission's definition of this term: 'Structural reforms tackle obstacles to fundamental drivers of growth by liberalising labour, product and service markets … to boost an economy's competitiveness, growth potential and adjustment capacity.'[33] But it must surely mean something much broader and indeed very different from that. The President himself has said that his government is 'resolved not merely to return our economy to where it was before the coronavirus but to forge a new economy in a new global reality'. This, he indicated, will be based on a new social compact between business, labour, community and government to 'restructure the economy and achieve inclusive growth … [based on] fairness, empowerment, justice and equality'.[34] Such a path to recovery will need a real stimulus, and will need also actively and deliberately to promote much more inclusivity in a context where it is the poor and the vulnerable that are most at risk from any prolonged contraction. It will also need specifically to build greater resilience to combat identifiable potential future emergencies. Directly and obviously, this must mean building more resilience in the health system, including through a decisive advance to the national health insurance (NHI) system. Here it is worth recalling that it was the 'Spanish flu' epidemic of 1918 that led to the establishment for the first time of a Ministry of Health in South Africa.[35] Surely the COVID-19 emergency needs to become recognised as an event that propelled the NHI forward. I have also suggested that one of the lessons from COVID-19 needs to be that greater resilience must be built against future foreseeable emergencies, including those arising from climate change (which is actually a much greater medium-term threat to human existence). The negative effect of overcrowding in townships and informal settlements in managing emergencies suggests an imperative for greater urgency in improving living conditions and municipal infrastructure. As in the 1930s, all of this, plus addressing backlogs in existing infrastructure, points to the imperative and possibility of a new deal driven initially by an infrastructure build programme rooted in public employment both to address real need and to drive economic recovery.

As indicated in chapters 8 and 10, the infrastructure build programme coordinated by the PICC contributed significantly to South Africa's ability to avoid joining peer countries in falling into recession in the years that followed the end of the commodity supercycle in 2012. But, despite a good beginning, it had been clear for years that PICC-monitored infrastructure projects were falling behind targets. Reports were also emerging of cost overruns and technically substandard delivery of key projects, amid increasingly evident financial and operational crises in several SOCs (linked, in part at least, to state capture and corruption). After being below the radar for some time, in July 2020 the Ramaphosa administration finally unveiled its plan to revive public infrastructure investment as a key driver of post-COVID recovery. The Strategic Integrated Projects (SIP) programme was gazetted on 24 July 2020. Of 276 projects that were submitted for consideration, 88 were at post-feasibility stage. The total investment value of all projects was estimated at R2.3 trillion. Of these, 50 projects, with a total investment value of R340 billion, were selected for fast-track implementation under the SIP programme. While some of the funding for the new infrastructure initiative was anticipated as coming from SOC balance sheets and pension funds, there was also a strong expectation that 'blended finance' would become a major driver.[36] Blended finance refers to the 'leveraging' of risk-absorbing public funds into financial instruments capable of attracting profit-seeking investors. Typically, it involves using securitisation – bundling individual project loans into financial instruments that can be bought by financial funds. Observers of attempts to use blended finance as a tool to raise funds to achieve the targets set by the 2015 Addis Ababa Action Agenda on Financing for Development, the targets of the United Nations Sustainable Development Goals (SDGs) or commitments under the 2015 Paris Climate Change Agreement have concluded that the total sum raised has been 'far too little' – less than $1 billion for all Least Developed Countries, in fact, compared to a funding gap of $2.5 trillion to meet the SDG targets alone. Critics have argued that the models of blended finance most commonly used have provided excessive guarantees for high returns to investors, and have therefore been high-cost, low-yield models rather than vehicles for 'financing that is not subject to capture by corruption and self-aggrandisement for short-term benefit'.[37] While an ambitious public infrastructure build programme is clearly pivotal to a post-COVID recovery, it remains to be seen to what extent the experience of blended finance will be any different from that of the financing of the SDGs and other development programmes.

At the same time as unleashing an infrastructure 'big push', a post-COVID recovery programme will also need to advance, with more energy and determination, a deeper transformation of the structure of the productive economy. As I have argued throughout this volume, South Africa emerged as a semi-peripheral economy through the development of its mineral economy, based initially on the mining of diamonds and gold. Gold has, however, been a waning asset for several decades, meaning that the once undisputed largest producer by far is now ranked only eighth in the world in terms of tonnage produced.[38] Despite this, South Africa will remain a mining economy for many years to come, with its mining sector resting on a range of industrial minerals, including platinum group metals, manganese, chrome, uranium, iron ore, titanium, zirconium and coal. Although South Africa commands significant percentages of the world's reserves in a number of these minerals, very little value addition (or beneficiation) takes place before these products are exported. The rise of the gold-mining industry led to the development of what has been called a 'mineral-energy complex',[39] where some mostly capital-intensive, upstream industries emerged providing inputs into mining but retarding broader industrialisation.

After the two world wars and significant contestation within capital, measures were taken to support the emergence of some consumer goods industries[40] geared towards the domestic market, leading later to the adoption by the apartheid regime of a strategy described as 'inward industrialisation'. As we have seen in previous chapters, many of these industries were sharply impacted by hyperglobalisation in the 1990s, while the effects of industrial policy pursued thereafter have had only a slight moderating impact on serious further pressures on the sector. The net effect is that South Africa remains integrated into the global economy predominantly as a producer and exporter of primary commodities – mainly minerals – but also including some agricultural and agro-processing products. This is only slightly modified by the fact that on the African continent, it is a supplier of value-added consumer goods.

Towards a developmental AfCFTA

In 1990 the United Nations Economic Commission for Africa (UNECA), then led by Professor Adebayo Adedeji, produced a paper titled 'African alternative framework to structural adjustment programmes for socio-economic recovery and transformation', widely known by its acronym AAF-SAP.[41] This became a major beacon looked to by many who doubted that externally imposed structural adjustment programmes were the best, or only, way forward. The first paragraph of AAF-SAP argued: 'The structure of the African economy defines the essential features of Africa's central problem of underdevelopment.'[42] It went on to identify what it saw as the structural weaknesses in most African economies. These included a 'weak productive base' characterised by low productivity and productive activities dominated by either subsistence or export-orientated primary product production. From this, AAF-SAP identified the central task as the structural transformation of African economies. One key element of this was that 'Africa has to break the apron strings of structural and relational dependence on producing a limited number of cheap primary commodities for export.'[43]

This highly pertinent observation remains as valid today as it was in 1990. It speaks to a reality highlighted by the experience of those very few countries that have transitioned from low to high income, or from underdeveloped to developed economies. The vast majority of these achieved this transition by passing through a stage of economic diversification involving a shift to higher value-added production. In a word, they industrialised. In Chapter 8, we outlined the contention of heterodox economists and economic historians that poor countries have stayed poor because they have remained trapped in their colonially defined role as producers and exporters of some primary product or products – agricultural or mineral – used in industrial production elsewhere. Developments that have unfolded in the period since the 1990s, including the rise of globally networked industries (or global value chains) and the emergence of more complex and knowledge-intensive products, have underlined this point even more starkly. The value of raw materials as a proportion of the price of final products is not only small, it is also declining. This is true even of products where little or no further physical transformation takes place. An example is that of African, Asian and Latin American coffee producers, who receive only seven per cent of the value of roasted coffee sold in super markets abroad.[44] In the case of highly knowledge-intensive products, the figures are even more stark. Take the case of the iPhone 6, which retails for US$649 in the US. The cost of the mineral products used in its manufacture totals a mere US$1.03 (0.16 per cent).[45]

In Chapter 8, we again referred to the writings of heterodox economists who argued that those few underdeveloped countries that have more recently emerged as high-income or 'moderately prosperous' countries have all followed the same path as earlier industrialisers. Whether they were the East Asian Newly Industrialising Economies in the 1960s and 1970s (Hong Kong, South Korea, Singapore, Taiwan) or, more recently, China, their governments pursued active industrial policies that promoted, nurtured and protected nascent industries.

Given the structural characteristics of the South African economy sketched out above, 'structural transformation' needs surely to involve moving the productive base away from the apron strings of merely supplying raw materials towards becoming a producer of higher value-added goods and services. These can include 'smart agriculture' – the production of quality products where premiums can be realised from quality, traceability, etc – and promoting higher levels of beneficiation of mineral products before they are exported. But it must also critically include an effort to halt premature deindustrialisation and a push towards deeper industrialisation. In pursuing this, South Africa, and indeed the continent as a whole, will need to contend with the technological transformations associated with the so-called fourth industrial revolution.

It is widely accepted that the world underwent a third industrial revolution at the end of the 20th century, with products such as the personal computer and the mobile phone giving rise to innovations such as the internet. This in turn facilitated an explosion of cross-border economic activities and the emergence of transnational corporations coordinating vast, globally networked industries (or global value chains) – phenomena associated with the term 'globalisation'. As I understand it, the years following the onset of the global economic crisis of 2008 saw digital technology advance in new directions and in ways that were set to bring about not just quantitative but qualitative change. Digital technologies began to advance into the realm of 'big data' management, mining and application. In 2016 Professor Klaus Schwab, founder of the World Economic Forum, argued that the world was on the cusp of a 'technology revolution ... unlike anything humankind has experienced before' and that this was set to bring about 'disruptive change' in practically all sectors of all economies.[46] Among the new technologies associated with the fourth industrial revolution, also known as the digital industrial revolution, are the internet of things, where machines will be able to pass on instructions to other machines via the internet; additive manufacturing, or 3D printing, that can be combined into global networks via the internet; autonomous vehicles; nanotechnology; and the greater application of robotics and artificial intelligence. On the frontier are developments such as quantum computing, which will totally revolutionise the speed of all computation – and incidentally also render all existing security codes obsolete. All of this will be enabled by the introduction of 5G (or fifth generation) mobile networks.

Many of these technologies have enormous potential to increase human welfare by increasing overall productivity. They also have potential to offer innovative solutions to a host of developmental challenges. On the African continent we have seen many innovative uses and adaptations, including cellphone banking, the use of drones to deliver medicines to remote areas and the development of apps to draw small producers and service providers into networks giving them access to larger markets. We need, however, to be aware that the roll-out of the very same technologies also poses enormous challenges. First, they have potential to widen inequalities both within and between countries. This arises, in part, through their exacerbating 'winner takes most' outcomes. MIT economists Erik Brynjolfsson and Andrew McAfee[47] explain this with an example. In the 19th century only a few hundred people could have attended performances by the best opera singer. This meant there was a market for the ninth, tenth and eleventh best singers. In the case of ICT apps, however, global networks provide access for the vast majority of consumers to the best, meaning there is no market for the 'also-rans'. The implication of this is that 'winners' begin to receive extraordinary rewards, while 'runners-up' get little or nothing.

For manufacturing, potential disruptive changes associated with the fourth industrial revolution look set not just to be confined to what happens within each domestic economy but also to impact on the location of industries around the world. Additive manufacturing, networked through the internet of things, looks poised to replace large assembly lines with smaller-scale processes located closer to the site of consumption. The potential implication of this was exemplified in 2017 when Adidas announced that it was relocating some of its production from Bangladesh to Germany on the grounds that a combination of 3D printing and robotics had lowered production costs far below those that could be obtained by paying low wages in Asia.[48] But disruptive changes are expected to go much further. They will impact on mining and agriculture, on financial services, legal services, the practising of medicine, education and a host of other public and private services. An early mover looks set to be wholesale and retail trade. Electronic commerce, both in intermediate products and in sales to final consumers, is taking off rapidly, with digitisation of processes within physical shops reducing demand for till clerks and other less skilled personnel.

Even global value chains look set to undergo radical reorganisation. Parminder Jeet Singh describes this as follows:

> As industrialisation placed machine power at the centre of the economy, digitalisation makes digital intelligence its new fulcrum. The factory as the site of mechanised production was the central economic institution of the Industrial Age. For the Digital Age, it is sectoral platforms that reorganise entire economic activities in any sector based on digital intelligence from data.[49]

A further reality is that the digital platforms emerging at the apex of digitally reorganising networks exhibit an exceptionally high degree of concentration and centralisation. According to UNCTAD, the top one per cent of technology, software and IT services companies globally increased their share of market capitalisation in the sector from 27 per cent in the period 1996–2000 to 52 per cent in 2009–2015. Over the same period, their share of revenues rose from

31 to 43 per cent, of physical assets from 31 to 47 per cent, while their share of employment remained flat at 27 per cent, compared to 25 per cent in the earlier period.[50] Kean Birch, Margaret Chiappetta and Anna Artyushina have argued further that the process of turning personal data into private assets is fuelling an innovation-finance nexus orientated to rent-seeking.[51]

It has long been argued that South Africa's destiny is inextricably interlinked with that of the African continent as a whole. Both the fourth industrial revolution and the green industrialisation associated with a move towards a lower-carbon economy will enhance the imperative as they raise the bar for Africa's drive to industrialise. If the continent remains marginalised as these developments unfold, the negatives of exclusion will outweigh the benefits of the introduction of products or systems based on the new technologies. Indeed, the continent's ability to create a scenario in which the positives or benefits outweigh the negatives or costs will depend on the extent to which it is able to industrialise. A key question, in this context, will be: can the continent develop its own niches and competitive advantages (perhaps at least initially in agro-processing and smart agriculture, mineral beneficiation and infrastructure-related industries, including those building resilience to withstand future emergencies)? The answer to this question will determine the extent to which the 21st century becomes the African century. Like every other industrialisation process before it, African industrialisation in the post-COVID-19 era, shaped as it will be by green industrialisation and the fourth industrial revolution, will depend on the successful implementation of industrial policy using all of the policy tools deployed by others to support, nurture and protect their emerging manufacturing industries. This, in turn, will depend on the extent to which the continent is able to defend access to the policy space used by earlier industrialisers and not have this curtailed by increasingly aggressive pressure to accept unfair trade rules.

What does all of this mean for one of the key issues that has rightly absorbed the attention of the continent, namely, the operationalisation of the African Continental Free Trade Area? I included a short chapter on this issue in a small volume I published in 2019.[52] In it, and more briefly in Chapter 9, I argued that whatever the pathway or pathways that led to the prioritisation of the broadening of integration by establishing an FTA reaching beyond existing RECs over the alternative of deepening integration within RECs by moving them into customs unions, common markets or monetary unions, that decision was both correct and appropriate to the circumstances in which we find ourselves.

Even before the COVID-19 crisis, it was becoming increasingly evident that the established order of hegemonic multilateralism that had driven the processes of uneven and unequal globalisation of the 1990s and early 2000s was under challenge. The roots of this lay in the growing discontent with widening inequality and a sense of economic insecurity among social forces in both the developed world and the developing world. While this took several forms, it included in the developed world, and in the United State in particular, the rise of a right-wing populist nationalism that is both sceptical of multilateralism and has underpinned a turn to outright mercantilism in matters of international trade that some have suggested is propelling an accelerating deglobalisation.[53]

A further key factor underpinning this challenge is that one of the major beneficiaries of the most recent phase of globalisation has been the latest economy to industrialise – China. It was not that China followed the policy prescriptions of neoliberalism proffered to the developing world during that era. It decidedly did not. China's industrialisation is much more recognisable as having proceeded along a path similar to that of other industrialisers before it. It implemented a clear industrial policy and calibrated its trade policy stance to this. It liberalised its economy selectively and strategically – beginning with liberalisation of investment in a network of defined Special Economic Zones. Only when its industries had achieved a level of competitiveness did it move towards a carefully calibrated liberalisation of trade. But, like others before it, China took advantage of any trade openings to expand its manufactured exports – beginning with clothing and textiles following the phasing out of the Multi-Fibre Arrangement.[54] China has now emerged not just as the world's second-largest economy and a major industrial producer, but also (and again as a result of its industrial policy choices) as a major innovator in the technologies of the fourth industrial revolution and indeed a leader (over its competitors) in a number of strategic areas.

Rather than accepting China's competitive challenge, some countries have responded with retaliatory measures justified on national security grounds. The so-called trade wars that began in 2018 are much more than a squabble over trade balances. They are, in the end, as Klaus Schwab has perceptively suggested, a struggle for mastery over the fourth industrial revolution,[55] and as such are likely to underpin a rivalry that looks set to shape international relations for some time to come. The COVID-19 crisis added further dimensions to this. It saw companies reassessing their dependence on supply chains reaching into countries affected by lockdowns and governments intervening to stop exports of medical equipment and indicating they would seek to localise production of key equipment in future. There were 'bizarre symptoms', including the Trump administration's attempt to insert the term 'Wuhan virus' into G20 declarations and then its withdrawal of funding from the WHO for allegedly being too soft on China at the start of the outbreak.

While all of this points, as suggested earlier, to the necessity of working for a different kind of multilateralism, it also suggests more immediately that even if we in Africa wanted to base an industrialisation effort on the production of value-added products for export to the markets of the developed world, that path is much less available than it was to previous industrialisers – even China. Under such circumstances, several of the more successful developing countries, China and India among them, have been turning to domestic consumption to drive the next phase of their development. The problem facing African countries seeking to move in a similar direction is that none of us – not even the largest – has a domestic market of sufficient scale to drive significant industrialisation. However, as indicated in Chapter 9, if we look to the continent as a whole, its 1.2 billion people and combined GDP of US$2.3 trillion do offer a base for significant diversification and potentially for deep industrialisation.

It is often said that the main benefit of the AfCFTA will be that it supports an increase in intra-regional trade – from the mere 17 per cent of total trade today to a level approaching that of other successful regions: 31 per cent in North America, 59 per cent in Asia or 69 per cent in Europe.[56] That of course would be an important gain and indication of success of the AfCFTA. But I would suggest that the AfCFTA's real prize would be if it supported the emergence of regional value chains involved in the production of higher value-added goods and services. Such an outcome could expect to see components and other intermediate inputs being produced in a number of countries before being assembled into 'products of Africa' consumed by the citizens of the continent and also exported. Under such a scenario we could expect to see not just a quantitative increase in intra-regional trade but a qualitative change in its character. This would involve a greater absolute and relative increase in intra-African trade in components and intermediate products, which is in fact the largest and fastest-growing part of global trade in goods.

For this to occur, it is important to recognise that trade integration is not a stand-alone. It must be an integral component of a broader economic integration process. Again, we can turn to AAF-SAP, which argues that African integration 'involves three mutually interdependent dimensions; namely, (a) the integration of the physical, institutional and social infrastructures; (b) the integration of the production structures; and (c) the integration of the African markets'.[57]

This speaks to the elements long argued by proponents of development integration.[58] A fundamental point of departure of the development integration perspective is that in developing country regions, low levels of intra-regional trade are not only, or even principally, a result of high customs tariffs or other regulatory barriers. Underdeveloped production structures and inadequate infrastructure are also critical factors. From this it is argued by proponents of development integration that trade liberalisation alone (reduction of tariffs and perhaps smoothing of other regulatory barriers) will only go so far. Two other pillars need to be integral to the integration effort. The first is infrastructure development, to connect the economies of the integrating region – physically and digitally – and address the massive deficit in this regard. The onset of climate change and medical pandemics adds a further imperative: we need to build our defences against predictable future challenges, including building greater resilience into traditional infrastructure so that we can defend roads and railway lines against floods or fires, ports against the effects of rising sea levels and storms, and people's access to water through better watercourse management.

The other essential pillar is to promote cooperation to support industrial development. As with industrialisation elsewhere, Africa's industrialisation will depend on strong policy-driven processes, including ensuring that local industries become involved in the infrastructure build, and that nascent industries in emerging value chains are supported through appropriate programmes such as localisation. The appropriate combination of industrial policy at national, REC and continental level is something still to be discovered. But one thing that is clear is that a united voice from the continent in defence of our right to access policy tools used by earlier industrialisers will strengthen our hand in circumstances where powerful external forces will seek to constrain this, not just to preserve their access to cheap raw materials but also to allow them to benefit from accessing growing consumer markets and mining the data generated on the continent, in the latter case by, among others, opposing any attempt to establish data sovereignty.

If the AfCFTA were to become reduced to a conventional trade integration arrangement, it would very likely entrench the competitive advantages and polarisation in favour of the very few countries currently having some capacity to export finished goods to the rest of the continent – South Africa, Egypt, Morocco and to a lesser extent Kenya. This could very likely provoke others to push for weak rules of origin that could lead to a proliferation of low value-added, screwdriver-type industries emerging in other countries. Under a worst-case scenario, this could result in a net lowering of the overall level of value addition on the continent. If this were to occur, it would mean that the main beneficiaries of the FTA would be those external parties producing goods subject only to nominal value addition on the continent.

It would be even worse if we were to succumb to the siren song of external forces urging that the AfCFTA become a stepping stone to greater liberalisation towards them. There are many external voices giving nominal support to the AfCFTA because they hope it will open up third-party access to a larger African market and thereby enxhance the value of any FTA they seek beyond that available with individual countries. The kind of supposedly 21st-century 'high quality' agreement envisaged by many would be only slightly asymmetrical or differentiated, and would include numerous trade-related chapters that would, without doubt, severely curtail the policy space essential for a drive to industrialise. The AfCFTA must, at the stage we find ourselves in, entrench a real advantage for continental producers over others. If it does not, it will be extra-regional rather than African producers that are the main beneficiaries of trade liberalisation in the AfCFTA.

If the AfCFTA is to fulfil its promise as a tool for inclusive development, industrialisation and diversification, it needs, therefore, to embrace more of the perspectives of a development integration

Wamkele Mene (left) is shown here in conversation with Lindiwe Sisulu, President Cyril Ramaphosa and me at the AU summit in Kigali, Rwanda, in March 2018. In February 2020, Mene became the first Secretary-General of the African Continental Free Trade Area (AfCFTA).

programme. This is not to suggest that the continent should pause to engage in a theoretical debate about paradigms. Even if this were desirable, which it is not, it could result merely in the formal adoption of wording in documents. What is needed as the AfCFTA moves into operationalisation is for practical implementation processes to become firmly rooted in addressing concrete development challenges and providing more opportunities for the continent to move towards higher value-added production. The insignificant progress recorded in industrial cooperation, whether at REC or AU level, should be a matter of concern. Industrial development cooperation needs to rise above the kind of consultancy-heavy scoping exercises that have dominated the work in formal bodies up to now, and to deliver forward-thinking proposals for sectorally specific, win-win outcomes, taking into account the AfCFTA.

Towards a New Deal for the New Dawn

South Africa's ability to play an appropriate role in driving such a process, as well as its ability to move its domestic economy out of stagnation, will depend on decisions taken in the near future. Over the past quarter of a century the NDR has recorded definite advances. But it is also a project that is now deeply wounded and more contested than at any time since 1994. The critical challenges confronting the movement now are to deal with the enormous damage caused by state capture and corruption, and to find a path beyond austerity that addresses both the concrete needs of the majority of its citizens in the circumstances they find themselves in and drives a truly inclusive economic recovery. To coin a phrase, there is an urgent need for the New Dawn to develop a genuine New Deal. The Ramaphosa administration is now well poised to lead such a process. But if it allows itself to remain trapped in austerity, its legacy could end up more like that of Herbert Hoover than the clearly more admired Franklin D Roosevelt. President Hoover's conservative policies, in the aftermath of the Wall Street crash of October 1929, are widely seen as having contributed to the journey from a stock market crash to a global economic depression. The circumstances the Ramaphosa administration finds itself in are neither of its making nor of its choosing. But prolonged economic stagnation will likely impact on more than reputations; it could indeed well erode the hegemony of the liberation alliance, to the detriment of the NDR.

The ANC-led alliance has already been eroded. Up to now this has been from two directions simultaneously: from the market-fundamentalist right and from a demagogic populism weaving together a narrow nationalism with a leftist populist rhetoric. This was reflected in the outcome of the 2016 local government elections, which in several metros saw the installation of unstable opposition coalitions that have now fallen apart. Right now, the erosion from the market-fundamentalist right looks likely to stall as its main expression, the Democratic Alliance, confronts its own internal crisis. The DA's attempt to grow beyond its base in minority communities has seen some of its African leaders attempting to develop positions that in some way acknowledge the need for specific programmes to address race-based disadvantage. In this, however, they have been thwarted by liberal fundamentalists who happen to be white. As recorded in Chapter 10, I saw something of the dress rehearsal for this close up, in the saga of the DA's positioning around the 2013 Broad-Based Black Economic Empowerment Amendment Act.

The real drama unfolded after the 2019 elections, which saw the DA losing a relatively small number of votes – probably most to a resurgent Freedom Front Plus. An internal review that placed a good deal of the blame for the election losses on then leader Mmusi Maimane was buttressed by an intervention from the South African Institute of Race Relations (where former leader Helen Zille was then based). This launched a campaign called '#Save The Opposition' in early October 2019 that called both on Maimane to step down as leader and for the DA to return to 'classically liberal' values. By this was meant the DA's recognising individual rights and responding to individual disadvantage rather than allowing the import of illiberal ideas of race-based redress.[59] That this was more than a theoretical debate became clear later that month when Zille made herself available for, and then won, the election for the position of Federal Chair of the DA. Within a week of Zille's election, Mmusi Maimane confronted his own 'off to Harvard' moment when he resigned first as leader and then as a member of the DA. He was preceded by a day by the DA Johannesburg mayor, Herman Mashaba. The DA's likely return to classical liberal positions on addressing individual disadvantage, as well as white leadership, will no doubt be accompanied by more explicit neoliberalism in respect of economic policy – including more strident calls for privatisation and labour market 'flexibility'. All of this seems unlikely to enhance the DA's prospects of gaining support among African voters, at least in the immediate future.

A long period of stagnation, accompanied by failure to advance programmes visibly seen to be leading to more inclusive future prosperity, could well underpin the materialisation of some combination of two of the scenarios envisaged in the Indlulamithi South African Scenarios 2030 project, a multi-stakeholder initiative examining alternative futures.[60] In one scenario, titled 'iSbhujwa – an enclave bourgeois nation', the country is torn by deepening social divides, daily protests and cynical self-interest, while that titled 'Gwara Gwara – the ups and downs of a false dawn' evokes a demoralised land of disorder and decay. The erosion that would be more likely to grow under such circumstances would be demagogic populism. This could take several forms. One could be the growing influence of such forces within the ANC. Another could be that the EFF continues to grow by positioning itself as a disruptive movement not playing the conventional game of parliamentary party politics.

The last point speaks to a reality underpinning the rise of populist movements and politicians across the world. The rise of neoliberalism supported the emergence of a particular form of state and style of politics. The agenda of neoliberalism (privatisation, liberalisation, the withdrawal of the state from the economy and light-touch regulation) was supposed to be applied in the same way by governments everywhere. Linked to this, the neoliberal governance model promoted the establishment of unelected 'independent' bodies of technocrats, not tied to the government of the day, to take charge of important decisions. This further limited the power of governments. In the neoliberal scheme of things, changes in government were not supposed to bring about profound changes in policy. Rather, weak governments were supposed to preside over weak states, with markets unleashed to operate with minimal constraints across the world. Democracy was professed, but the understanding of this concept was reduced to regular elections bringing about frequent changes in government. These elections were supposed to be contests involving parties with very little significant policy difference, as they were all supposed to be united about the fundamentals of neoliberalism. One colleague from Mozambique, observing a US presidential election in the 1980s, described it as a contest between brands – Colgate or Pepsodent – but however you voted you could only get toothpaste. In some parts of the developed world, this led to one weak coalition following another, with electorates unable to discern much difference between them. In one extreme example, Belgium had no government for 15 months without anyone much noticing.

By the late 1990s it was already apparent that this model was facing a backlash within electorates. The first signs were growing apathy and even antipathy towards 'politics and politicians'. In one EU country after another, it was reported that more people were voting in celebrity television contests than in elections that were supposed to determine who would govern them. Periodic spectacular rises of perceived anti-systemic forces, generally on the right championing some kind of anti-immigrant, xenophobic agenda, were a further symptom of widespread alienation from this type of politics in parts of the developed world.

By the middle of the second decade of the 21st century, it had become clear that established neoliberal politics was entering an even deeper crisis. Politicians and parties able to excite any kind of popular support were increasingly those seen as 'anti-politics politicians', while regular 'establishment politicians' of all hues were being shunned. In the developed world, this phenomenon had predominantly a right-wing face. Its manifestations included the rise of neo-fascist parties in Europe and of a 'celebrity' non-politician such as Donald Trump,

ousting mainstream Republican Party insiders on a populist platform
with a strong anti-immigrant and narrow nationalistic agenda.

There is a saying that the centre in Latin America is left. What
this means is that the majority of the people of the continent are
more inclined to a political project that is able to present itself as
left. The same is true in South Africa, and probably also in the rest of
the continent. Populist 'anti-politics politics' in South Africa is much
more likely to be viable putting forward a left face, but that doesn't
mean it could not eventually spawn the emergence of a neo-fascist
movement pursuing what might ultimately become an authoritari-
an narrow-nationalist agenda. Nicos Poulantzas[61] has argued that the
fascist parties that rose to power in Europe in the 1930s were petty
bourgeois movements. Their petty bourgeois leaderships 'borrowed'
elements from the ideologies of the fundamental classes – capital
and the working class – that varied at different stages of their rise
to power. During the first phases of mobilisation, the 'borrowings'
from working-class militancy were more prominent, and it should
not be forgotten that the term 'socialist' in National Socialist German
Workers' Party (the full name of the Nazi Party) was not there by
accident. When they got closer to power, fascist movements forged
an alliance with monopoly capital around a programme of militarism
and expansion. At this stage, elements of 'socialistic' populism were
rapidly ditched.

There can be no doubt that the emerging conjuncture in South
Africa will pose real challenges of a level and seriousness not previously confronted. If the false dawn of populist demagogy is to
be avoided, it is imperative that the national liberation movement
decisively self-corrects, seizes the moment and drives a genuine
New Deal that propels recovery in a way that manifestly prioritises
the needs and interests of the working class and the poor. In this
quest it is imperative that the image of aloof politicians indifferent to the challenges facing ordinary people be decisively turned
round and that the alliance recover its historical role as a popular

campaigning movement rooted among the people. It is imperative also that popular mobilisation embrace more of the heterodox perspectives on the structural characteristics of underdevelopment that ultimately constrain the ability to address real issues facing the people of the country. If this occurs, the crisis may yet become not just a challenge but an opportunity – an opportunity that, if seized, could indeed ensure that the next ten years are better than the last.

ACKNOWLEDGEMENTS

I have prepared this work after completing 40 years' uninterrupted membership of the ANC. I have also been a member of the SACP for well over 30 years. Before that I was involved in one way or another in the anti-apartheid struggle, bringing my total years of support and/or active struggle for national liberation to over half a century. For half of that time, I was a public representative of the movement, serving as an MP without interruption from the time of the installation of our first democratic Parliament in May 1994 until May 2019. In the decade before my retirement, I served as Minister of Trade and Industry.

I am extremely grateful to Jeremy Cronin, Faizel Ismail, Nimrod Zalk and Xavier Carim for taking the time to make very useful and pertinent comments on an earlier draft of this work. Nkanyezi Tshabalala, Alfred LeMaitre and the team at Jonathan Ball were a source of great encouragement and very professional in all the processes involved in preparing the manuscript for publication. I am sincerely grateful for the opportunity I had to work with a fantastic cohort of dedicated public servants at the Department of Trade and Industry. Everything achieved during my time as Minister was the product of collective effort by Team DTI. Lionel October was an exceptional Director-General, recognised as such in winning several awards. There were also many other skilled and dedicated public servants in the department and agencies reporting to it. For fear of leaving anyone out, I will not try to list all the names here, but simply acknowledge the real privilege it was to have worked with an exceptional team.

At a personal level, I need to record the support of three wonderful women who partnered me at various stages of my life's journey. Marge Urban was my wife and partner in Botswana and during our time in Sussex in the UK. We also went together to Mozambique. In Mozambique I met and married Judith Head. Two of our children were born while we lived in Mozambique. They definitely benefited during the early years of their lives from living in an environment without many of the trappings of capitalist consumerism, and which emphasised non-racialism and multiculturalism. Our third child was born in Cape Town. All three of them have grown into fine human beings, finding some way to serve their people and country. The oldest, Joe, is a diplomat who served his first posting in Kinshasa, DRC, and his second in the South African Mission to the United Nations in New York. Ellen has developed a passion for development issues and the green economy while working at the World Wide Fund for Nature (WWF) and continues to engage in research on issues of climate change and development while living with her partner in Niger and Senegal. Matthew, the youngest, became an activist in youth formations of the movement while a student at the University of Cape Town.

Later in life I met and married Grace Constable. Together now for more than a decade and a half, I have found in Grace an extraordinary life partner who has enabled me to know the full meaning of love, companionship and support. As I put it on our wedding day, paraphrasing Marx, with her I feel myself, without her outside of myself. Through Grace I have also had the opportunity to relate to black South Africans as family and community members, giving me insight into both the resilience and the challenges faced by people still grappling with the legacy of apartheid discrimination. Also through Grace I now have a stepdaughter, Naomi, who is a source of much pride and joy as I watch her growing into a fine young woman.

Rob Davies
Velddrif
September 2020

NOTES

Introduction

1 Among Marcuse's works much read at the time were *An Essay on Liberation* (1969) and *One-Dimensional Man: Studies in the Ideology of Advanced Industrial Society* (1964).

2 HJ and RE Simons, *Class and Colour in South Africa 1850–1950*, Penguin, Harmondsworth, 1969.

3 'The White Working-Class in South Africa', *New Left Review*, 82, November–December 1973.

4 Published by Harvester Press, Brighton, in 1979.

5 For a comprehensive account of the life of the ANC community in Mozambique, including more details of my own role there, see Nadja Manghezi, *The Maputo Connection: ANC Life in the World of Frelimo*, Jacana, Auckland Park, 2009.

6 See, for example, Chinyamata Chipeta and Robert Davies, 'Regional Relations and Cooperation Post-Apartheid: A Macro Framework Study Report', consultancy study for the Southern African Development Community, 1993; and Robert Davies, Dot Keet and Mfundu Nkuhlu, 'Reconstructing Economic Relations with the Southern African Region', discussion document prepared for Macro-Economic Research Group, March 1993.

Chapter 1

1 See tributes to Harold Wolpe by Dan O'Meara, Harold Wolpe Papers, University of Cape Town Libraries, www2.lib.uct.ac.za/mss/existing/Finding%20Aids/bc1150_harold_wolpe_papers.htm; and by Michael Burawoy, 'From liberation to reconstruction: Theory and practice in the life of Harold Wolpe', *Review of African Political Economy*, Vol 31, No 102, 2004, pp 657–675 (also available at wolpetrust.org.za/lectures/ML2004Burawoy_pdf.pdf); and Steven Friedman, *Race, Class and Power: Harold Wolpe and the Radical Critique of Apartheid*, University of KwaZulu-Natal Press, Pietermaritzburg, 2015.

2 For an outline and critique see Martin Legassick, 'The Rise of Modern South African Liberalism: Its Assumptions and its Social Base', University of Sussex seminar paper, 1974. For an explicitly reformist perspective of this type, see Merle Lipton, *Capitalism and Apartheid: South Africa 1910–1986*, David Philip, Cape Town, 1986.

3 For a fairly recent review, including a bibliography of many of the major contributions, see Friedman, op cit.

4 Frederick A Johnstone, *Class, Race and Gold: A Study of Class Relations and Racial Discrimination in South Africa*, Routledge and Kegan Paul, London, 1976.

5   See note 1.

6   Harold Wolpe, 'Capitalism and cheap labour-power in South Africa: From segregation to apartheid', *Economy and Society*, Vol 1, No 4, 1972.

7   Harold Wolpe, *Race, Class and the Apartheid State*, James Currey, London, 1988.

8   For the definitive account of this, see Dan O'Meara, *Forty Lost Years: The Apartheid State and the Politics of the National Party 1948–1994*, Ravan Press, Randburg, 1996, and *Volkskapitalisme: Class, Capital and Ideology in the Development of Afrikaner Nationalism*, Cambridge University Press, 1983.

9   See Rob Davies, Dan O'Meara and Sipho Dlamini, *The Struggle for South Africa: A Reference Guide to Movements, Organizations and Institutions*, Vol 1, Zed Books, London, 1984, p 21.

10   Francis Wilson, *Labour in the South African Gold Mines 1911–1969*, Cambridge University Press, Cambridge, 1972.

11   'The Freedom Charter', www.historicalpapers.wits.ac.za/inventories/inv_pdfo/AD1137/AD1137-Ea6-1-001-jpeg.pdf.

12   See Davies, O'Meara and Dlamini, op cit, pp 37–47.

Chapter 2

1   See Immanuel Wallerstein and Sérgio Vieira, 'Historical Development of the Region in the Context of the Evolving World-System', in Sérgio Vieira, William G Martin and Immanuel Wallerstein (coordinators), *How Fast the Wind? Southern Africa 1975–2000*, Africa World Press, Trenton, New Jersey, 1992.

2   Colin Murray, 'From Granary to Labour Reserve: An Economic History of Lesotho', conference paper No 28, SALDRU Farm Labour Conference, September 1976.

3   See Ruth First, *Black Gold: The Mozambican Miner, Proletarian and Peasant*, St Martin's Press, New York, 1983.

4   See 'Maputo', www.wikizero.com/en/History_of_Maputo.

5   See 'Operation Gordian Knot', en.wikipedia.org/wiki/Operation_Gordian_Knot.

6   See Robert Davies and Dan O'Meara, 'Total strategy in southern Africa: An analysis of South African regional policy since 1978', *Journal of Southern African Studies*, Vol 11, No 2, 1985.

7   See Robert Davies, 'The SADF's Covert War Against Mozambique', in Jacklyn Cock and Laurie Nathan (eds), *War and Society: The Militarisation of South Africa*, David Philip, Cape Town, 1989, pp 108–109.

8   'About SADC', sadc.int/about-SADC.

9   Davies, 'The SADF's Covert War Against Mozambique'.

10   Ibid.

11   Joseph Hanlon, *Beggar Your Neighbours: Apartheid Power in Southern Africa*, Catholic Institute for International Relations, James Currey, Indiana University Press, 1986, chapter 11.

12   Ibid, Appendix 1.

13   Roy Stacey, Deputy Assistant Secretary of State for African Affairs, interview 1988, quoted in 'The Cold War's Final Battle', twnafrica.org/wp/2017/?p=489.

14   The Truth and Reconciliation Commission called for further investigation on this matter and there have been numerous similar calls since then.

15   See Thomas Ohlson, 'The Cuito Cuanavale Syndrome: Revealing SADF Vulnerabilities', *South African Review 5*, Ravan Press, Johannesburg, 1989.

16   'Battle of Cuito Cuanavale 1988', www.sahistory.org.za/article/battle-cuito-cuanavale-1988.

17   See Ronnie Kasrils, 'Historic Turning Point at Cuito Cuanavale', address at Rhodes University, 28 May 2008.

Chapter 3

1   See Truth and Reconciliation Commission Amnesty Committee AC/2000/082.

2   See First, op cit.

3   Marc Wuyts, 'Camponeses e Economia Rural em Moçambique (Peasants and Rural Economy in Mozambique)', Centro de Estudos Africanos, Universidade Eduardo Mondlane, 1978.

4   The CEA's research on the cotton sector in Nampula province was carried out in 1979. The report I was involved in preparing was entitled 'O Descaroçamento de Algodão na Provincia de Nampula' (Cotton Ginning in the Province of Nampula), CEA Relatorio, 79/9.

5   See, among others, Centro Estudos Africanos (CEA), 'O Desemprego e a sua ligação com o campo' (Unemployment and its link to the countryside), 1979; 'Problemas de transformação rural na provincia de Gaza: Um estudo sobre a articulação entre aldeias comunais selecionadas, cooperativas agricolas e a unidade de produção do baixo Limpopo' (Problems of rural transformation in Gaza province: A study of the articulation between selected communal villages, agrarian cooperatives and the lower Limpopo unit of production), unpublished study, 1979; 'O trabalhador sazonal na transformação duma economia de plantações' (The seasonal worker in the transformation of a plantation economy), 1981.

6   Published in John Suckling and Landeg White (eds), *After Apartheid: Renewal of the South African Economy*, James Currey, London, 1988.

7   For a description, see Joseph Lelyveld, 'Mozambique ousts jobless from cities', *The New York Times*, 1 October 1983.

8   'Accord of Nkomati signed by the Honourable Pieter Willem Botha and His Excellency Samora Moises Machel at the Common Border on the Banks of the Nkomati River on 16 March 1984 on behalf of the Republic of South Africa and the People's Republic of Mozambique', mimeo, Articles 2 and 3.

9   'Press Conference on Gorongosa documents', Maputo, 30 September 1985, peacemaker.un.org/mozambique-southafrica-nkomati84.

10   Ohlson, op cit.

11   Rob Davies, Dan O'Meara and Sipho Dlamini, *The Struggle for South Africa: A Reference Guide to Movements, Organizations and Institutions*, two vols, Zed Books, London, 1984 and 1988.

12   Vieira, Martin and Wallerstein, op cit.

13   It was repeated and further elaborated in Jacques Pauw, *In the Heart of the Whore: The Story of Apartheid's Death Squads*, Southern Book Publishers, Johannesburg, 1991.

Chapter 4

1   Gorbachev, uniquely for a national leader, went into retreat to write a book that was published in English as Mikhail Gorbachev, *Perestroika: New Thinking for our Country and the World*, John Curley and Associates, South Yarmouth, MA, 1988.

2   Manuel Castells, *The Information Age: Economy Society and Culture, Vol III: End of Millennium*, Blackwell, Oxford, 2000, Chapter 1.

3   See Howard Barrell, 'Soviet Policy in Southern Africa', *Work in Progress*, 48, July 1987.

4   Joe Slovo, 'Has Socialism Failed?', SACP discussion paper, published in *South African Labour Bulletin*, Vol 14, No 6, February 1990. My own reflection on this issue was published as 'Rethinking socialist economics for South Africa', *African Communist*, No 125, second quarter 1991.

5   Francis Fukuyama, 'The end of history', *The National Interest*, No 16, Summer 1989, pp 3–18.

6   UNDP, *Human Development Report 1997*, Oxford University Press, New York, 1997.

7   These points were all elaborated on and referenced in my *The Politics of Trade in the Era of Hyperglobalisation*, South Centre, Geneva, 2019, pp 11–14.

8   Manuel Castells, *The Information Age: Economy, Society and Culture, Vol I: The Rise of the Network Society*, Blackwell, Oxford, 2000.

9   UNDP, op cit, p 82.

Chapter 5

1   Published as Avril Joffe, David Kaplan, Raphael Kaplinsky and David Lewis, *Improving Manufacturing Performance in South Africa: Report of the Industrial Strategy Project*, UCT Press and International Development Research Centre, Cape Town and Ottawa, 1995.

2   *Making Democracy Work: A Framework for Macroeconomic Policy in South Africa*, A Report from the Macro-Economic Research Group (MERG) to Members of the Democratic Movement of South Africa, Centre for Development Studies, University of the Western Cape, 1993.

3   Ibid, pp 277–281.

4   See note 6 of Introduction.

5   See Chapter 9, where this approach is briefly outlined.

6   African National Congress, 'Ready to Govern: ANC Policy Guidelines for a Democratic South Africa', adopted at the National Conference, 28–31 May 1992.

7   African National Congress, *The Reconstruction and Development Programme*, Umanyano Publications, Johannesburg, 1994.

Chapter 6

1   'President Nelson Mandela Inauguration Speech May 10, 1994', SABC Digital News, 8 May 2015, youtu.be/pJiXu4q__VU.

2   Republic of South Africa, *The Constitution of the Republic of South Africa, 1996*, Chapter 2: Bill of Rights.

3   Ibid, Chapter 13: Finance, and Chapter 9: State Institutions Supporting Constitutional Democracy (Auditor-General).

4   This issue is substantively analysed in Vishnu Padayachee and Robbie van Niekerk, *Shadow of Liberation: Contestation and Compromise in the Economic and Social Policy of the African National Congress 1943–1996*, Wits University Press, Johannesburg, 2019.

5   Republic of South Africa, *The Constitution of the Republic of South Africa, 1996*, Chapter 13, clauses 223–225.

Chapter 7

1   These figures are from ANC, *The Reconstruction and Development Programme*, op cit.

2   Department of Trade and Industry, *White Paper on National Strategy for the Development and Promotion of Small Businesses in South Africa*, 1995.

3   Figures given in SONA address by President Kgalema Motlanthe, 6 February 2009, www.sanews.gov.za/south-africa/over-26mil-houses-built-1994.

4   *Engineering News*, 28 February 2014.

5   RC Nnadozie, 'Access to adequate water in post-apartheid South African provinces: An overview of numerical trends', *WaterSA*, Vol 37, No 3, 2011.

6   See Hein Marais, *South Africa Pushed to the Limit: The Political Economy of Change*, UCT Press, Cape Town, 2011, Chapter 7.

7   Hernando de Soto, *The Mystery of Capital: Why Capitalism Triumphs in the West and Fails Elsewhere*, Basic Books, New York, 2000.

8   The small loan taken out by the De Klerk government was not a 'structural adjustment facility' and was also not of a size that would create policy leverage for the IMF.

9   Iraj Abedian, 'Balancing the Nation's Books', in Raymond Parsons (ed),

Manuel, Markets and Money: Essays in Appraisal, Double Storey Books, Cape Town, 2004, p 49.

10   See Pippa Green, *Choice Not Fate: The Life and Times of Trevor Manuel*, Penguin Books, Johannesburg, 2008, p 434.

11   Significantly, this document was subjected to a trenchant critique in an ANC NEC statement (9 March 1996), which described its provisions as 'a recipe for disaster'.

12   Thomas Friedman, *The Lexus and the Olive Tree*, Farrar, Straus and Giroux, New York, 1999.

13   Joseph Stiglitz, *Globalisation and its Discontents*, Allen Lane/The Penguin Press, London, 2002.

14   Department of Finance, *Growth, Employment and Redistribution: A Macroeconomic Strategy*, 1996.

15   Pippa Green, op cit, p 442.

16   Hein Marais, op cit, pp 131, 117.

17   Ibid, p 131.

18   See note 11 above.

19   Marais, op cit, pp 112–115.

20   Justin Barnes and Anthony Black, 'The Motor Industry Development Programme 1995–2012: What have we learned?', conference paper, International Conference on Manufacturing-led Growth for Employment and Equality, Johannesburg, May 2013; Department of Trade and Industry, *Industrial Policy Action Plan 2014/5–2016/7*, p 86.

21   Nedlac Fund for Research into Industrial Development, Growth and Equity (FRIDGE), 'China: The Textile, Clothing, Footwear and Leather Sectors', report No 7, April 2006, paragraph 71.

22   Etienne Vlok, 'The Textile and Clothing Industry in South Africa', in Herbert Jauch and Rudolf Traub-Merz (eds), *The Future of the Textile and Clothing Industry in Sub-Saharan Africa*, Friedrich-Ebert Stiftung, Bonn, 2006.

23   Marais, op cit, p 217.

24   I drafted an SACP discussion paper, 'Engaging with GEAR', in 1997. Some of the points made above draw on that paper.

25   UNCTAD, *Trade and Development Report 2019: Financing a Global Green New Deal*, United Nations, Geneva, 2019.

26   Robert Brenner, 'The economics of global turbulence', *New Left Review*, 229, Special Edition, May/June 1998.

27   The National Credit Act 34 of 2005 allowed transactions to be declared null and void if it could be shown that they amounted to 'reckless lending'. There was some international interest in this Act in the immediate aftermath of the global financial crisis of 2008.

28   Marais, op cit, p 130.

29   See, eg, DG Clarke, 'The South African Chamber of Mines: Policy and Strategy with Reference to Foreign African Labour Supply', Development Studies

Research Group, University of Natal, Pietermaritzburg, 1977; R First and RH Davies, *Migrant Labour to South Africa: A Sanctions Programme?*, Economic Sanctions Against South Africa series, International University Exchange Fund, Geneva, 1980.

30   See 'South Africa: Mining since 1980', in Kevin Shillington (ed), *Encyclopedia of African History 3*, Routledge, New York, 2013.

31   See, for example, Haroon Bhorat, 'Skills-biased labour demand and the pursuit of inclusive growth in South Africa', WIDER Working Paper 2014/130, October 2014, and other articles authored or co-authored by Haroon Bhorat. Low levels of fixed investment in most sectors of manufacturing outside of heavy industry also meant that job opportunities (maybe even at a higher level of fixed investment per job) were not created on a sufficient scale in manufacturing. In other words, there was insufficient investment in machinery that could have created jobs. I owe this point to Nimrod Zalk.

32   Dale Benton, 'Top 10 mining companies in the world', www.miningglobal.com.

33   Republic of South Africa, Economic Sectors and Employment Cluster, *2010/11–2012/13 Industrial Policy Action Plan*, February 2010, p 4, paragraph 2.1

34   Department of Trade and Industry, 'Trade and Industry Department Budget Vote 2015/16', 21 May 2015.

Chapter 8

1   See UNAIDS, South Africa country overview, www.unaids.org/en/regionscountries/countries/southafrica.

2   See Marais, op cit, pp 279–228, 410–412.

3   See Vishwas Satgar, 'Thabo Mbeki and the South African Communist Party' and other contributions in Sean Jacobs and Richard Calland (eds), *Thabo Mbeki's World: The Politics and Ideology of the South African President*, University of Natal Press, Pietermaritzburg, 2002. See also William Mervin Gumede, *Thabo Mbeki and the Battle for the Soul of the ANC*, Zebra Press, Cape Town, 2005, Chapter 12.

4   Jeremy Cronin, 'Palace Politics or People's Politics? The Challenges Facing the ANC-led Alliance', in Ben Turok (ed), *Wealth Doesn't Trickle Down: The Case for a Developmental State in South Africa*, New Agenda, Cape Town, 2008.

5   Ibid, and Ebrahim Harvey, *Kgalema Motlanthe: A Political Biography*, Jacana Media, Auckland Park, 2012, pp 205–207.

6   See 'excerpts from 2007 Conference Documents', in Turok (ed), op cit.

7   Resolution on Economic Transformation, ANC 53rd National Conference, Mangaung, 6–20 December 2012, paragraph 3.

8   See Ha-Joon Chang, *Kicking Away the Ladder: Development Strategy in Historical Perspective*, Anthem Press, London, 2002; Erik Reinert, *How Rich Countries got Rich ... and Why Poor Countries Stay Poor*, Carroll & Graf, New York, 2007.

9   Reinert, op cit, p 168.

10   Ibid, Chapter 5.

11   Ibid, pp 1–2.

12   World Bank, *The East Asian Miracle: Economic Growth and Public Policy*, World Bank Policy Research Report, Oxford University Press, Oxford, 1993.

13   Marais, op cit, p 130.

14   Ha-Joon Chang, 'An Industrial and Trade Strategy for Inclusive Growth', presentation.

15   Karl Marx, *Capital Vol III*, Progress Publishers, Moscow, 1971, Chapter XIV, Part II.

16   José Gabriel Palma showed that the stock of global financial assets grew ninefold between 1980 and 2007 from a ratio of 1.2 to global GDP to 4.4 times global GDP. See José Gabriel Palma, 'The Revenge of the Market on the Rentiers: Why neo-liberal reports of the end of history turned out to be premature', Cambridge Working Papers in Economics (CWPE) 0927, June 2009.

17   Peter Hain recalls that his colleague, Stephen Byers, Industry Secretary in the first administration of Tony Blair, operated on a mantra that his role was to be 'active but not interventionist'; see Peter Hain, *Outside In*, Biteback Publishing, London, 2012, p 434.

18   Department of Trade and Industry, *National Industrial Policy Framework*, no date, www.thedti.gov.za.

19   Ibid.

20   See Bhorat, op cit, and Benton, op cit.

21   See, for example, International Monetary Fund, *South Africa 2011 Article IV Consultation Report*, IMF Country Report No 11/258; and *South Africa 2012 Article IV Consultation Report*, IMF Country Report No 12/247, International Monetary Fund, Washington, DC.

22   See Chapter 7.

23   Justin Barnes, 'A Strategic Assessment of the South African Clothing Sector', report prepared for Nedlac, 29 July 2005.

24   Department of Economic Development, *The New Growth Path: Framework*, 2010.

25   South African Government, 'National Infrastructure Plan', no date.

26   Department of Trade and Industry, *Industrial Policy Action Plan 2014/5–2016/7*, p 51.

27   See Chapter 12 and also my input into the SONA debate, 8 February 2019.

Chapter 9

1   Department of Trade and Industry, 'A South African Trade Policy and Strategy Framework', May 2010; and 'South Africa's Trade Policy and Strategy Framework (TPSF): An Update', November 2012.

2   Department of Trade and Industry, 'South Africa's Trade Policy and Strategy Framework (TPSF): An Update', paragraph 45.

3   Department of Trade and Industry, 'A South African Trade Policy and Strategy Framework', under section headed 'A Strategic Tariff Policy: Future Perspectives'.

4   Department of Trade and Industry, 'South Africa's Trade Policy and Strategy Framework (TPSF): An Update', paragraph 48.

5   Ibid, paragraph 54.

6   Rob Davies, *The Politics of Trade in the Era of Hyperglobalisation: A Southern African Perspective*, South Centre, Geneva, 2019, Chapter 5.

7   See, for example, C Fred Bergsten, 'Open Regionalism', Peterson Institute for International Economics, Working Paper 97-3, January 1997.

8   See Robert Davies, 'Promoting regional integration in Africa: An analysis of prospects and problems from a South African perspective', *African Security Review*, Vol 5, No 5, 1996; S Adejumobi and Z Kreter, 'The Theory and Discourse on Developmental Regionalism', paper prepared for Regional Forum on Developmental Regionalism organised by ECA-SRO-SA and APN-SSRC together with SADC Secretariat, Swaziland, 28–30 September 2016; and UNCTAD, *Economic Development in Africa Report 2013*, United Nations, Geneva, 2013. This report 'recommends that African governments should promote intra-African trade in the context of developmental regionalism. In particular, it stresses the need for a shift from a linear and process-based approach, which focuses on elimination of trade barriers, to a more development-based approach to integration, which pays as much attention to the building of productive capacities.' See also Faizel Ismail, 'A "Developmental Regionalism" Approach to the AfCFTA', Trade and Industrial Policy Strategies, Working Paper in celebration of the 90th birthday of Chief Olu Akinkugbe CFR CON, Tshwane, 5 December 2018.

9   Ibid.

10   Keynes' famous quotation reads, 'Practical men, who believe themselves to be quite exempt from any intellectual influence, are usually the slaves of some defunct economist.'

11   Southern African Development Community, 'Protocol on Trade', 1996.

12   Southern African Development Community, 'Regional Indicative Strategic Development Plan', 2003.

13   Development Network Africa, 'Evaluation of an Appropriate Model for a SADC Customs Union Section H', report commissioned by the SADC Secretariat, 3 September 2007.

14   Southern African Development Community, 'SADC Facts and Figures', 2012.

15   Department of Trade and Industry, 'Ratification of COMESA-EAC-SADC Tripartite Free Trade Area (TFTA)', presentation to Portfolio Committee on Trade and Industry, 13 June 2018.

16   African Union, 'CFTA – Continental Free Trade Area', no date.

17   East African Community, 'Communique of the first COMESA-EAC-SADC Tripartite Summit', 22 October 2008.

18   South African Government, 'Communique of the second COMESA-EAC-SADC Tripartite Summit', 13 June 2011.

19   See Intergate Immigration, 'The Guidelines for Good Business Practice in Africa', no date.

20   For various views on the operation of SACU on the eve of South Africa's transition to democracy, see Max Sisulu, Morley Nkosi, Bethuel Sethai and Rosalind H Thomas (eds), *Reconstituting and Democratising the Southern African Customs Union: Report of the Workshop held in Gaborone, Botswana, March 1994*, National Institute of Economic Policy, Braamfontein, 1994.

21   Southern African Customs Union, '2002 Southern African Customs Union (SACU) Agreement'.

22   Former Finance Minister Nhlanhla Nene, briefing to Parliament, 3 August 2017.

23   Davies, *The Politics of Trade*, op cit, Chapters 2–4.

24   Jim O'Neill, 'Building Better Global Economic BRICs', Global Economic Paper no 66, Goldman Sachs, 30 November 2001.

25   European Union, 'Agreement on Trade, Development and Cooperation between the European Community and its Member States and the Republic of South Africa', 4 December 1999, document 1999A1204 (02).

26   IMA Europe, 'Raw Materials Initiative', no date.

27   ACP-EU Joint Parliamentary Assembly, 'Draft Report of the Joint Co-Vice President for Human Rights on the Human Rights Challenges facing the ACP-EU Partnership', mimeo, 2004.

28   See, for example, numerous reports from the European Research Office, headed by Paul Goodison.

29   These figures, supplied by the DTI, were included in a 'Status Report on Trade Negotiations' I made to the Economic Transformation Committee of the ANC on 2 December 2016.

30   See *Engineering News*, 28 September 2007. Mandelson made these remarks in a briefing to a committee of the European Parliament.

31   See European Commission, trade statistics, ec.europa.eu/trade/policy/countries-and-regions/statistics/.

32   For the figures for 2018, see Office of the United States Trade Representative, 'Countries & Regions', no date.

33   Office of the US Trade Representative, *Beyond AGOA: Looking to the Future of US-Africa Trade and Investment*, September 2016.

Chapter 10

1   Enacted as the Broad-Based Black Economic Empowerment Amendment Act 46 of 2013, *Government Gazette* no 37271, 27 January 2014.

2   Ibid, section 1 (e).

3   Ibid, Broad-Based Black Economic Empowerment Act 53 of 2003, as amended, section 13 F (1).

4   Ibid, section 10 (1).

5   Helen Zille, *Not without a Fight: The Autobiography of Helen Zille*, Penguin Random House, Johannesburg, 2016.

6   Enacted as the Intellectual Property Laws Amendment Act 28 of 2013, *Government Gazette* no 37148, 10 December 2013.

7   WIPO defines this as 'a living body of knowledge passed on from generation to generation within a community. It often forms part of a people's cultural and spiritual identity.' See World Intellectual Property Organization, 'Traditional knowledge', no date, www.wipo.int/tk/en.

8   See, for example, Dr Marisella Ouma, 'Traditional knowledge: The challenges facing international lawmakers', *WIPO Magazine*, January 2017.

9   The EU was the main demandeur on this. On the issue of geographical indications in our own bilateral relations with the EU, see Chapter 9.

10   Enacted as the Protection, Promotion, Development and Management of Indigenous Knowledge Act 6 of 2019, *Government Gazette* no 42647, 19 August 2019.

11   See, among other sources, 'Brief: New Draft Traditional Knowledge Bill published in South Africa', *Intellectual Property Watch*, 10 April 2013.

12   See remarks from members on UN agencies consulted in the process in Linda Daniels, 'South Africa approves new IP policy with guidance from UN agencies', *Intellectual Property Watch*, 27 May 2018.

13   Department of Trade and Industry, 'Intellectual Property Policy of the Republic of South Africa: Phase 1', 2018.

14   Lotteries Amendment Act 32 of 2013; *Government Gazette* no 37171, 18 December 2013.

15   For example, the address by then Western Cape MEC for Finance Alan Winde in 2013: 'There has also been excellent coordination with our national departments, particularly the DTI. I'd also like to highlight the coordination with our national departments, particularly the DTI, which has seen several billion rands of incentives flowing into sectors such as clothing and textiles and aquaculture.' See Alan Winde, 'Minister Alan Winde's address on key achievements of the Western Cape's biggest sectors', 28 November 2013.

16   Enacted as the Protection of Investment Act 22 of 2015, signed into law December 2015, *Government Gazette* no 39514, 15 December 2015. Signed into operation on 18 June 2018 by President Ramaphosa.

17   See, for example, Armen Abagyan, 'Weapons of Legal Destruction: ISDS lawsuits and Lydian International's Assault on Armenian Sovereignty', Committee for the Abolition of Illegitimate Debt, 23 September 2019.

18   Protection of Investment Act, op cit, section 12.

19   Ibid, sections 6 and 10.

20   Ibid, sections 8 and 11.

21   Ibid, section 9.

22   Ibid, section 13.

23 'Promotion and Protection of Investment Bill in line with global trends', TRALAC News, 4 September 2015.

24 See, for example, James Noyes, 'Britain's betting industry is out of control. A new gambling act must curb it', *The Guardian* 21 January 2020; Callum Tulley, 'Online gambling: Former addicts worry for next generation', *BBC News*, 27 February 2019; Mark D Griffiths and Jonathan Parke, 'The Social Impact of Internet Gambling', *Social Science Computer Review* 20, No 3, 1 August 2002; 'Sports Minister Tracey Crouch resigns over 'delay' to betting crackdown', *BBC News*, 1 November 2018; Phil Mercer, 'Australia's escalating addiction to gambling', *BBC News*, 18 December 2017; and 'Gen Bet: Has gambling gatecrashed our teens?', discussion paper, Victorian Responsible Gambling Foundation, March 2017, responsiblegambling.vic.gov.au/documents/16/gen-bet-has-gambling-gatecrashed-our-teens_SIPh7sd.pdf, reporting that one in ten young people in Australia gamble online and one in five adolescents have played social casino games.

25 Charlotte Probst, Charles DH Parry, Hans-Ulrich Wittchen and Jürgen Rehm, 'The socioeconomic profile of alcohol-attributable mortality in South Africa: A modelling study', *BMC Medicine*, Vol 16, No 97, 25 June 2018.

26 RG Matzopoulos, S Truen, B Bowman and J Corrigall, 'The cost of harmful alcohol abuse in South Africa', *South African Medical Journal*, Vol 104, No 2, February 2014.

27 *Government Gazette* no 40319, 30 September 2016.

28 See, for example, Suzanne Hiller-Sturmhofel and H Scott Swartzwelder, 'Alcohol's effects on the adolescent brain: What can be learned from animal models', *Alcohol Research & Health*, Vol 28, No 4, 2004, pp 213–221.

29 Anne T McCartt, Laurie A Hellinga and Bevan B Kirley, 'The effects of minimum legal drinking age 21 laws on alcohol-related driving in the United States', *Journal of Safety Research*, Vol 41, No 2, April 2010, pp 173–181.

30 Paul J Gruenewald, Andrew J Treno, Sally Casswell et al, 'Impacts of New Zealand's lowered minimum purchase age on context-specific drinking and related risks', *Addiction*, Vol 110, No 11, November 2015, pp 1757–1766.

31 Copyright Amendment Bill B13B-2017, Performers' Protection Amendment Bill B24-2016.

32 Department of Trade and Industry, *Copyright Review Commission Report (2011)*.

33 Ibid, Executive Summary, paragraph ii.

34 Ibid, paragraph 3.5.4.

35 Ibid, paragraph 3.6.1.

36 Copyright Amendment Bill B13B-2017, clause 25.

37 Ibid, clauses 5 and 9.

38 Ibid, clauses 30 and 31.

39 Ibid, Memorandum, paragraph 1.2

40 Ibid, clause 13, 'General exceptions from copyright protection'.

41 Ibid.

42   See South African Government, 'President Cyril Ramaphosa refers Copyright and Performers' Protection Amendment Bills to Parliament', 23 June 2020.

Chapter 11

1   Slide presentation on IPAP 2016/7–2017/8, April 2016.

2   Department of Trade and Industry, *Industrial Policy Action Plan 2013/4–2015/6*, p 6, reiterating a point made in several prior and later iterations of the IPAP.

3   Ibid, p 8.

4   Rebecca Davis, 'Marikana: The debt-hole that fuelled the fire', *Daily Maverick*, 12 October 2012.

5   This is something that the Farlam Commission investigated and explicitly rejected.

6   See Terence Creamer, 'ANC Mining policy should focus on "capturing rents" not nationalisation', *Polity*, 25 June 2012.

7   National Planning Commission, *National Development Plan 2030: Our future – make it work*, Executive Summary, 15 August 2012.

8   South African Communist Party, 'Let's not monumentalise the NDP – SACP', SACP discussion document, politicsweb, 14 May 2013.

9   African National Congress, 'Resolution on Economic Transformation', ANC 53rd National Conference, Mangaung, 16–20 December 2012, section under heading 'The National Development Plan', paras 1–2.

10   Ibid, paragraph 3.

11   See African National Congress, 'The ANC's 2014 election manifesto', politicsweb, 11 January 2014.

Chapter 12

1   'President Jacob Zuma: Address during 2014 Presidential Inauguration', GovernmentZA, 27 May 2014, youtube.com/watch?v=g6jVZzXGass&feature=youtu.be.

2   See Jeremy Cronin, 'Legislative disruptions: From the Nazis to the EFF', 20 February 2015.

3   Sébastien Dessus, World Bank Senior Economist and Program Leader for Southern Africa, submission to Standing Committee on Appropriations, South African Parliament, 15 February 2017, Parliamentary Monitoring Group, pmg.org.za/committee-meeting/23954/.

4   After a Competition Commission inquiry, 21 large construction companies admitted to a parliamentary committee that they had been involved in bid-rigging to a combined value of R26 billion; see, for example, Dennis Cruywagen, 'Big construction firms admit to bid-rigging', SA News, 23 April 2013.

5   See, for example, Jabu Moleketi, 'Is a retreat from National Democratic Revolution to National Bourgeois Revolution imminent?', *African Communist*,

No 133, second quarter 1993.

6   See Harvey, op cit, pp 174–176.

7   On the 'relationship' between DA politicians and property developers in Cape
     Town, see Crispian Olver, *A House Divided: The Feud that Took Cape Town to
     the Brink*, Jonathan Ball, Johannesburg, 2019.

8   Public Protector South Africa, 'Secure in Comfort', Report No 25 of 2013/14,
     19 March 2014.

9   See US Department of Transportation, Federal Railroad Administration, 'Buy
     America', 31 March 2020.

10   Figures provided by the DTI, quoted in my input to the SONA debate,
     8 February 2019.

11   See Department of Trade and Industry, *Industrial Policy Action Plan 2014/5–
     2016/7*, p 82.

12   See South African Government, 'Minister Rob Davies: South African
     Automotive Masterplan and Extension of Automotive Production and
     Development Programme', 23 November 2018, www.gov.za/speeches/
     minister-rob-davies-media-statement-south-african-automotive-master-
     plan-2035-and-extension.

13   See my contribution to the SONA debate, February 2019, pmg.org.za/
     hansard/28329/.

14   See *BusinessTech*, 'Yekani unveils new R1 billion electronics factory in East
     London that will create 1 000 jobs', 5 June 2018.

15   See Linda Ensor, 'Minister Davies says Jonas is a man of integrity', *TimesLive*,
     17 March 2016.

16   Jan Gerber, 'Hawks investigate cases related to Gupta-loot worth more than
     R40 billion', *News24*, 15 August 2018.

17   Public Protector South Africa, 'State of Capture', Report No 6 of 2016/17.

18   Gareth van Onselen, 'Political Musical Chairs: Turnover in The National
     Executive and Administration Since 2009', report by the Institute of Race
     Relations, August 2017.

19   Chandré Gould, Conrad Barberton and Carmen Abdoll, 'What is at stake for
     new councils in South Africa?', *ISS Today*, 17 August 2016.

20   'Read: Alleged full report of Bell Pottinger's Gupta PR plan', *The Citizen*,
     4 April 2017.

Chapter 13

1   See Adriaan Basson, 'Ramaphosa's straight talk refreshing and frightening',
     News24, 9 March 2020.

2   See *BusinessTech*, 'Ramaphosa speaks of Zuma exit and corruption at Davos',
     24 January 2018.

3   See SA News, 'SA hard at work to clear path for investment', 26 October 2018.

4   See James de Villiers, 'Foreign direct investment in SA rocketed by 446% in 2018 – these were the hottest sectors', *Business Insider South Africa*, 22 January 2019.

5   Downloadable at www.treasury.gov.za/comm_media/press/2019/Towards%20an%20Economic%20Strategy%20for%20SA.pdf.

6   In the colloquium held in December 2018 at the start of this process, the DTI tabled a paper entitled, 'Placing Structural Transformation at the Centre of Economic Revival under the New Dawn'. This argued that a carefully structured and targeted fiscal stimulus was both possible and necessary.

7   See speech and supporting documents downloadable at www.treasury.gov.za/documents/mtbps/2019/.

8   Asghar Adelzadeh, 'Economic Policy Scenarios for Growth and Development of South Africa: 2019–2030', Applied Development Research Solutions, mimeo, 2019.

9   Political Report to SACP Central Committee meeting, 29 November to 1 December 2019.

10   Interview with Gilad Isaacs, *Daily Maverick*, 20 November 2019.

11   Ibid.

12   Natasha Marrian, 'Dead end for government's public wage bill plan?', *Financial Mail*, 12 March 2020.

13   See Statistics South Africa (Stats SA), 'Press Statement: GDP in the fourth quarter of 2019 decreased by 1.4%', 3 March 2020.

14   *BusinessTech*, 1 July 2020, quoting Statistics South Africa.

15   See Stats SA, 'Media Release: Quarterly Labour Force Survey – Q3:2019', 29 October 2019.

16   *BusinessTech*, 23 June 2020.

17   See, for example, *BusinessLive*, 6 March 2020, quoting Eskom press briefing.

18   UNCTAD, 'The economic impact of COVID-19: Can policy makers avert a multi-trillion dollar crisis?', press release, 9 March 2020.

19   UNCTAD, 'UN calls for $2.5 trillion support package for developing countries to deal with Coronavirus shock', press release, 30 March 2020.

20   Adam Behsudi, 'IMF predicts global contraction on par with Great Depression', *Politico*, 14 April 2020.

21   The World Bank forecast released on 9 June 2020 was minus 7.1 per cent (*BusinessTech*), while that of National Treasury was minus 7.2 per cent (Supplementary Budget Speech, 24 June 2020).

Chapter 14

1   See, for example, Ezra Klein, 'How the COVID-19 recession could become a depression', *Vox*, 23 March 2020. This article was based on interviews with economists from Moody's and Goldman Sachs, among others, agreeing that the impact would be worse than the 2008 financial crisis and could lurch into a depression. See also Nouriel Roubini, 'A Greater Depression?', *Project*

Syndicate, 24 March 2020.

2   'Value of COVID-19 fiscal stimulus packages in G20 countries as of July 2020, as a share of GDP', graphic, statista.com, 15 August 2020.

3   The official budget forecast was 0.9 per cent for the 2020/1 financial year. The IMF and private banks all had forecasts below this before any impact of COVID-19 was anticipated.

4   Stats SA, 'Statistical release: Mid-year population estimates 2019', 31 July 2020, p 8.

5   Minister of Finance, Supplementary Budget Speech, 24 June 2020.

6   See Ferial Haffajee, 'Stage 4 load shedding hits as Cabinet divide on energy deepens', *Daily Maverick*, 10 March 2020, on the South African Energy Forum and Transform SA, black business lobby groups, she argues, that are 'growing as patronage networks are weeded out at Eskom'.

7   'Severe acute respiratory syndrome', Wikipedia.

8   Naledi Mashishi, 'History Check: Did 1918 Spanish flu "decimate more than 300 000" South Africans in just two years?', Africa Check, 21 May 2020.

9   Science Daily, 'New data confirm increased frequency of extreme weather events', 21 March 2018, www.sciencedaily.com/releases/2018/03/180321130859.htm.

10   'Instrumental temperature record', Wikipedia.

11   *The New York Times*, 'Extreme weather displaced a record 7 million in first half of 2019', 12 September 2019.

12   *The Guardian*, 'Climate emergency: global action is "way off track" says UN head', 10 March 2020.

13   Downloadable at www.marxists.org/archive/marx/works/1845/condition-working-class/.

14   Figures provided by the Special Inspector General for the Troubled Asset Relief Program (TARP); see Mike Collins, 'The big bank bailout', *Forbes*, 14 July 2015.

15   UNCTAD, *Trade and Development Report 2019*, p viii.

16   Ibid, p iii.

17   Sergei Klebnikov, 'Here are the countries on the brink of recession going into 2020', *Forbes*, 28 October 2019.

18   UNCTAD, *Trade and Development Report 2017: Beyond Austerity, Towards a Global New Deal*, United Nations, Geneva, 2017, p vii.

19   Ibid, p xii.

20   Ibid, p 42.

21   I referred to studies by both the OECD and the IMF in my *The Politics of Trade in the Era of Hyperglobalisation*, op cit, pp 39–40.

22   Studies by Niall Reddy and Phillip Burger, quoted in 'Serve the People as a Whole, Build a People's Economy', *Bua Komanisi*, 4th Special National Congress edition, December 2019, pp 23–24.

23   Even the World Economic Forum bases its prediction, that the recession will

not lead to a depression, on the assumption that the world has learnt that 'measures introduced after the Great Depression have proved powerful'; see Reuters, 'A US recession? Probably. Depression? Only if the virus is untamed', World Economic Forum, 28 March 2020.

24   UNCTAD, *Trade and Development Report 2019*, op cit, p 34.

25   UNCTAD, *Trade and Development Report 2017*, op cit, pp xiii–xiv, 152–164.

26   Kevin P Gallagher and Richard Kozul-Wright, *A New Multilateralism for Shared Prosperity: Geneva Principles for a Global Green New Deal*, UNCTAD, Geneva, and Boston University Global Development Policy Center, 2019. The Acknowledgements record that I participated in a discussion group that led to the formulation of these principles.

27   See 'Value of COVID-19 fiscal stimulus packages', op cit. According to this source, the US stimulus package is the largest at 10 per cent of its GDP, followed by Australia (9.7 per cent), Germany (4.5 per cent) and Canada (3.6 per cent). China's was 1.2 per cent, Brazil's 2.5 per cent and Russia's 0.3 per cent. South Africa's was 0.2 per cent, followed only by Japan and India at 0.1 per cent each.

28   See, among others, Gilad Isaacs, 'COVID-19: Unpacking President Ramaphosa's rescue package', GroundUp, 22 April 2020; South African Communist Party, 'SACP welcomes pro-poor and pro-worker interventions', SACP statement, 22 April 2020, www.sacp.org.za.

29   See Neil Coleman, 'Supplementary Budget puts South Africa on the edge', *Daily Maverick*, 7 July 2020.

30   See National Treasury, 'Supplementary Budget Review 2020', 24 June 2020, Chapter 1. The quotation is the heading of the paragraph that precedes the spending proposals.

31   Mike Davis, 'We can't go back to normal: How will coronavirus change the world?', *The Guardian*, 31 March 2020.

32   See, for example, Anthony Squazzin and Prinesha Naidoo, 'Ramaphosa has window to reform South Africa as twin crises hit', *Bloomberg*, 31 March 2020.

33   European Commission, 'Structural reforms for economic growth', no date.

34   'Statement by President Cyril Ramaphosa on Further Economic and Social Measures in Response to the COVID-19 Epidemic', Union Buildings, Tshwane, 21 April 2020.

35   Howard Phillips, 'Black October: The Impact of the Spanish Influenza Epidemic of 1918 on South Africa', PhD thesis, University of Cape Town, 1984.

36   Dr Kgosientsho Ramokgopa, Head of Investment & Infrastructure Office: Presidency, 'Unlocking Private Capital for Public Infrastructure Development in South Africa', slide presentation to University of the Witwatersrand webinar, 13 August 2020.

37   Gary A Dymski, Professor of Applied Economics, University of Leeds, 'Blended Finance as Finance for Development: Lessons from 40 Years of Financial Transformation', presentation to UNCTAD Intergovernmental Group of Experts Meeting on Financing for Development, Geneva, 4–6 November 2019.

38   According to US Global Investors, Inc (www.usfunds.com), the eight largest

gold producers are now China, Australia, Russia, USA, Canada, Indonesia, Peru and South Africa.

39   Ben Fine and Zavareh Rustomjee, *The Political Economy of South Africa: From Minerals-Energy Complex to Industrialisation*, C Hurst and Co, London, 1996.

40   On this, see DE Kaplan, 'Class Conflict, Capital Accumulation and the State: An Historical Analysis of the State in Twentieth-Century South Africa', DPhil thesis, University of Sussex, 1977.

41   AAF-SAP can be downloaded from repository.uneca.org/bitstream/handle/10855/5670/Bib-44783.pdf.

42   Ibid, paragraph 1.

43   Ibid, paragraph 43.

44   Roman Grynberg, 'African coffee isn't worth a bean', *Mail & Guardian*, 10 May 2013.

45   'Data Story: An iPhone costs hundreds of dollars but its raw material costs just over $1', moneycontrol.com, 21 August 2017.

46   Klaus Schwab, *The Fourth Industrial Revolution*, Crown Business and World Economic Forum, Geneva, 2016.

47   Erik Brynjolfsson and Andrew McAfee, *The Second Machine Age: Work, Progress and Prosperity in a Time of Brilliant Technologies*, WW Norton & Co, New York, 2014.

48   See report by Dan Alexe, 'Adidas is moving production from China back to Germany … to be made by robots', *New Europe*, 11 April 2017.

49   Parminder Jeet Singh, 'Digital Industrialization in Developing Countries: A Review of the Business and Policy Landscapes', Commonwealth Secretariat, 2017, p 4.

50   UNCTAD, *Trade and Development Report 2018: Power, Platforms and the Free Trade Delusion*, United Nations, Geneva, 2018, p 80.

51   Kean Birch, Margaret Chiappetta and Anna Artyushina, 'The Problem of Innovation in Technoscientific Capitalism: Data Rentiership and the Policy Implications of Turning Personal Data into a Private Asset', mimeo, 2020.

52   Davies, *The Politics of Trade in the Era of Hyperglobalisation*, op cit, Chapter 5.

53   See Andrew Browne, 'How the coronavirus is accelerating deglobalization', *Bloomberg*, 29 February 2020, www.bloomberg.com.

54   It is widely agreed that China's liberalisation 'reforms' took place in phases starting under the leadership of Deng Xiaoping in 1978. Local experimentation, the construction of Special Economic Zones and liberalisation of entry of foreign investment before trade liberalisation were all features of this process. China benefited enormously from the process of phasing out of quotas under the Multi-Fibre Arrangement that began with the establishment of the WTO in 1994 and was completed in 2005. This enabled Chinese clothing and textile products, initially produced in Special Economic Zones, to capture an increasing percentage of world markets, thereby providing a major boost to the country's industrialisation. Serious trade liberalisation only really began after China joined the WTO in 2001. See, among others, Barry Naughton and Kellee S Tsai (eds), *State*

Capitalism, Institutional Adaptation, and the Chinese Miracle, Cambridge University Press, Cambridge, 2015.

55 This remark was made at a WEF-sponsored investment conference in South Africa in early 2018.

56 Vera Songwe, 'Intra-African trade: A path to economic diversification and inclusion', report, Foresight Africa 2019, Brookings Institution, 11 January 2019.

57 AAF-SAP, op cit, para 47.

58 See Robert Davies, 'Promoting regional integration in Africa: An analysis of prospects and problems from a South African perspective', *African Security Review*, Vol 5, No 5, 1996; S Adejumobi and Z Kreter, 'The Theory and Discourse on Developmental Regionalism', paper prepared for Regional Forum on Developmental Regionalism, organised by ECA-SRO-SA and APN-SSRC together with SADC Secretariat, Swaziland, 28–30 September 2016; UNCTAD, *Economic Development in Africa Report 2013*, op cit. This report 'recommends that African governments should promote intra-African trade in the context of developmental regionalism. In particular, it stresses the need for a shift from a linear and process based approach, which focuses on elimination of trade barriers, to a more development-based approach to integration, which pays as much attention to the building of productive capacities ...' See also Faizel Ismail, 'A "Developmental Regionalism" Approach to the AfCFTA', Trade and Industrial Policy Strategies, Working Paper in celebration of the 90th birthday of Chief Olu Akinkugbe CFR CON, Tshwane, 5 December 2018.

59 See 'DA "needs our honesty", insists IRR's Hermann Pretorius', *TimesLive*, 8 October 2019.

60 See 'Indlulamithi South Africa Scenarios 2030: Look Above the Trees', June 2018, sascenarios2030.co.za.

61 Nicos Poulantzas, *Fascism and Dictatorship*, New Left Books, London, 1974.

SOURCES

Unpublished sources

Centro de Estudos Africanas (CEA). 'Problemas de transformação rural na provincia de Gaza: Um estudo sobre a articulação entre aldeias comunais selecionadas, cooperativas agricolas e a unidade de produção do baixo Limpopo' (Problems of rural transformation in Gaza province: A study of the articulation between selected communal villages, agrarian cooperatives and the lower Limpopo unit of production). Unpublished study, 1979.

Kaplan, DE. 'Class Conflict, Capital Accumulation and the State: An Historical Analysis of the State in Twentieth-Century South Africa'. DPhil thesis, University of Sussex, 1977.

Phillips, Howard. 'Black October: The Impact of the Spanish Influenza Epidemic of 1918 on South Africa'. PhD thesis, University of Cape Town, 1984. open.uct.ac.za.handle/11427/7852/thesis_hum_1984_phillips_h.pdf.

Public documents

'Accord of Nkomati signed by the Honourable Pieter Willem Botha and His Excellency Samora Moises Machel at the Common Border on the Banks of the Nkomati River on 16 March 1984 on behalf of the Republic of South Africa and the People's Republic of Mozambique'.

ACP-EU Joint Parliamentary Assembly. 'Draft Report of the Joint Co-Vice President for Human Rights on the Human Rights Challenges facing the ACP-EU Partnership'. Mimeo, 2004.

African National Congress. 'Ready to Govern: ANC Policy Guidelines for a Democratic South Africa'. Adopted at the National Conference, 28–31 May 1992.

African National Congress, *The Reconstruction and Development Programme*. Umanyano Publications, Johannesburg, 1994.

African National Congress. 'Resolution on Economic Transformation'. ANC 53rd National Conference, Mangaung, 16–20 December 2012.

African National Congress. 'The ANC's 2014 election manifesto'. Politicsweb, 11 January 2014. www.politicsweb.co.za/documents/the-ancs-2014-election-manifesto.

African National Congress. 'The Year of Unity, Socio-Economic Renewal and Nation Building: January 8th Statement 2020'.

African Union. 'CFTA – Continental Free Trade Area', no date. www.au.int/en/ti/cfta/about.

275

European Union. 'Agreement on Trade, Development and Cooperation between the European Community and its Member States and the Republic of South Africa', 4 December 1999. Document 1999A1204 (02). eur-lex.europa.eu/legal-content/EN/TXT/PDF/?uri=CELEX:01999A1204(02)-20160301&from=HR.

Department of Economic Development. *The New Growth Path: Framework*, 2010.

Department of Finance. *Growth, Employment and Redistribution: A Macroeconomic Strategy*, 1996.

Department of Trade and Industry. *National Industrial Policy Framework*, no date. www.thedtic.gov.za/wp-content/uploads/NIPF_r2.pdf.

Department of Trade and Industry. *White Paper on National Strategy for the Development and Promotion of Small Businesses in South Africa*, 1995.

Department of Trade and Industry. 'A South African Trade Policy and Strategy Framework', May 2010.

Department of Trade and Industry. *Copyright Review Commission Report (2011)*. www.publishsa.co.za/file/1532283873rsg-copyrightreviewcommissionreport2011.pdf.

Department of Trade and Industry. 'South Africa's Trade Policy and Strategy Framework (TPSF): An Update', November 2012

Department of Trade and Industry. *Industrial Policy Action Plan 2014/5–2016/7*.

Department of Trade and Industry. 'Trade and Industry Department Budget Vote 2015/16'. Politicsweb, 21 May 2015. www.politicsweb.co.za/opinion/value-of-agoa-is-diminishing-while-its-costs-are-r.

Department of Trade and Industry. 'Intellectual Property Policy of the Republic of South Africa: Phase 1', 2018. www.gov.za/sites/default/files/gcis_document/201808/ippolicy2018-phasei.pdf.

Department of Trade and Industry. 'Ratification of COMESA-EAC-SADC Tripartite Free Trade Area (TFTA)'. Presentation to Portfolio Committee on Trade and Industry, 13 June 2018.

East African Community. 'Communique of the 1st COMESA-EAC-SADC Tripartite Summit', 22 October 2008. www.eac.int/documents/category/comesa-eac-sadc-tripartite.

European Commission. 'Structural reforms for economic growth', no date. ec.europa.eu/info/business-economy-euro/growth-and-investment/structural-reforms/structural-reforms-economic-growth_en.

IMA Europe. 'Raw Materials Initiative', no date. www.ima-europe.eu/content/raw-materials-initiative.

International Monetary Fund. *South Africa 2011 Article IV Consultation Report*. IMF Country Report No 11/258. International Monetary Fund, Washington, DC.

International Monetary Fund. *South Africa 2012 Article IV Consultation Report*. IMF Country Report No 12/247. International Monetary Fund, Washington, DC.

National Planning Commission. *National Development Plan 2030: Our future – make it work*, Executive Summary, 15 August 2012.

National Treasury. 'Supplementary Budget Review 2020', 24 June 2020. www.treasury.gov.za/documents/national%20budget/2020S/review/FullSBR.pdf.

Office of the United States Trade Representative. 'Countries & Regions'. No date. ustr.gov/countries-regions.

Office of the US Trade Representative. *Beyond AGOA: Looking to the Future of US-Africa Trade and Investment.* September 2016. www.tralac.org/images/docs/10526/beyond-agoa-report-ustr-september-2016.pdf.

Public Protector South Africa. 'Secure in Comfort: Report on an investigation into allegations of impropriety and unethical conduct relating to the installation and implementation of security measures by the Department of Public Works in the private residence of President Jacob Zuma at Nkandla in the KwaZulu-Natal province'. Report No 25 of 2013/14, 19 March 2014.

Public Protector South Africa. 'State of Capture'. Report No 6 of 2016/17, 14 October 2016.

Republic of South Africa. *The Constitution of the Republic of South Africa, 1996, Act 108 of 1996.*

Republic of South Africa, Economic Sectors and Employment Cluster. *2010/11–2012/13 Industrial Policy Action Plan*, February 2010.

South African Government. 'National Infrastructure Plan', no date, www.gov.za/issues/national-infrastructure-plan.

South African Government. 'Communique of the second COMESA-EAC-SADC Tripartite Summit', 13 June 2011. www.gov.za/communiqu%C3%A9-second-comesa-eac-sadc-tripartite-summit-sandton-convention-centre-johannesburg-south.

South African Government. 'Minister Rob Davies: South African Automotive Masterplan and Extension of Automotive Production and Development Programme', 23 November 2018.

South African Government. 'President Cyril Ramaphosa refers Copyright and Performers' Protection Amendment Bills to Parliament', 23 June 2020.

Southern African Customs Union. '2002 Southern African Customs Union (SACU) Agreement'. www.sacu.int/show.php?id=566.

Southern African Development Community. 'Protocol on Trade', 1996. www.sadc.int/files/4613/5292/8370/Protocol_on_Trade1996.pdf.

Southern African Development Community. 'Regional Indicative Strategic Development Plan', 2003.

Southern African Development Community. 'SADC Facts and Figures', 2012.

'Statement by President Cyril Ramaphosa on Further Economic and Social Measures in Response to the COVID-19 Epidemic'. Union Buildings, Tshwane, 21 April 2020.

Statistics South Africa (Stats SA). 'Media release: Quarterly Labour Force Survey – Q3:2019', 29 October 2019.

Stats SA. 'Press Statement: GDP in the fourth quarter of 2019 decreased by 1.4%', 3 March 2020. www.statssa.gov.za/?p=13065.

Stats SA. 'Statistical release: Mid-year population estimates 2019', 31 July 2020.

Truth and Reconciliation Commission Amnesty Committee AC/2000/082. www.justice.gov.za/Trc/decisions/trc-adt-2000.pdf.

United Nations Conference on Trade and Development (UNCTAD). *Economic Development in Africa Report 2013*. United Nations, Geneva, 2013.

UNCTAD. *Trade and Development Report 2017: Beyond Austerity, Towards a Global New Deal*. United Nations, Geneva, 2017.

UNCTAD. *Trade and Development Report 2018: Power, Platforms and the Free Trade Delusion*. United Nations, Geneva, 2018.

UNCTAD. *Trade and Development Report 2019: Financing a Global Green New Deal*. United Nations, Geneva, 2019.

UNDP. *Human Development Report 1997*. Oxford University Press, New York, 1997.

UNECA. 'African alternative framework to structural adjustment programmes for socio-economic recovery and transformation', 1990. repository.uneca.org/bitstream/handle/10855/5670/Bib-44783.pdf.

US Department of Transportation, Federal Railroad Administration. 'Buy America', 31 March 2020. cms8.fra.dot.gov/legislation-regulations/buy-america/buy-america.

World Bank. *The East Asian Miracle: Economic Growth and Public Policy*. World Bank Policy Research Report. Oxford University Press, Oxford, 1993.

World Intellectual Property Organization. 'Traditional knowledge', no date. www.wipo.int/tk/en.

Published sources

Abagyan, Armen. 'Weapons of Legal Destruction: ISDS lawsuits and Lydian International's Assault on Armenian Sovereignty'. Committee for the Abolition of Illegitimate Debt, 23 September 2019. www.cadtm.org/Weapons-of-Legal-Destruction-ISDS-lawsuits-and-Lydian-International-s-Assault.

Abedian, Iraj. 'Balancing the Nation's Books'. In Raymond Parsons (ed), *Manuel, Markets and Money: Essays in Appraisal*. Double Storey Books, Cape Town, 2004.

Adejumobi, S and Z Kreter. 'The Theory and Discourse on Developmental Regionalism'. Paper prepared for Regional Forum on Developmental Regionalism, organised by ECA-SRO-SA and APN-SSRC together with SADC Secretariat, Swaziland, 28–30 September 2016.

Adelzadeh, Asghar. 'Economic Policy Scenarios for Growth and Development of South Africa: 2019–2030'. Applied Development Research Solutions, mimeo, 2019.

Alexe, Dan. 'Adidas is moving production from China back to Germany ... to be made by robots'. *New Europe*, 11 April 2017. www.neweurope.eu/article/adidas-is-moving-production-from-china-back-to-germany-to-be-made-by-robots/.

Barnes, Justin. 'A Strategic Assessment of the South African Clothing Sector'. Report prepared for Nedlac, 29 July 2005.

Barnes, Justin and Anthony Black. 'The Motor Industry Development Programme 1995–2012: What have we learned?' Conference paper, International Conference on Manufacturing-led Growth for Employment and Equality, Johannesburg, May 2013.

Barrell, Howard. 'Soviet Policy in Southern Africa'. *Work in Progress*, 48, July 1987.

Basson, Adriaan. 'Ramaphosa's straight talk refreshing and frightening'. *News24*, 9 March 2020.

Behsudi, Adam. 'IMF predicts global contraction on par with Great Depression'. *Politico*, 14 April 2020.

Bergsten, C Fred. 'Open Regionalism'. Peterson Institute for International Economics. Working Paper 97-3, January 1997.

Bhorat, Haroon. 'Skills-biased labour demand and the pursuit of inclusive growth in South Africa'. WIDER Working Paper 2014/130, October 2014. www.wider.unu.edu/sites/default/files/wp2014-130.pdf.

Birch, Kean, Margaret Chiappetta and Anna Artyushina. 'The Problem of Innovation in Technoscientific Capitalism: Data Rentiership and the Policy Implications of Turning Personal Data into a Private Asset'. Mimeo, 2020.

Brenner, Robert. 'The economics of global turbulence'. *New Left Review*, 229, Special Edition, May/June 1998.

'Brief: New Draft Traditional Knowledge Bill published in South Africa'. *Intellectual Property Watch*, 10 April 2013. www.ip-watch.org/2013/04/10/new-traditional-knowledge-bill-published-in-south-africa/.

Browne, Andrew. 'How the coronavirus is accelerating deglobalization'. *Bloomberg*, 29 February 2020. www.bloomberg.com/news/newsletters/2020-02-29/why-deglobalization-is-accelerating-bloomberg-new-economy.

Brynjolfsson, Erik and Andrew McAfee. *The Second Machine Age: Work, Progress and Prosperity in a Time of Brilliant Technologies*. WW Norton & Co, New York, 2014.

BusinessTech. 'Ramaphosa speaks of Zuma exit and corruption at Davos', 24 January 2018.

Castells, Manuel. *The Information Age: Economy, Society and Culture, Vol I: The Rise of the Network Society*, Blackwell, Oxford, 2000.

Castells, Manuel. *The Information Age: Economy Society and Culture, Vol III: End of Millennium*. Blackwell, Oxford, 2000.

Centro de Estudos Africanos (CEA). 'O Descaroçamento de Algadão na Provincia de Nampula' (Cotton Ginning in the Province of Nampula), CEA Relatorio, 79/9.

CEA. 'O Desemprego e a sua ligação com o campo' (Unemployment and its link to the countryside), 1979.

CEA. 'O trabalhador sazonal na transformação duma economia de plantações' (The seasonal worker in the transformation of a plantation economy), 1981.

Chang, Ha-Joon. *Kicking Away the Ladder: Development Strategy in Historical Perspective*. Anthem Press, London, 2002.

Chipeta, Chinyamata and Robert Davies. 'Regional Relations and Cooperation Post-Apartheid: A Macro Framework Study Report'. Consultancy study for the Southern African Development Community, 1993.

Clarke, DG. 'The South African Chamber of Mines: Policy and Strategy with Reference to Foreign African labour supply'. Development Studies Research Group, University of Natal, Pietermaritzburg, 1977.

Coleman, Neil. 'Supplementary Budget puts South Africa on the edge'. *Daily Maverick*, 7 July 2020.

Collins, Mike. 'The big bank bailout'. *Forbes*, 14 July 2015.

Creamer, Terence. 'ANC Mining policy should focus on "capturing rents" not nationalisation'. *Polity*, 25 June 2012.

Cronin, Jeremy. 'Palace Politics or People's Politics? The Challenges Facing the ANC-led Alliance'. In Ben Turok (ed), *Wealth Doesn't Trickle Down: The Case for a Developmental State in South Africa*. New Agenda, Cape Town, 2008.

Cronin, Jeremy. 'Legislative disruptions: From the Nazis to the EFF'. Politicsweb, 20 February 2015. www.politicsweb.co.za/opinion/legislative-disruptions-from-the-nazis-to-the-eff-.

Cruywagen, Dennis. 'Big construction firms admit to bid-rigging'. SA News, 23 April 2013. www.sanews.gov.za/south-africa/big-construction-firms-admit-bid-rigging.

Daniels, Linda. 'South Africa approves new IP policy with guidance from UN agencies'. *Intellectual Property Watch*, 27 May 2018. www.ip-watch.org/2018/05/27/south-africa-approves-new-ip-policy-guidance-un-agencies/.

'Data Story: An iPhone costs hundreds of dollars but its raw material costs just over $1'. Moneycontrol.com, 21 August 2017. www.moneycontrol.com/news/business/companies/data-story-it-takes-hundreds-of-dollars-to-buy-an-iphone-but-just-over-a-dollar-to-make-one-2365065.html.

Davies, Robert. 'The White Working-Class in South Africa'. *New Left Review*, No 82, November–December 1973.

Davies, Robert. 'The SADF's Covert War Against Mozambique'. In Jacklyn Cock and Laurie Nathan (eds), *War and Society: The Militarisation of South Africa*. David Philip, Cape Town, 1989.

Davies, Robert. 'Rethinking socialist economics for South Africa'. *African Communist*, No 125, second quarter 1991.

Davies, Robert. 'Promoting regional integration in Africa: An analysis of prospects and problems from a South African perspective'. *African Security Review*, Vol 5, No 5, 1996.

Davies, Robert. *The Politics of Trade in the Era of Hyperglobalisation: A Southern African Perspective*. South Centre, Geneva, 2019.

Davies, Robert and Dan O'Meara. 'Total strategy in southern Africa: An analysis of South African regional policy since 1978'. *Journal of Southern African Studies*, Vol 11, No 2, 1985.

Davies, Rob, Dan O'Meara and Sipho Dlamini. *The Struggle for South Africa: A Reference Guide to Movements, Organizations and Institutions*. Two volumes. Zed Books, London, 1984.

Davies, Robert, Dot Keet and Mfundu Nkuhlu. 'Reconstructing Economic Relations with the Southern African Region'. Discussion document prepared for Macro-Economic Research Group, March 1993.

Davis, Mike. 'We can't go back to normal: How will coronavirus change the world?'. *The Guardian*, 31 March 2020.

Davis, Rebecca. 'Marikana: The debt-hole that fuelled the fire'. *Daily Maverick*, 12 October 2012.

De Soto, Hernando. *The Mystery of Capital: Why Capitalism Triumphs in the West and Fails Elsewhere*. Basic Books, New York, 2000.

Development Network Africa. 'Evaluation of an Appropriate Model for a SADC Customs Union Section H'. Report commissioned by the SADC Secretariat, 3 September 2007. www.dnaeconomics.com/assets/dlas/FILE_063020080157_FILE_062520080525_SADC_CU_Study_Final.pdf.

Ensor, Linda. 'Minister Davies says Jonas is a man of integrity'. *TimesLive*, 17 March 2016.

Fine, Ben and Zavareh Rustomjee. *The Political Economy of South Africa: From Minerals-Energy Complex to Industrialisation*. C Hurst and Co, London, 1996.

First R and RH Davies. *Migrant Labour to South Africa: A Sanctions Programme?* Economic Sanctions Against South Africa series. International University Exchange Fund, Geneva, 1980.

First, Ruth. *Black Gold: The Mozambican Miner, Proletarian and Peasant*. St Martin's Press, New York, 1983.

Friedman, Steven. *Race, Class and Power: Harold Wolpe and the Radical Critique of Apartheid*. University of KwaZulu-Natal Press, Pietermaritzburg, 2015.

Friedman, Thomas. *The Lexus and the Olive Tree*. Farrar, Straus and Giroux, New York, 1999.

Fukuyama, Francis. 'The end of history'. *The National Interest*, No 16, summer 1989, pp 3–18.

Gallagher, Kevin P and Richard Kozul-Wright. *A New Multilateralism for Shared Prosperity: Geneva Principles for a Global Green New Deal*. UNCTAD, Geneva, and Boston University Global Development Policy Center, 2019.

Gerber, Jan. 'Hawks investigate cases related to Gupta-loot worth more than R40 billion'. *News24*, 15 August 2018.

Gorbachev, Mikhail. *Perestroika: New Thinking for our Country and the World*. John Curley and Associates, South Yarmouth, MA, 1988.

Gould, Chandré, Conrad Barberton and Carmen Abdoll. 'What is at stake for new councils in South Africa?' *ISS Today*, 17 August 2016.

Green, Pippa. *Choice Not Fate: The Life and Times of Trevor Manuel*. Penguin Books, Johannesburg, 2008

Gruenewald, Paul J, Andrew J Treno, Sally Casswell et al. 'Impacts of New Zealand's lowered minimum purchase age on context-specific drinking and related risks'. *Addiction*, Vol 110, No 11, November 2015, pp 1757–1766.

Grynberg, Roman. 'African coffee isn't worth a bean'. *Mail & Guardian*, 10 May 2013.

Gumede, William Mervin. *Thabo Mbeki and the Battle for the Soul of the ANC*. Zebra Press, Cape Town, 2005.

Haffajee, Ferial. 'Stage 4 load shedding hits as Cabinet divide on energy deepens'. *Daily Maverick*, 10 March 2020.

Hain, Peter. *Outside In*. Biteback Publishing, London, 2012.

Hanlon, Joseph. *Beggar Your Neighbours: Apartheid Power in Southern Africa*. Catholic Institute for International Relations, James Currey, Indiana University Press, 1986.

Harvey, Ebrahim. *Kgalema Motlanthe: A Political Biography*. Jacana Media, Auckland Park, 2012.

Hiller-Sturmhofel, Suzanne and H Scott Swartzwelder. 'Alcohol's effects on the adolescent brain: What can be learned from animal models'. *Alcohol Research & Health*, Vol 28, No 4, 2004, pp 213–221.

'Indlulamithi South Africa Scenarios 2030: Look Above the Trees', June 2018. sascenarios2030.co.za/wp-content/uploads/2018/02/SA-Scenarios-Layout_SMALL.pdf.

Intergate Immigration. 'The Guidelines for Good Business Practice in Africa', no date. corporate.intergate-immigration.com/news/guidelines-good-business-practice-africa/.

Isaacs, Gilad. 'COVID-19: Unpacking President Ramaphosa's rescue package'. GroundUp, 22 April 2020. www.groundup.org.za/article/unpacking-president-ramaphosas-rescue-package/.

Ismail, Faizel. 'A "Developmental Regionalism" Approach to the AfCFTA'. Trade and Industrial Policy Strategies, Working Paper in celebration of the 90th birthday of Chief Olu Akinkugbe CFR CON, Tshwane, 5 December 2018.

Joffe, Avril, David Kaplan, Raphael Kaplinsky and David Lewis. *Improving Manufacturing Performance in South Africa: Report of the Industrial Strategy Project*. UCT Press and International Development Research Centre, Cape Town and Ottawa, 1995.

Johnstone, Frederick A. *Class, Race and Gold: A Study of Class Relations and Racial Discrimination in South Africa*. Routledge and Kegan Paul, London, 1976.

Kasrils, Ronnie. 'Historic Turning Point at Cuito Cuanavale'. Address at Rhodes University, 28 May 2008. www.61mech.org.za/uploads/mediafiles/files/238.pdf.

Klebnikov, Sergei. 'Here are the countries on the brink of recession going into 2020'. *Forbes*, 28 October 2019.

Klein, Ezra. 'How the COVID-19 recession could become a depression'. *Vox*, 23 March 2020.

Legassick, Martin. 'The Rise of Modern South African Liberalism: Its Assumptions and its Social Base'. University of Sussex seminar paper, 1974.

Lelyveld, Joseph. 'Mozambique ousts jobless from cities'. *The New York Times*, 1 October 1983.

Lipton, Merle. *Capitalism and Apartheid: South Africa 1910–1986*. David Philip, Cape Town, 1986.

Manghezi, Nadja. *The Maputo Connection: ANC Life in the World of Frelimo*. Jacana, Auckland Park, 2009.

Marais, Hein. *South Africa Pushed to the Limit: The Political Economy of Change*. UCT Press, Cape Town, 2011.

Marcuse, Herbert. *One-Dimensional Man: Studies in the Ideology of Advanced Industrial Society*. Beacon Press, Boston, 1964.

Marcuse, Herbert. *An Essay on Liberation*. Beacon Press, Boston, 1969.

Marrian, Natasha. 'Dead end for government's public wage bill plan?'. *Financial Mail*, 12 March 2020.

Marx, Karl. *Capital Vol III*. Progress Publishers, Moscow, 1971.

Matzopoulos, RG, S Truen, B Bowman and J Corrigall. 'The cost of harmful alcohol abuse in South Africa'. *South African Medical Journal*, Vol 104, No 2, February 2014.

McCartt, Anne T, Laurie A Hellinga and Bevan B Kirley. 'The effects of minimum legal drinking age 21 laws on alcohol-related driving in the United States'. *Journal of Safety Research*, Vol 41, No 2, April 2010, pp 173–181.

MERG. *Making Democracy Work: A Framework for Macroeconomic Policy in South Africa*. A Report from the Macro-Economic Research Group (MERG) to Members of the Democratic Movement of South Africa, Centre for Development Studies, University of the Western Cape, 1993.

Moleketi, Jabu. 'Is a retreat from National Democratic Revolution to National Bourgeois Revolution imminent?' *African Communist*, No 133, second quarter 1993.

Murray, Colin. 'From Granary to Labour Reserve: An Economic History of Lesotho'. Conference paper No 28, SALDRU Farm Labour Conference, September 1976. opensaldru.uct.ac.za/bitstream/handle/11090/495/1976_murry_sflcp28.pdf.

Naughton, Barry and Kellee S Tsai (eds). *State Capitalism, Institutional Adaptation, and the Chinese Miracle*. Cambridge University Press, Cambridge, 2015.

Nedlac Fund for Research into Industrial Development, Growth and Equity (FRIDGE). 'China: The Textile, Clothing, Footwear and Leather Sectors'. Report No 7, April 2006.

Nnadozie, RC. 'Access to adequate water in post-apartheid South African provinces: An overview of numerical trends'. *WaterSA*, Vol 37, No 3, 2011.

Ohlson, Thomas. 'The Cuito Cuanavale Syndrome: Revealing SADF Vulnerabilities'. In *South African Review 5*. Ravan Press, Johannesburg, 1989.

Olver, Crispian. *A House Divided: The Feud that Took Cape Town to the Brink*. Jonathan Ball, Johannesburg, 2019.

O'Meara, Dan. *Volkskapitalisme: Class, Capital and Ideology in the Development of Afrikaner Nationalism*. Cambridge University Press, Cambridge, 1983.

O'Meara, Dan. *Forty Lost Years: The Apartheid State and the Politics of the National Party 1948–1994*. Ravan Press, Randburg, 1996.

O'Neill, Jim. 'Building Better Global Economic BRICs'. Global Economic Paper no 66, Goldman Sachs, 30 November 2001.

Ouma, Dr Marisella. 'Traditional knowledge: The challenges facing international lawmakers'. *WIPO Magazine*, January 2017.

Padayachee, Vishnu and Robbie van Niekerk. *Shadow of Liberation: Contestation and Compromise in the Economic and Social Policy of the African National Congress 1943–1996*. Wits University Press, Johannesburg, 2019.

Palma, José Gabriel. 'The Revenge of the Market on the Rentiers: Why neo-liberal reports of the end of history turned out to be premature'. Cambridge Working Papers in Economics (CWPE) 0927, June 2009. www.econ.cam.ac.uk/research-files/repec/cam/pdf/cwpe0927.pdf.

Pauw, Jacques. *In the Heart of the Whore: The Story of Apartheid's Death Squads*. Southern Book Publishers, Johannesburg, 1991.

Poulantzas, Nicos. *Fascism and Dictatorship*. New Left Books, London, 1974.

Probst, Charlotte, Charles DH Parry, Hans-Ulrich Wittchen and Jürgen Rehm. 'The socioeconomic profile of alcohol-attributable mortality in South Africa: A modelling study'. *BMC Medicine*, Vol 16, No 97, 25 June 2018. bmcmedicine.biomedcentral.com/articles/10.1186/s12916-018-1080-0.

'Promotion and Protection of Investment Bill in line with global trends'. TRALAC News, 4 September 2015. www.tralac.org/news/article/8020-promotion-and-protection-of-investment-bill-in-line-with-global-trends-dti.html.

'Read: Alleged full report of Bell Pottinger's Gupta PR plan'. *The Citizen*, 4 April 2017.

Reinert, Erik. *How Rich Countries got Rich ... and Why Poor Countries Stay Poor*. Carroll & Graf, New York, 2007.

Reuters. 'A US recession? Probably. Depression? Only if the virus is untamed'. World Economic Forum, 28 March 2020. www.weforum.org/agenda/2020/03/a-u-s-recession-probably-depression-only-if-the-virus-is-untamed.

Roubini, Nouriel. 'A Greater Depression?'. *Project Syndicate*, 24 March 2020.

Satgar, Vishwas. 'Thabo Mbeki and the South African Communist Party'. In Sean Jacobs and Richard Calland (eds), *Thabo Mbeki's World: The Politics and Ideology of the South African President*. University of Natal Press, Pietermaritzburg, 2002.

Schwab, Klaus. *The Fourth Industrial Revolution*. Crown Business and World Economic Forum, Geneva, 2016.

'Serve the People as a Whole, Build a People's Economy'. *Bua Komanisi*, 4th Special National Congress edition, December 2019.

Shillington, Kevin (ed). *Encyclopedia of African History 3*. Routledge, New York, 2013.

Simons, HJ and Simons, RE. *Class and Colour in South Africa 1850–1950*. Penguin, Harmondsworth, 1969.

Singh, Parminder Jeet. 'Digital Industrialization in Developing Countries: A Review of the Business and Policy Landscapes'. Commonwealth Secretariat, 2017.

Sisulu, Max, Morley Nkosi, Bethuel Sethai and Rosalind H Thomas (eds). *Reconstituting and Democratising the Southern African Customs Union: Report of the Workshop held in Gaborone, Botswana, March 1994*. National Institute of Economic Policy, Braamfontein, 1994.

Slovo, Joe. 'Has Socialism Failed?'. SACP discussion paper. *South African Labour Bulletin*, Vol 14, No 6, February 1990.

Songwe, Vera. 'Intra-African trade: A path to economic diversification and inclusion'. Report, Foresight Africa 2019, Brookings Institution, 11 January 2019.

South African Communist Party. 'Let's not monumentalise the NDP – SACP'. SACP discussion document. Politicsweb, 14 May 2013. www.politicsweb. co.za/documents/lets-not-monumentalise-the-ndp--sacp.

South African Communist Party. 'SACP welcomes pro-poor and pro-worker interventions'. SACP statement, 22 April 2020. www.sacp.org.za/content/sacp-welcomes-pro-poor-and-pro-worker-interventions-announced-president-ramaphosa-tuesday.

Squazzin, Anthony and Prinesha Naidoo. 'Ramaphosa has window to reform South Africa as twin crises hit'. *Bloomberg*, 31 March 2020. www.bloomberg.com/news/articles/2020-03-31/ramaphosa-has-window-to-reform-south-africa-as-twin-crises-hit.

Stiglitz, Joseph. *Globalisation and its Discontents*. Allen Lane/The Penguin Press, London, 2002.

Suckling, John and Landeg White (eds). *After Apartheid: Renewal of the South African Economy*. James Currey, London, 1988.

Turok, Ben (ed). *Wealth Doesn't Trickle Down: The Case for a Developmental State in South Africa*. New Agenda, Cape Town, 2008.

'Value of COVID-19 fiscal stimulus packages in G20 countries as of July 2020, as a share of GDP'. Graphic, statista.com, October 2020. www.statista.com/statistics/1107572/covid-19-value-g20-stimulus-packages-share-gdp/.

Van Onselen, Gareth. 'Political Musical Chairs: Turnover in The National Executive and Administration Since 2009'. Report by the Institute of Race Relations, August 2017. irr.org.za/reports/occasional-reports/files/irr-political-musical-chairs.pdf.

Vlok, Etienne. 'The Textile and Clothing Industry in South Africa'. In Herbert Jauch and Rudolf Traub-Merz (eds), *The Future of the Textile and Clothing Industry in Sub-Saharan Africa*. Friedrich-Ebert Stiftung, Bonn, 2006.

Wallerstein, Immanuel and Sergio Vieira. 'Historical Development of the Region in the Context of the Evolving World-System'. In Sergio Vieira, William G Martin and Immanuel Wallerstein (coordinators), *How Fast the Wind? Southern Africa 1975–2000*. Africa World Press, Trenton, New Jersey, 1992.

Wilson, Francis. *Labour in the South African Gold Mines 1911–1969*. Cambridge University Press, Cambridge, 1972.

Winde, Alan. 'Minister Alan Winde's address on key achievements of the Western Cape's biggest sectors', 28 November 2013. www.gov.za/minister-alan-windes-address-key-achievements-western-capes-biggest-sectors.

Wolpe, Harold. 'Capitalism and cheap labour-power in South Africa: From segregation to apartheid'. *Economy and Society*, Vol 1, No 4, 1972.

Wolpe, Harold. *Race, Class and the Apartheid State*. James Currey, London, 1988.

Wuyts, Marc. 'Camponeses e Economia Rural em Moçambique' (Peasants and Rural Economy in Mozambique). Centro de Estudos Africanos, Universidade Eduardo Mondlane, 1978.

Zille, Helen. *Not without a Fight: The Autobiography of Helen Zille*. Penguin Random House, Johannesburg, 2016.

Other

'About SADC'. sadc.int/about-SADC.

'Battle of Cuito Cuanavale 1988'. www.sahistory.org.za/article/battle-cuito-cuana-vale-1988.

'Maputo'. www.wikizero.com/en/History_of_Maputo.

'Operation Gordian Knot'. www.wikipedia.com/en.wikipedia.org/wiki/Operation_Gordian_Knot.

'President Jacob Zuma: Address during 2014 Presidential Inauguration'. GovernmentZA, 27 May 2014. youtube.com/watch?v=g6jVZzXGass&feature=youtu.be.

'President Nelson Mandela Inauguration Speech May 10, 1994'. SABC Digital News, 8 May 2015. youtu.be/pJiXu4q__VU.

'The Cold War's Final Battle'. twnafrica.org/wp/2017/?p=489.

'The Freedom Charter'. www.historicalpapers.wits.ac.za/inventories/inv_pdfo/AD1137/AD1137-Ea6-1-001-jpeg.pdf.

INDEX

CPSIA information can be obtained
at www.ICGtesting.com
Printed in the USA
LVHW052006220321
682109LV00023B/1612